RUMBA RULES

RUMBA RULES

The Politics of Dance Music in Mobutu's Zaire

Bob W. White

Duke University Press | Durham and London | 2008

© 2008 Duke University Press

All rights reserved.

Printed in the United States of America on acid-free paper ∞

Designed by Heather Hensley

Typeset in Quadratt by Tseng Information Systems, Inc.

Library of Congress Cataloging-in-Publication Data appear

on the last printed page of this book.

To Lucie, Jeremy, Aria, and Piccolo

Since he has taken us by the hand, let him not forget about us! Let him make it possible for us to play music! That will enable us to take care of ourselves, instead of him using all his energy to take care of us. Let him always think of us, because sometimes we forget to finish what we started! Let us continue to sing and live in the best of conditions! We live for music. Let our music find a place in the history of Zaire for the generations of our children and our grandchildren! We will be unified to be strong and to defend the rights of our ancestors, just as we seek friendship with others who are sincere.

"MESSAGE FROM ARTISTS TO
PRESIDENT MOBUTU SESE SEKO," 1974

À travers la vision du monde de l'artiste, un spécialiste du beau, du sublime, de la jouissance, est offerte une perspective esthétique sur l'expérience et sur le savoir.

BOGUMIL JEWSIEWICKI

CONTENTS

PREFACE
Condemned to Find the Formula

WHEN ONE OF THE SINGERS OF THE BAND I WAS working with sat down next to me and began to read my field notes from over my shoulder, I looked up at him, smiling slightly, so he would not feel that he was intruding, and continued writing in my notebook. After a few minutes filled with nothing but the sound of my scribbling, he discreetly cleared his throat and began by asking me a question: "Monsieur Bob, excuse me, I know that curiosity is an ugly habit, but can I ask you a few questions?" At first I was surprised, since in all the time I had spent with this band, no one had ever seemed particularly interested in what I was writing in my notebook or why. Of course there were the endless requests by fellow band members that I put their name in my book ("Monsieur Bob, don't forget me!"), but this never involved any interest in what exactly the book was about or what had driven me to want to write a book about them in the first place. For most of the musicians, I was simply another member of the band.

"Go ahead," I said to Makuta, intrigued by his interest, "What would you like to know?" He began by asking me some general questions about life in the United States: Do blacks and whites live in the same neighborhoods? How much does it cost to buy a car? Had I ever met Michael Jackson? And then, as if it were the most logical next question: "When you're in the States, do you spend your time with people like this?" He was referring to our fellow band members, many of whom he found to be somewhat rough around the edges. Makuta came from Matadi, a port city much smaller than Kinshasa, and as the newest member of the band, he often seemed overwhelmed by his new environment. I stared at him for a minute and then realized that I had never been asked a question like this. In fact, I had never even taken the time to reflect on how my life "in the field" was similar to or different from my lifestyle at home, or even why I chose this particular lifestyle as a topic for doctoral research. "Actually, no," I answered. "My life is very different here. At home I mostly hang out with university types, but here I spend my time with musicians. Here I am a musician. I kind of like that."

In retrospect I am not sure if Makuta's question was an innocent one, or if he was indirectly commenting on the strange fact of my presence among them. Makuta himself, as someone who had actually been living in Kinshasa for less time than I had, was still an outsider to the city. It was probably this outsider position that made him interested in my status as an outsider and inspired him to ask such a question, and his polite demeanor made me think that he had more education than most people in the band. Makuta's curiosity was the rare exception among the people with whom I worked, but it could be that he only articulated a question that other band members had wondered about but not bothered (or dared) to ask. In most cases, the musicians I worked with were more concerned with how I would fit into their networks of sociability and exchange, and very few of them ever asked me why a foreigner might be interested in their music. Indeed, for many musicians my presence simply confirmed its importance.

"We are condemned to find the formula . . . ," wrote Michel Lonoh in a handwritten dedication on the inside cover of his pamphlet *Négritude, africanité et musique africaine* (1990). The sense of heroism in Lonoh's statement is oddly appropriate since even today, more than thirty years after his groundbreaking essay on "la musique congolaise moderne" (1969), the literature on the Congo has produced surprisingly little scholarship on this privileged form of cultural expression. As I set out to find my own "formula," some part of me knew that the heroism I felt was mostly in my head since no one ever asked me to do research on Congolese popular dance music, and no one was waiting for me when I got off the plane. Perhaps *heroism* was not the right word. It was certainly not the word chosen by the Congolese philosopher V. Y. Mudimbe, who on meeting me and hearing about my research stepped back and exclaimed with a tone somewhere between amazement and horror: "Martyr!"

When I first arrived in the region in 1995, I was excited about beginning my research, but I was also apprehensive about doing work on popular music in a country in which many people have a hard time getting something to eat. Among the people I encountered, most were pleased—though not necessarily surprised—that I had come from so far away to study their music. Some Congolese even expressed the idea that the Congo should learn from the experience of the United States, which they perceived as building an economic and political empire on a very solid base of cultural production for export. Only rarely did they openly question the value of doing research on popular music. On more than one occasion I was jokingly accused of wanting to learn about the local music scene so I could exploit this valuable natural resource and make money from selling records abroad. On other occasions I was teased for having the luxury of being able to do research on music; as one friend commented wryly: "I have to do things that put food on the table." But even these reactions—which I assume were much more common when I was not within hearing range—do not in themselves undermine the importance that people in Kinshasa attribute to popular music as a social and cultural phenomenon. Rather, they call attention to the privilege inherent in doing something that does not "feed its man."

Technically speaking, popular music in Kinshasa does put food on the table, and this is one of the aspects that I found most intriguing about the topic: given the ongoing political and economic crisis, how can popular dance music continue to flourish? A senior researcher working in Kinshasa at about the same time as I prepared to begin my fieldwork wrote me a letter in March 1995 concerning my plans to conduct research on popular music:

> Now major parts of the city have become mute. Dozens of bars and nightclubs are turned into healing churches, private schools or maternities. Paradoxically, while it is gaining importance in Brussels or Paris, Zairian music here has lost very much of its appeal, and somehow be-

comes secondary ("hors-scène"), even obscene for many people; the euphoric anomie is over and turned into some kind of violence or flight into the sacred. . . . Some colleagues and collaborators in Kinshasa were quite resentful when hearing about your research. "Kinshasa the Beautiful has become Kinshasa the Garbage Can," as it is commonly said. "Who can improve their situation by doing research on music?"

On reading this letter, I was struck with a sudden feeling of paralysis. It began to grate on my nerves, resonating in my head in the final weeks leading up to fieldwork. With some hindsight I can see that these words probably helped me articulate how popular dance music actually formed part of the problem with Mobutu's Zaire, not only because it promoted a certain degree of hedonism and escapism but also because of the ways in which it had become implicated in the performance of state-based forms of power and authority, a topic at the center of my analysis. As an ethnography of popular dance music at the end of the Mobutu regime, this book attempts to show why popular music continues to have relevance for so many people in Kinshasa and how, at the same time, it has come to be synonymous with bad leadership and various forms of economic and moral decay. From my point of view, this paradox is not simply a sad fact of Congo's particular trajectory of modernity; it is something that needs to be explained.

Initial research for this book was conducted as part of my doctoral dissertation between May 1995 and June 1996, with a series of monthlong return trips in 1996, 1999, 2002, 2003, and 2004. After some initial fact-finding among Congolese and friends of Congolese in Brussels and Paris, I began the actual field research in Brazzaville to ease my arrival into Kinshasa, but also because I wanted to gather information about the distribution networks that at the time constituted an important aspect of the music industry on the other side of the river. Several months after arriving in Brazzaville, I moved permanently to Kinshasa, but I had been there previously on several visits varying from one day to one week. Once in Kinshasa, I continued to conduct research on industry-related issues, but also became much more focused on the activities of musicians and the music lifestyle. It was here that I approached a local music group and underwent an extended apprenticeship as a musician and member of the group. In Kinshasa I made living arrangements similar to those in Brazzaville, renting a room in the compound of a large family in a middle-class neighborhood. Bandalungwa (Bandal-

Moulaert) was centrally located and relatively new compared to some of the neighborhoods in other sections of the city. Living in a Zairian neighborhood gave me access to general cultural information about family relations and the challenges of everyday life in Kinshasa, but it also ensured that I was close to the band, which practiced close by and performed on a regular basis. Initially I divided my fieldwork into three basic units of inquiry: the music industry, musicians and the world of performance, and the music's audience. I intended to divide my time in the field equally among these three aspects, but somewhere in the middle of the second I realized that I would not have enough time to complete the third. Although the finished product does not exactly reflect this three-part division, these categories (industry, musicians, audience) are still present in the structure and logic of the book.

Before beginning fieldwork, my research project was much more focused on the question of cultural commodities, a topic brilliantly articulated in a recent text by Timothy Taylor (2006). I was interested in looking at the emergence of cultural products and their relationship to national identity, and while there is clearly a relationship between cultural production and national identity in Mobutu's Zaire (see chapter 3), what resulted from my field research is a series of reflections on power and its entanglement with popular music. Once back from the field, it became increasingly clear to me that my book was not about cultural commodities (see White 2000b) but about political culture, or more precisely, about the relationship between popular music and politics. Thus one of the challenges with this book is the question of time. Not only because the popular music scene is changing so quickly but also because so much time has lapsed between the initial field research and the publication of this book (see "Note to the Reader"), I decided to limit my analysis to a particular period in Congolese cultural history—the better part of the 1990s—and that the book should be as much about this historical moment as it should about the genre of popular music.

If, as Ellen Corin once told me, writing a book is a form of arrogance, then the best antidote to this arrogance is to acknowledge the people who in one way or another contributed to the completion of this project. First and foremost I would like to thank my Ph.D. advisor John Galaty and the members of my doctoral dissertation committee—Ellen Corin, Kristin Norget, and Johannes Fabian—for their ongoing support of this project and for their generosity and patience, which have gone far beyond the time they spent with my writing. Since I began working on a revised version of the manuscript I have received thoughtful comments from a number of friends and colleagues who have given generously of their time and expertise. Of these people I especially acknowledge Nancy Rose Hunt and Corinne Kratz (my closest and most precious readers), Bogumil Jewsiewicki, Michael McGovern, Dieudonné Mbala Nkanga, Vinh-Kim Nguyen, Gilles Bibeau, John Leavitt, Peter Seitel, John Grinling, and Yoka Lye Mudaba. My research and writing has also benefited from exchanges and conversations with Mariella Pandolfi, Christine Jourdan, Peter Geschiere, Leonard Buleli N'sanda, Lomomba Emongo, Kamari Clarke, Bernard Gendron, Phil Tagg, Kelly Askew, Steven Feld, Tim Taylor, Denis-Constant Martin, Don Brenneis, Dan Linger, Susan Harding, Louis Chude-Sokei, Shelly Errington, Nancy Chen, Diane Gifford Gonzales, Nyunda ya Rubango, Ngwarsungu Chiwengo, Kazadi wa Mukuna, Olema Debhonvapi, Lomomba Emongo, Eric Worby, Blair Rutherford, Eric Gable, Filip De Boeck, Bennetta Jules-Rosette, Michael Schatzberg, Janet MacGaffey, Ivan Karp, Chris Waterman, Stephen Jackson, and the late T. K. Biaya. In terms of making the perilous transition from dissertation to manuscript to book, I am especially grateful to my editor Ken Wissoker, whose judicious comments and thoughtful advice defy the gravity of publishing. Our periodic exchanges taught me a great deal about writing and about myself, and I feel extremely fortunate to have been able to work with him. Duke University Press's three anonymous readers proved instrumental in helping me refine the argument and better understand my potential audiences. Readers such as these, who engage with an author's writing not as a text but as an intellectual project, are rare, and I am grateful for their input. I also thank Courtney Berger, who brought her insight and experience to the final stages of editing and production, as well as Fred Kameny. A special thanks goes to my other editor (and father), Will White, for whom I was writing during the final stages of revisions and for whom I have probably been writing for a long time. He gave me the gift of his time and experience during a crucial period of rethinking, and I will always treasure this moment in our relationship.

A number of people helped with my research in the field, not only before and during but also after. Among those I especially thank my friends, collaborators, and teachers Manda Tchebwa, John "Grand Maracuja" Grinling, General Defao, Chef Maneko (na leli yo mabe), Ladi Son, Bébé Atalaku, Ya Lidjo, Lofombo "Kamola Basse," (le grand frère) Djuna Mumbafu, and the late T. K. Biaya. If the names of these people roll from my tongue every time I have the pleasure to say or write them, it is because they are more than interlocutors—in some sense they were my "field." I am deeply indebted to them for their friendship and their involvement. I also wish to express my gratitude to Matt Bergbusch (who helped me tremendously both before and after the writing phase), Avi Goldberg, David Macaulay, Patricia Foxen, Christine Zarowsky, Titus Moser, Raj Gandesha, Rose-Marie Stano, The BulaBula family of Bukavu, Thierry from Lumumbashi (wapi yo?), Césarine Boliya, Vincent Kenis, Didier de Lannoy and Ana Lanzas, Jean-Pierre Jacquemin, Jerome and Anthuya Deye, Mama Lutiya Barazani, Nicolas Martin-Granel, Lascony Balloux, the Ingila family of Bandal, Jose Kamwena and his family, Pieter Remes and Hilkka Rosa Abicht, Docteur Kikudi, John Loftin, Christine Krotzer and my colleagues at the Zaire American Language Institute, Max Makiadi and Lydie, Ilunga Bukasa, Michel Lonoh, Liliane Kasanda, Mama Odia, Mama Rebecca, Tatou, Nlandu, Almaz (Mazanza Maurice), Socrates, Mampasa, Gaby Shabani, Wendo Kolosoy, Lutumba Simaro, Jean-Serge Essous, Philippe "Rossignol" Lando, Augustin "Roitelet" Moniania, Antoine "Brazzos" Armando, the late Roger Izeidi, Charles Mwamba "Dechaud," Tabu Ley Rochereau, Sam Manguana, Papa Noel, Kiamanguana Verckys, Bombolo wa Lokole "Bholen," the late Pépé Kallé, Lokassa ya Mbongo, Ben Nyamabo, Ilo Pablo, the late Lengi Lengos, Nyoka Longo, Fely Manwaku, Papa Wemba, Reddy Amisi, Donat, Manda Chante, Lambio Lambio, Kester Emeneya, Blaise Bula, Rasta Bob, Shora Mbemba, Montana, Kabosé Makuta, Jean-Louis, Theo Mbala, Burkina Faso, Bleu de Bleu, Koyo, Cheri Samba, Chris McCarus, Seth Cashman, John Nimis, and Martin Sinnock.

Research assistants in Montreal (Doudou Madoda and Boniface Bahi) and Kinshasa (Jean-Claude Diyongo, Leon Tsambu, Jean Liyongo, Rigobert Mbila, and Henry Mubenga) were extremely helpful in later stages of the research. Two people in particular deserve special mention. Jean-Pierre Busé (formerly of Zaiko Langa Langa) has been a close friend and a wonderfully rich source of information about the history of his country and his music, and I will forever be grateful for his involvement in my research. My principal research assistant, Serge Makobo Kalala, has literally become my eyes and ears on the ground in Kinshasa. Much of what I have accomplished would have been impossible without his assistance, and I look forward to our future discoveries, both in the Congo and farther abroad.

Funding for the initial phase of this research was made possible by the

Centre for the Study of Society, Technology, and Development (STANDD) at McGill University, the McGill Associates, the McGill Graduate Faculty, and the Zeller Family Foundation. Professor Peter Johnson was instrumental in helping me organize the initial funding of the project. I also thank the Wenner-Gren Foundation for its support with a dissertation write-up grant, and Anthony Seeger and Atesh Sonneborn of Folkways Records who supervised my research during a postdoctoral fellowship made possible by the Smithsonian Institution. I am particularly grateful to Ivan Karp and Corinne Kratz who took me under their huge wings during a postdoctoral fellowship at the Center for the Study of Public Scholarship. I cannot thank them enough for their ongoing support of my work, and I continue to believe that my career began under their watch. Some of the material in this book was collected during return visits to Kinshasa funded by the Social Sciences and Humanities Research Council of Canada (SSHRC), the Fonds Québécois de la Recherche sur la Société et la Culture (FQRSC), and the International Collaborative Research Grant of the Wenner-Gren Foundation. I also benefited from colleagues' comments during invited presentations at York University (Department of Anthropology) and Carleton University (Department of Sociology and Anthropology). Earlier versions of certain sections of this text have appeared elsewhere. My description of the *atalaku* phenomenon first appeared in the journal *Research in African Literatures* (see White 1999) and later in a volume edited by John Conteh-Morgan and Tejumola Olaniyan (see White 2004b). Some of the material in chapter 5 appears in a volume edited by Theodore Trefon (see White 2004a). My material on cultural policy under Mobutu appears in a more elaborate form in the Quebec-based journal *Anthropologie et sociétés* (see White 2006a). I am grateful to the editors of these publications for their assistance and the opportunity to publish the material.

A number of important people have been involved in my research only indirectly, but this has not kept them from having a profound impact on my thinking, both professionally and personally. Dave Rearick, who told me to do two things in life: have a child and write a book; Dorothy Holland, who directed my first independent research project and passed on her passion for cultural analysis; Don Nonini, who taught me the importance of asking questions; Dan Aronson, who took a chance on me as a graduate student; Johannes Fabian, who blazed the trail for much of the work I do today;

Luambo Makiadi "Franco," who better than any other musician embodies the ambiguity and the power of Congolese popular dance music and whose music continues to haunt me; Björk, without whose music I could never have finished writing; and finally Dr. Martin Luther King Jr., for his commitment to compassion even in the presence of hate and contempt. I also thank my mother, an out-of-place girl from Hurley, Mississippi, who lovingly gave me my first book and my first guitar, and of course I thank my chair (an early model Steelcase "Criterion"), for supporting me throughout this entire process.

I consider myself terribly fortunate to have had all this time to do something as self-indulgent and antisocial as writing a book. Of all the people who helped me by giving of themselves and their time, the most important are my wife Lucie and our two children. Neither Jeremy nor Aria seems to understand why I spend so much time in my office, and neither has ever known anything different, but as they grow older, they each in their own way inspire me to do something about it. In some sense I do not know how to separate Lucie from Zairian popular dance music since from the project's very inception she has been with me, gently prodding and deeply present, especially during those moments in which I most needed someone to help me untie the intellectual and psychological knots keeping me from telling this story. And even though this book gradually became something of a mistress, she somehow found the energy to urge me on. One night, as I found myself in the throes of final revisions, she stood behind me and wrapped her arms around my neck to see what I was working on. "It's going to be a nice book," I said, staring at the screen, very excited about the idea of finishing. "C'est un peu notre histoire," she answered. "Yeah," I said, with a lump in my throat, "c'est un peu notre histoire."

NOTE TO THE READER

AT VARIOUS PLACES IN THE TEXT THE READER will notice audio and video cues (for example, " 'The next morning they woke up and decided that this would be their new musical signature [audio]."). These cues correspond to material that can be accessed through links at the web site www.atalaku.net and will be organized according to the chapter in the book where they appear, and also by type of media (image, audio, video, text). Material and analysis will be available in English, French, and Lingala.

It is not at all uncommon, especially in the context of Congolese popular dance music, for people in Kinshasa to mix in elements of French with the city's most commonly spoken language, Lingala. Foreign words that recur often or play a central role in the text (for example *atalaku* or *animation politique*) are italicized. Unless otherwise indicated, all translations are those of the author.

Throughout this text, place names are used to indicate historical periods that correspond to particular political regimes. For example, the term "Belgian Congo" refers to the country during the colonial period, "Congo" to the period following independence, and "Zaïre" most commonly to the Mobutu period. The term "Congo-Zaïre" is also used to refer to the post-colonial period, without reference to a particular regime. Upon seizing power from Mobutu in May 1997, Laurent Kabila changed the name of the country once again, this time reverting to the form used during the period immediately following independence: Democratic Republic of Congo, or more commonly DRC.

Since the initial research for this book was completed, the political situation in the Congo has become increasingly volatile. After assuming control of the country, Kabila's relations with his allies in Kigali and Kampala soured, and the eastern part of D.R.C. plunged deeper into political insecurity and violence. Beginning in 1998 the Rwanda-backed rebel movement RCD (Rassemblement Congolais pour la Démocratie) and the Uganda-backed MLC (Mouvement pour la Libération du Congo)—themselves plagued with factionalism and in-fighting—represented a serious threat in the region, not only for the Congolese government and military but also for local populations who in many ways have been held hostage by the conflict.

Even with support from several other nations in the region (most notably Zimbabwe, Namibia, and Angola), Kabila's forces were not able to defeat the various rebellions, and a bloody stalemate ensued. In July 1999 several of the warring parties finally came together around a first ceasefire agreement in Lusaka, Zambia. The Lusaka Accords resulted in the establishment of an extended UN peacekeeping mission (MONUC) and a call by the United Nations for the withdrawal of all foreign troops from Congolese soil, but fighting continued in the region, much of it fueled by the ongoing threat of Hutu militias based in the DRC (those having fled from the genocide in Rwanda in 1994) and the competition for access to land and valuable mining resources.

In January 2001 Laurent Kabila was assassinated under mysterious circumstances and succeeded by his son Joseph, who early on made clear his intentions to revive the peace process. In July 2002 another peace agreement was signed between Rwanda and DRC (including a provision for the official withdrawal of Rwanda's more than thirty thousand troops), and in April 2003 a transitional government was formed with Kabila as head of state and four vice-presidents (including the leaders of the MLC and the RCD), as well as an interim constitution with provisions for multiparty elections. Despite this progress, armed conflict and violence had become so endemic that in

March 2005 the United Nations described the conflict in eastern Congo as "the world's worst humanitarian crisis," and a report by the International Rescue Committee showed the crisis in the DRC to be the bloodiest conflict in history since the Second World War, with the number of deaths generally estimated at four million.

In July 2006 multiparty elections were finally held, the first since independence in 1960. Results from the first round of voting gave the majority of votes to President Joseph Kabila and the MLC rebel leader Jean-Pierre Bemba. In the second-round runoff Kabila gained 58 percent of the vote, results that did not go uncontested despite a consensus among international observers that the elections were substantially free and democratic. The period following the elections saw a slight increase in stability throughout the region, even though the IRIN news service was reporting over a million internally displaced persons (IDPs) and widespread sexual violence against women and children.

The year 2007 was marked by a series of confrontations in the Kivu region of the Congo between the Congolese national army and the rebel forces of Laurent Nkunda (Congrès National pour la Défense du Peuple), a former DRC army general who stands accused of war crimes. In January 2008 the government in Kinshasa and various remaining rebel movements in the east of the country signed a peace agreement that opened the possibility of amnesty for insurgency, but not for war crimes or crimes against humanity. At this writing many observers are hopeful that the agreement will mark the end of a long period of displacement and insecurity in the region, but the situation remains tense, and it is too early to say whether the conflict is over for good.

1

POPULAR CULTURE'S POLITICS

IN OCTOBER 1996, WHEN LAURENT DÉSIRÉ KABI-
la's rebel movement began to gain momentum, many
people in Kinshasa found it hard to believe that the rebels
would push as far as the nation's capital: "He might take
Zaire," a young man told me, "but he'll never take Kinshasa." President Mobutu Sese Seko's declining state of
health (he was said to suffer from prostate cancer) and
Kabila's military and financial support from other African leaders in the region (especially Paul Kagame of
Rwanda and Yoweri Museveni of Uganda) proved these
predictions wrong. When Kabila's name began to circulate as the leader of an emerging rebel movement in
the east, the Alliance des Forces Démocratiques pour la
Libération du Congo-Zaïre (AFDL), relatively little was
known about him. A journalist I spoke with told me that
people in Kinshasa were ready for Mobutu to go, but that
in their hearts they wanted their next leader to be a *kinois*
(someone from Kinshasa). Nonetheless, as Kabila and
his troops marched triumphantly into Kinshasa in May
1997, the capital was buzzing with excitement. From
loudspeakers and radios all over the city, the musicians
of the popular music group Wenge Musica could be heard

singing: "Louis de Funès! I saw Fantomas! He was running away! Running Away!"[1] Young people in Kinshasa were quick to make a link between the villain of French popular cinema and Mobutu, who apart from being diabolical was also being chased out of town.

While most people in Kinshasa expressed excitement and optimism about the idea of a Zaire without Mobutu, some of the musicians I spoke with during the transition seemed ambivalent, even confused. Under Mobutu, who ruled Zaire from 1965 to 1997, popular musicians had become accustomed to a system of politics that rewarded them for making public displays of loyalty or for staying out of politics altogether. In response to this system, popular musicians gradually developed a series of strategies (public praise, self-censorship, and new forms of showmanship) that enabled them to thrive both as artists and as international stars. Over time, these strategies became an integral part of the aesthetics and performance of their music, so integral, in fact, that some musicians no longer saw their relationship with the people and institutions of power as problematic. By the middle of the 1990s popular music had become more than just a form of mass entertainment. It had turned into a means of social mobility and self-protection for those willing to immortalize the wealthy and powerful by citing their names in their music. As it became increasingly obvious that Mobutu's days were numbered, many musicians felt nervous because this meant that the intricate networks of patron-client relations built around his powerful presence would be destabilized if not completely overturned.

At first Kabila seemed to have no interest in being the object of musicians' praise. In the weeks following his arrival, rumors circulated that a number of popular musicians had offered compositions in honor of the newly formed government, but that Kabila was ignoring them. People in Kinshasa understood this as an attempt to distance himself from Mobutu and his system of rule, and no one seemed particularly surprised. After all, it was Kabila himself who had been heard saying that people in Kinshasa did nothing but listen to music and that one of the objectives of his leadership would be to get the Congo back to work. Musicians, especially those making a living through music, found this situation unsettling. Walking back from a concert in Montreal in the summer of 1997, I asked a Congolese musician who was touring Canada with his group what he thought about the rumors, and he expressed a sense of frustration with the new regime's stance: "It's no good, mon cher. Kabila doesn't want us to sing him. What are we supposed to do now?" Kabila was either uninterested in playing the old game or unable to understand it, a situation that clearly made musicians insecure about the future.

La Guidomanie

Within Africa, the Congo is known primarily for two things: music and Mobutu. While Congolese music is known for its seductive combination of melancholy and joie de vivre, the legacy of Mobutu's political system is much more sinister (White 2005). A wealth of scholarship exists on political developments in the Congo, especially during the years leading up to and following independence in 1960, and much of it is available in English.[2] I refer readers to this literature for a more detailed analysis of the sequence of events surrounding and following independence: the end of colonial rule, the rise and fall of Lumumba, Mobutu's seizure of power in 1965, the formation of the MPR (Mouvement Populaire de la Révolution) as the country's only officially recognized political party and later as the "supreme institution of the Republic," the nationalization schemes of the early 1970s (Zaïri-anization, radicalization, retrocession), changes in international markets for copper and oil in the mid-1970s, and in the early 1980s the beginning of a difficult period of democratic denial surrounding the formation of the first opposition party, Étienne Tshisekedi's Union pour la Démocratie et le Progrès Social.

Ongoing concern about the status of opposition politics, along with the controversy surrounding the Bindo lottery scheme (see Jewsiewicki 1992b) and the dismantling of the Berlin Wall in 1989, contributed to widespread frustration, especially in the capital, and in 1991 Kinshasa exploded in riots. Referred to sardonically as le pillage, this period of only a few days left an indelible mark on the memory of many Congolese as a low point in economic and political history and as a symbol of how deeply le mal zaïrois ("the Zairian condition") had penetrated society. A similar series of riots occurred in 1993, but this time the civil unrest seemed both more organized and more brutal, primarily due to the role played by disgruntled members of the military. During the 1990s, Mobutu kept a safe distance from Kinshasa, preferring to divide his time between Gbadolite (the presidential village in the north central part of the country) and various villas in Europe. His famous speech in Kinshasa on April 24, 1990, in which, crying, he announced his resignation as the head of the MPR, marked for many people the beginning

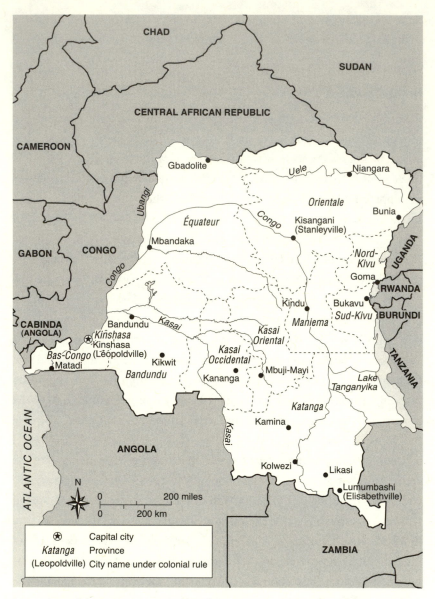

Map 1. Map of the Democratic Republic of Congo.

of the end of *mobutisme*. Mobutu's decision to retract this decision several days later would confirm for many that the tears shed during this speech (after which he uttered the famous words "understand my emotion") were those of a crocodile and not a leopard.

This period also saw important changes in the music scene. Since the early

1990s, the musical group Wenge Musica has been held up as the flagship of the fourth generation of Congolese popular dance music. Unlike most well-known groups in Kinshasa, Wenge was formed by a group of cofounders instead of by a single charismatic leader. This organizational structure (which is rare, but not without precedent) enabled Wenge to hold audiences' attention for a number of years, but in many ways Wenge was also a disaster waiting to happen. For a long time the musicians of Wenge Musica maintained close ties with Mobutu's son Mwenze Kongolo (also known by his nickname, "Saddam Hussein"), who in addition to being a high-ranking officer in the Zairian army was probably the most powerful figure in the music industry of the 1990s. Like his father, Kongolo combined the lure of money with the threat of violence to control musicians' movements and words. As long as musicians continued to sing his name on records and during concerts, they would benefit from political protection and financial support. Kongolo was known to have a special affinity for Wenge, and his position as the honorary "president" of the group served as a constant reminder that it was in the group's best interest to stay together. In fact, Kongolo had intervened in the past by physically threatening anyone who tried to break up or separate from the group. With the release of the first Wenge solo album in 1996 (*Feux de l'amour*), however, the singer J. B. M'piana drove a decisive wedge between himself and his longtime rival and fellow band member Werra Son. Furthermore, increasing political tension in the eastern part of the country meant that Kongolo was often absent from Kinshasa and no longer in a position to mediate conflict within the group. In the fall of 1997, after an altercation during a concert at Kinshasa's prestigious Intercontinental Hotel, it became clear that Wenge was breaking up, and rumors about the group's fragile future began to spread across the city like wildfire.

The next day fans organized a protest in front of the band's headquarters, and as the conflict with Kabila's new government intensified, there was increasing concern that the situation with Wenge might lead to civil unrest in Kinshasa. Finally in December 1997 the newly installed minister of information and cultural affairs, Raphael Ghenda, called a special meeting with the conflicting parties in hopes of brokering an agreement that would lead to reconciliation. Ghenda's chief of staff announced to the press that "there were some serious problems within Wenge due to an absence of consultation, but we are not yet talking about the possibility of separating. Furthermore, the musicians have been asked to not let themselves be distracted at a time when what we need most is unity in order to ensure national reconstruction" (qtd. in Kasongo 1997).

According to the author Manda Tchebwa, who together with the famous singer Tabu Ley was approached by the minister to facilitate the meeting, the closed-door session lasted nearly six hours, with each musician expressing his grievances, and resulted in a heated exchange of personal accusations and a fragile consensus to keep the group together (personal communication, May 2, 2005). While the two rivals left the minister's office shaking hands in front of the cameras, in only a matter of days Wenge had officially split into two: J. B. M'piana's Wenge Musica BCBG (for the group's original name, Bon chic, Bon genre) and Werra Son's Wenge Musica Maison Mère. This separation led to a series of secondary offshoots in the months to come, and the dream of a reunited Wenge quickly became a thing of the past. Perhaps Werra Son himself said it best when he announced to the local media that "there are too many Wenges in the Congo."

During this period it seemed that everyone in Kinshasa was talking about the conflict between the two musicians. Most people had an opinion about what had happened and continue to remember this period as a time during which friends, families, and neighbors became increasingly divided over the issue of the group's separation. A young man in his mid-twenties told me, "J. B.'s album really marked a turning point in terms of politics. . . . From that point on the conflict between the musicians got worse and for the first time in our neighborhood we were able to see who was who" (group interview, May 15, 2005). When another young man told me that he had "lost a lot of friends during that period" (ibid.), he was referring not only to friends who left the Congo because of increasing political instability but also to the fact that the Wenge controversy was slowly starting to cause division among fans along ethnic lines, with people from Kasai supporting J. B. M'piana and people from the Kikongo-speaking areas around Kinshasa supporting Werra Son. Wenge Musica's ethnic makeup had never surfaced as an issue in the group's past, and the fact that Wenge's problems were being read in ethnic terms seemed to signal a structural shift not only in popular music but in national politics as well.

One thing that was not new in Congolese popular dance music was the internal dynamic of *dislocation* ("splintering") that occurs whenever a disgruntled member of a group (generally one of the lead singers or guitarists) decides to strike out on his own and establish his own authority as a musical and artistic leader. Splintering has been a central dynamic in the management and performance of popular music in Kinshasa since its very beginnings, and it may or may not be explained by looking to an equatorial tradition of "big man" politics in various regions of the Congo basin (see chapter 8). What is clear is that throughout his political career Mobutu modeled a style of political leadership that made strategic use of divisiveness, most often as a means of consolidating authority, and this aspect of his leadership also became common in social organization outside of the political sphere. Mobutu's status as "president for life" was only reinforced by the series of honorific titles that became part of his propaganda campaigns in the 1970s: "Helmsman," "Founding President," "Father of the Nation," and "Revolutionary Guide." Many popular musicians, also deeply concerned with their status as leaders, adopted this aesthetic of authority by playing on the imagery of military strongmen to assert their power as artists. This preference for strong, charismatic leadership and the tendency toward splintering as a means of establishing political authority led to what people in Kinshasa today refer to as *guidomanie* (from Mobutu's use of the term *guide*), or the obsessive preoccupation with having a following and becoming a *leader*.[3]

One of the most striking examples of this *guidomanie* is the title track from J. B. M'piana's 2000 album T.H., which was seen not only as a response to Werra Son's *Solola Bien* (1999) but also as an important follow-up to M'piana's own *Titanic* (1998).[4] The music video for the song "T.H." is typical of most music videos produced in Kinshasa. There is no story line or scenario: the song consists of a series of choreographed dance sequences, and the musicians are dressed in coordinated outfits (in this video the latest gear from the hip-hop fashion designer FUBU), with M'piana ("The no. 1 Sovereign") dressed differently from the other musicians in the band. M'piana is surrounded by a dozen or so musicians arranged in a pyramid formation behind him singing the praises of their leader, who is visibly excited to be dancing in spite of what seems like a feigned indifference in the lyrics:

Souverain azali champion, solo tokobanga te

Souverain azali champion, solo tokobanga te . . .

The Sovereign is champion, we have nothing to fear

The Sovereign is champion, we have nothing to fear . . .

Souverain a bangi naye baye kobenga ye	He was keeping to himself and they called him
Souverain a bangi naye baye kobenga ye	He was keeping to himself and they called him
Po na nini?	Why?
A beti liboso Zenith	First he played the Zenith [theater in Paris]
A beti lisusu Olympia	Then he played the Olympia
Bapesi ye disque d'or, match esili	Next a gold record and then he won the match
Biso tozali *humble* . . .	We are humble . . .

The song's introduction borrows musical elements from the performances accompanying the state-sponsored political rallies that during the 1970s and 1980s intended to show the "unconditional support" of the Zairian people for their nation and its leader, a genre of political propaganda that became known as *animation politique et culturelle* (see chapter 3). The irony of this video is not that it borrows from the aesthetics of cultural propaganda under the Mobutu regime, since as I will discuss later this particular performative genre had become ubiquitous in the national media by the early 1980s. What is ironic is that M'piana would surround himself with such ceremony, bragging about his accomplishments and demonstrating the loyalty of his followers, while making a claim about his leadership qualities based on his ability to remain "always humble"; the title of the song "T.H." stands for the French expression *toujours humble*" (figure 1). This is the kind of doublespeak for which Mobutu became famous, and the celebrities of the popular music scene of the 1990s mobilized similar rhetorical strategies to the point where it was unclear whether they themselves were fully conscious of their actions.

Popular Culture and Politics

As the dominant form of popular cultural production in Zaire since at least the 1940s, popular dance music in Kinshasa is an excellent example of the privileged form of cultural expression that becomes instrumental in the articulation of national identities (Abu-Lughod 2005). If music from the Congo is often touted as "Africa's most influential pop music" (Barlow and Eyre 1995, 27), and the Congo's "richest and most distinctive gift to the con-

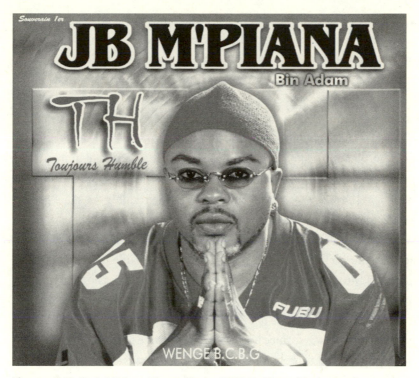

Figure 1. T. H. (J. B. M'piana, Wenge Musica B.C.B.G., Simon Music, 2000).

tinent" (Fabian 1998, 82), it is not because of the music's politics. Indeed, the joyful sound of the music and the playful eroticism of the choreographed dance sequences can easily suggest the complete absence of politics in Congolese popular music. Through stereotypes about singing, dancing, and having a good time, the words and sounds of Congolese popular music—and by extension Congolese popular musicians themselves—have come to stand for Congolese identity far beyond the Congo's borders. A Congolese music promoter, Socrates, with whom I worked in Kinshasa explained that the stereotypes about Congolese he encountered while traveling in other parts of Africa were very often related to music: "'You work?' people used to say to me, 'We thought you guys didn't work. We thought you just sing and dance all the time.' They must think we eat music," he said, visibly amazed that anyone could be so ignorant about his country (interview with Socrates, December 21, 1995).

In fact, popular music is hard work, especially in the contexts of economic crisis and political instability that came to characterize Zaire. One of the things that this book will show is how musicians under Mobutu developed a way of organizing and performing music that enabled them to compensate for the effects of the crisis. For example, consider Congolese music's unique two-part song structure: a slow lyrical section followed by a fast-paced dance sequence. This structural innovation, which did not clearly emerge until the 1970s, made it possible for musicians to extend the period of time for choreographed dancing, an aspect of live performance that assured musicians a regular clientele in concerts following the dramatic decrease of record sales in the middle part of the decade. In addition to these changes in the structure of the music, and during roughly the same period, popular music in Kinshasa witnessed the emergence of a phenomenon known as *libanga*, where wealthy patrons and public figures offer money to musicians in exchange for being cited or sung by name. Beginning in the 1980s and throughout the 1990s, *libanga* became an increasingly important source of income for Kinshasa's most well-known musicians, but it also became a way for musicians to urge those in positions of power to act in socially responsible ways, since *libanga* aims to activate patron-client relations and references the fear of abandonment that can exist in economies with structural limits on the redistribution of wealth.

The question of socially responsible leadership is one that will appear frequently in my analysis, not only because musicians are preoccupied with this issue but also because the question of leadership is one that symbolically links politics and popular music in this context. During a return visit to Kinshasa, I was traveling in a taxi with several friends and having a conversation about bandleaders, a common topic among musicians. The conversation began as do most good conversations about music in Kinshasa: "Les musiciens sont bizarres!" (Musicians are bizarre!). Then my friends began to share stories about musicians' jealousy, vanity, extravagance, and hunger for power. One friend, who up until that point had been mostly listening, decided to share some aspects of his personal experience, in particular the attitude of his bandleader. He spoke about the fact that musicians were rarely paid, suffered insults in front of peers and fans, and were left in the dark about the band's movements or the bandleader's strategies. As he vented his frustration, I could see that our conversation had touched on a sensitive topic and that he was dealing with strong feelings of resentment: "The way they act is just like Mobutu, exactly like Mobutu." His voice filled with anger, almost visibly shaking, as he tried to come to terms with his own band-leader's indifference. "It's the same thing; they make all these decisions and they don't listen to anyone, no one!" Indeed, in the minds of many people in Kinshasa, musicians and politicians resemble each other in a number of important ways: They are gluttonous, not only with food and money, but also in their relations with the opposite sex. They have a fixation with imported luxury items. They speak in an aggressive manner to avoid appearing weak-minded or feeble. They are intolerant of dissent and opposed to the idea of sharing power.

The links between popular music and politics, however, go deeper than the image that musicians portray in public: they are also located in the social organization, the performance, and the sound of the music. Take for example the *atalaku*, the musician in every dance band who brings live performance to life by singing and shouting the short percussive phrases that have come to stand for the sound of modern Congolese dance music. As a necessary element of every self-respecting dance band, and yet a musician who invariably finds himself at the bottom of the band hierarchy, the *atalaku* plays a crucial but ambiguous role in the music. The story of the emergence of the *atalaku* is important, especially because of the *atalaku*'s relationship to cultural policy under Mobutu. While not an invention of the propaganda machine of the Mobutu regime, the *atalaku* was a product of the political culture in which propaganda thrived and thus retains important elements of the cultural propaganda initiatives of the 1970s and 1980s. An ethnographic analysis of the *atalaku* phenomenon enables us to see the larger context of this political reality: how cultural policy under Mobutu encouraged the objectification of tradition, how economic policy during the same period caused musicians to remain dependent on the state, and how authoritarian rule in the Congo reproduced itself through a culture of praise and self-promotion.

The *atalaku*'s primary instrument, apart from his voice, is a hollowed-out metal insecticide spray can that is modified to be used as a maracas (figure 2). This instrument has always been a part of Congolese popular music, but in the early years musicians used imported gourd-style maracas (as those common in Afro-Cuban music of the period). Young musicians in the 1970s, faced with an increasingly precarious economy and a music scene controlled by older musicians with close ties to the regime, struggled to gain

Figure 2. Insecticide
maracas. PHOTO:
BOB W. WHITE.

access to professional-quality instruments. This, they say, was the primary
reason they began fabricating spray-can maracas, which over time have become an iconic symbol of the popular dance music in Kinshasa. From the
atalaku's point of view, the choice of this particular type of can—one made of
a high-quality, durable metal that resonates loudly enough to eliminate the
need for its own microphone—is not random. Most *atalaku* prefer it over a
myriad of other cans (for example perfume spray, powdered milk, sardines,
etc.), primarily because of its sound [audio], but also because the production of this instrument stands as a sign of resourcefulness (*débrouillardise*).
The musician who presented me with my first spray can maracas was visibly
proud of his recycling skills. He explained how he had removed the nozzle,
perforated each line of sound holes, and opened a small triangular door on
the bottom for inserting the hardwood tree seeds that we would look for
together. I have held onto the image of this instrument not only because it

CHAPTER ONE

represents the *atalaku*, a central character in my story, but also because of how the maracas evoke a time of crisis, when Kinshasa's mosquito problem became a metaphor for economic and political insecurity.[5]

Attempts to understand the significance of music in non-Western societies are generally associated with ethnomusicology and with research that focuses on the role of musical performance in relatively isolated classless societies, primarily outside of western Europe and North America. Early studies in this area set out to catalogue cultural diversity by documenting stylistic and instrumental variation, and they tended to view music as an external expression of a cultural core or sensibility (Chernoff 1979). At least as far back as the 1960s ethnomusicology was plagued by an almost existential dilemma that pitted the study of music against the study of culture, and the social sciences against the humanities (Merriam 1964). But as Steven Feld carefully points out (2001), the field of ethnomusicology emerged primarily within the institutional context of musicology, a fact ignored even by many anthropologists. Before the 1980s there was very little research and writing on popular music, which many ethnomusicologists still considered a deracinated, contaminated form of "traditional" music (Barber 1997, 1). But in the late 1980s and early 1990s the first in-depth ethnographies of popular music began to appear (Coplan 1985; Waterman 1990), and by the mid-1990s an important number of books were published on popular music outside the West (Guilbault 1993; Averill 1997; Erlmann 1996), most of them written by scholars with training in ethnomusicology. During this period, while the anthropological study of music still tended to be confused with ethnomusicology, there was at least a growing acceptance of the idea that the study of popular music, and popular culture more generally, could tell us something about the complex relationship between culture and politics.

The term *popular culture* always runs the risk of being confused with *popular arts* (White 2006c). The latter term refers to any form of cultural activity or cultural production framed in terms of its status as a cultural product or performance. This includes but is not limited to the performing arts (dance, theater, music, storytelling, comedy), the visual arts (painting, sculpture, handicrafts, cartoons, music videos), certain forms of popular fiction and film, and certain forms of decoration (including graffiti, houses, taxis, coffins, bodies). These categories thus form a subset of the larger category of popular culture, which in addition to everything mentioned above also includes orally based forms of cultural expression (rumors, sayings, language, jokes, prayers), public forms of festivity and competition (sports, carnival, beauty pageants), and everyday practices and gestures that transcend ethnic categories of folklore or tradition. The particular case of popular culture presented in this monograph—Congolese popular dance music—shares two important characteristics with other forms of popular culture. First, it is commercially robust, meaning that it is integrated into large-scale social and commercial networks and therefore contributes and perpetuates the circulation of cultural products in general. Second, it is supra-ethnic, meaning that by virtue of its extended visibility (and audibility), it is accessible to a large number and wide variety of consumers, regardless of their ethnic or linguistic origin.

With this definition it is possible to distinguish popular culture from culture in a strictly anthropological sense, where the latter is generally associated with a system of beliefs, values, and practices, and the former most often takes the form of a product or performance. Because popular culture is often implicated in large-scale networks of commercial production and distribution, it enables us to see larger structural processes such as the formation of national identities, the movement of international capital, and the commercialization of cultural products and performances (Hunt 2002). Its ability to circulate widely makes popular culture a kind of trace element for thinking beyond local boundaries (White 2002). At the same time, the study of popular culture gives us privileged access to information about how identities are constructed and constrained within these larger global structures (Jules-Rosette and Martin 1997). In this sense popular culture can be seen as a corrective to received cultural theory (Fabian 1998), not only because it sheds light on new areas of cultural production but also because it forces us to think of culture as something that takes place at the intersection of local experience and "larger impersonal systems" (Marcus and Fischer 1986, 77). The challenge from the point of view of anthropology is not only to show "how the powerful moments in popular music are accomplished" (Walser and McClary 1990, 289) but also how the power of these moments is related to the music's ability to reference things outside of itself, what Tsitsi Dangaremba refers to as music's capacity to "point unsystematic fingers at the conditions of the times" (1988, 4).

The study of political culture—a relatively recent phenomenon in anthropological literature—attempts to apply anthropological research methods to the structures and discourses of the modern state.[6] The turn toward a more empirically grounded qualitative approach has meant that anthropological and historical accounts have played a prominent role in this emerging scholarly literature.[7] While studies of political culture do not form a coherent body of writing or research, many of these analyses share the basic premise that nation-states are always situated in history: "Instead of talking about the state as an entity that always, already consists of certain features, functions, and forms of governance, let us approach each actual state as a historically specific configuration of stateness" (Hansen and Stepputat 2001, 7). This "stateness" comes in many shapes and sizes, but in many parts of sub-Saharan Africa it is often grounded in complex dialectics of authoritarian rule (Mbembe 1992a), though the analysis of state formation as a historical process enables us to see how these dynamics are entangled in the history of colonial rule (Mamdani 1996). With the proliferation of new types of "invisible governance" (Hecht and Simone 1994), local ideas about extralocal identities are increasingly articulated through singing (Askew 2002; Meintjes 2003), dancing (Castaldi 2006; Durham 2002; Taylor 1998), painting (Fabian 1996; Jewsiewicki 1995), and other forms of popular cultural performance.

Thus popular culture represents a powerful analytical tool for understanding political culture, which I define simply as the culturally patterned beliefs and practices that inform the way that power is sought after, yielded, and understood. Using examples from my fieldwork with musicians in Kinshasa, I will try to paint a portrait of how popular culture and political culture have held each other up and fixed each other in place, not only through tangible relations of clientelism and praise but also through a common idiom of big man–style leadership. Is it going too far to suggest that popular dance music can reveal something new about politics in Mobutu's Zaire? Possibly. But some twenty years after Johannes Fabian's important early article on popular culture, I believe that we still "must ask ourselves whether the concept of popular culture (and especially our emphasis on its originality and vigor) does not lead to a surreptitious denial of the political processes of class struggle and its neo-colonial suppression" (1978, 329). Popular music in Kinshasa is interesting not only because of its "power and beauty" (Fabian 1998, 86) but also because of how it uses—and is used by—the institutions of power. It is a mediating force that provides us with new ways of understanding politics and popular consciousness: how expressions of power are embodied in the act of performance, how officialdom makes use of the voices of music, how structural and stylistic elements of artistic expression are tied to long-term political delinquency and neglect.[8] And these factors—to be seen as more of an agonistic dance with power than a resistance to it (Mbembe 2001)—are part of what makes popular dance music so political.

Ultimately, however, popular culture is more than just a solution to theoretical problems. It is a way of bringing anthropologists closer to the political implications of the work they do as self-appointed observers of other people's cultures. By its very nature, popular culture leads us to ask difficult questions about relations of power, unequal access to resources, the role of the state, and the complex processes by which culture is produced, reproduced, and made public. It urges us to confront our discomfort with the products of mass commercial desire and with cultural practices too often dismissed as derivative or inauthentic. It compels us to critically examine the decisions we make before we ever get to the field, decisions concerning what type of phenomena are to be considered "cultural" and our options concerning how to engage with them (Hannerz 1992, 251). Following Lila Abu-Lughod I want to argue that the most important reason for studying popular culture is that it belongs to a world in which, in some sense, anthropologists are also natives (2005, 52).

From Brazzaville to Kinshasa

At roughly the same time as Max Gluckman and a team of scholars affiliated with the Rhodes-Livingstone Institute in Northern Rhodesia (later to become known as the Manchester School), Georges Balandier was conducting research on cities and urban phenomena in West and Central Africa. Like Gluckman, Balandier was at the center of a network of Africanist scholars (he became the first director of the Centre d'Études Africaines at the École des Hautes Études en Sciences Sociales in Paris in 1957), and his teaching and research influenced an entire generation of young scholars in Europe and Africa. Balandier was well read in British social anthropology, especially that of Gluckman and his followers, with whom he shared an emphasis on whole, interrelating systems and on the centrality of conflict in the analysis of social change. Balandier's work is especially relevant to my research, not

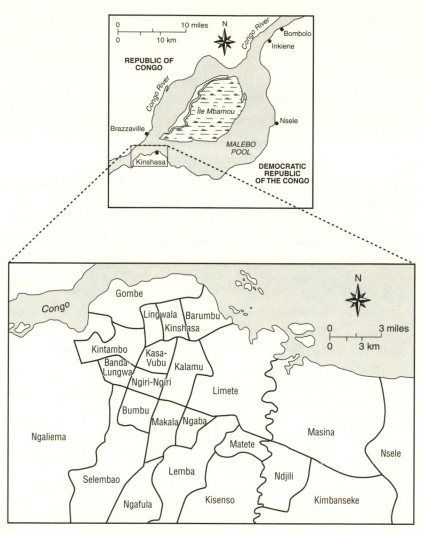

Map 2. Map of Kinshasa and the Malebo Pool.

only because he spent considerable time in the Pool region that both separates and unites Kinshasa and Brazzaville (see map 2) but also because his
writing gives a sense of why people go to a city, what they do there, and why
they stay. "For better or worse," Balandier wrote in the opening lines of his
now classic monograph, "the fabric of the new Africa is the city" (1985, vii).
Indeed, it was Balandier's reading of African urban life in the late colonial
period, wonderfully condensed in his expression la *passion moderniste*, that
served as the intellectual frame for my doctoral dissertation. Balandier's re-

search is also important because it served as a counterweight to the Manchester School, which, it can be argued, was limited by too narrow a focus on historically unique urban labor arrangements, such as those that predominated in the copper belt region of southern Central Africa, and by an overreliance on the determinacy of structure.

I spent the first two months of my research in Brazzaville, looking at Kinshasa through the eyes of Balandier. I had read *Sociologie des Brazzavilles noires* from cover to photocopied cover, and I was fully prepared to see the city not as a place, but as a process, one that was contingent and incomplete. Even after the first phase of my research was underway, I remained open to the idea that if for some reason Kinshasa was too dangerous or too big, I would always have Brazzaville, and I would always have Balandier. He, too, had one eye on the other Congo:

> "Across the way," to use a stock phrase, is a real city. Leopoldville lies in a fine mist, lifting a single tall building. From a distance, the comparison with the French capital is still a harmless game. . . . Up close, the inferiority complex of certain Brazzavillians is easy to understand: concrete roads, numerous commercial buildings, modern hotels with noiseless servants and the latest mechanical gadgets; finally, the avenue congested with American cars. Impressions of opulence, speculation, of the bold persistence of a capitalism that is off to a new start, unlike French colonial capitalism, which has surrendered all risks to the public powers. The Congolese Belgians reveal a certain upstart's arrogance: optimism, a sense of superiority, and an unshakable confidence in the future of their system. (1985, 180–81)

It is difficult to resist the temptation to read this passage as an allegory of Franco-American relations. Balandier's vision of the Congolese from "across the way" sounds strikingly similar to the way that the French describe the United States: possessing the latest technology, widespread opulence, "a certain upstart's arrogance," unshakable confidence in its capitalism, and of course cars everywhere. I hardly think that this reading would surprise Balandier, who began his 1957 *Ambiguous Africa* with the daring proposition that to explain other cultures is inevitably to explain oneself. Perhaps such a reading is obvious to me because as an American I felt strangely at home in Kinshasa. The people I met in Kinshasa were friendly, bold, and proud to be *zaïrois*. Unlike people in Brazzaville, who assume that you prefer to be spoken to in French, people in Kinshasa are not reluctant to speak to foreigners in Lingala. Much like Americans, they hold deep and often uncritical convictions about their country's importance—both geographically and geopolitically—and the presence of foreigners in the Congo only serves to reinforce their ideas about the Congo's place in the world.

Since I had no contacts in Kinshasa, I had prepared myself for the possibility that my fieldwork would begin and end in Brazzaville, where I had the names of two people, a customs officer who worked at the airport and an administrator at the Zairian embassy. When I arrived at the airport in Brazzaville, the customs officer found me before I found her. She was tall, neatly pressed, and a bit gruff, but when her subordinates were out of our sight she gave me a complicit grin as she whisked me through the airport and put me in an "express" taxi (meaning no other passengers and no stops along the way) to the Zairian embassy. At the embassy no one was expecting me. The only introduction I had was a note from a close friend in Brussels, whose aunt worked at the embassy and who I was told could help me find a place to stay on arrival. The aunt in question agreed to rent me a small studio in the family's compound in Poto Poto, which was very close to Mbakas Street where most of the city's music distributors were based. From this base I divided my time between interviewing a handful of first-generation musicians still based in Brazzaville (Jean-Serge Essous, Edo Nganga, Nino Malapet, and others), attempting to establish contact with officials from the Ministry of Culture, and trying to track down music producers and distributors. Working in Brazzaville was difficult. Not many people seemed genuinely enthusiastic about my project, and the work I was doing lacked focus and energy, so I decided to make a trip to Kinshasa.

Crossing the river was short work. In fact, people living in the Pool region often remind visitors that Brazzaville and Kinshasa, separated by a mere twenty-minute ferry ride, are the two closest capitals in the world. What is difficult about this ride is the fear of what waits on the other side. In the days leading up to my trip I heard countless horror stories about the *zaïrois* and their corruption, and about how *le beach* (the place where the ferry lands) is a viper's nest of officials and fake officials whose only goal is to strip you of everything you have. "If you know someone, or if you have a lot of money you can make it through okay," a friend in Brazzaville told me; "otherwise forget it." Unfortunately, I had neither. As the ferry started out against the current, I was taken with a feeling of excitement about the idea of having my own Congo River crossing story. My excitement turned to anxiety when we got close enough to see people on the opposite shore pushing and shoving to get a good position on the dock. I tried to remain calm by focusing on the sound of the ferry motor and the rushing water, but with little success. As soon as the ferry touched the dock, people from both sides started scrambling in every direction, and from that moment on the rest became a blur. Somehow I managed to get through customs with my belongings and what was left of my savings, but once away from the beach, Kinshasa seemed like a totally different city.

It became obvious relatively soon that a lot of research needed to be done on music in Kinshasa. The first few people I met in the Kinshasa music scene (Ilo Pablo and Claude Lengos from Zaiko Familia Dei, the music chronicler and television personality Manda Tchebwa, and Lofombo from Empire Bakuba) were extremely helpful, and they also put me in contact with other people from the business. Here music presented itself as a source of livelihood for many people, a fact that would prove beneficial for my research. During the week there were bands practicing all over the city. Throughout the long Kinshasa weekend (Thursday to Sunday), it was possible to see any number of top-billed groups playing live in concert. Wherever there was electricity there was loud music blaring into the night, especially the sound of the new dance step *kitisela* that would later mutate into *ndombolo* and dominate the music scene for nearly a decade. Musicians were a visible part of the urban landscape; they were painted on storefronts, plastered on billboards, filling the television screens, driving by in expensive cars. Kinshasa was not simply filled with music; it seemed held together by music. A taxi driver told me something that I would hear again and again in the following months: "If you want to understand the music, you have to understand this city."

Looking back on this period, I am not entirely sure why I was reluctant to begin my research in Kinshasa. Maybe because Brazzaville, which is one-fifth the size of Kinshasa, seemed more navigable than the Zairian capital. Or maybe because so many people had told me that Kinshasa was spiraling out of control and that the idea of doing research there seemed dangerous, if not impossible. Or maybe because in the late 1980s and early 1990s a number of important producers and distributors had been based in Kinshasa, but

Figure 3. Place des Artistes, Matonge, Kinshasa. PHOTO: SERGE MAKOBO.

when I arrived the region's most important recording studio was located just outside of Brazzaville. Whatever the reason, as soon as I set foot in Kinshasa, I immediately knew that I had to get out of Brazzaville. The musical activity in Brazzaville was limited to a few nightclubs and large-scale music distributors, elements that failed to give an accurate sense of the dynamics of the music industry as a whole. With the exception of the occasional group on tour from Kinshasa, there was almost no live music scene in Brazzaville. Kinshasa, on the other hand, was alive, and despite what many foreigners to the region had told me before leaving, the music scene was on fire.

As are most cities of more than five million, Kinshasa is overflowing with automobiles, billboards and neon signs, tall buildings, satellite dishes, and cellular phones (figure 3). People in Kinshasa show their urban colors through a whole series of cultural markers such as language (Lingala with bits of French is the language of choice), dress (women combine high heels with three-piece traditional dresses made of local or imported wax cloth; men wear dress slacks, dress shirts, and imported leather shoes), and education (apart from politics and music, this is still the primary means of social status and advancement). The particular neighborhood they call home can

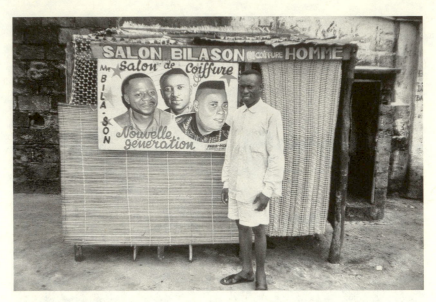

Figure 4. Salon Bilason, men's hair salon with picture of Papa Wemba, Reddy Amisi, and Kester Emeneya. PHOTO: BOB W. WHITE.

be a marker of social status just as it can be a source of silence or shame (since those from the poor areas of the city tend not to draw attention to their place of residence), but it is also a place of comfort. For many young people in Kinshasa, however, the best place to find a livelihood is abroad, presumably somewhere in Europe (*poto* or *Miguel*) or North America (*Super Miguel*), almost always with the intention of a glorious return to the black man's Europe (*poto mwindo*), Kinshasa.

While it may be a cliché to say that music occupies a special place in Kinshasa's urban landscape, it still needs to be said. Music animates households, taxis, storefronts, and bars (figures 4 and 5). It floods the airwaves of local television and radio stations, regardless of their religious or political affiliation. In the morning, storekeepers begin their day by putting out the loudspeakers. The music they choose attracts customers, but it also helps them wake up and find the energy to begin sweeping last night's leftovers and yesterday's waste. The music played will change throughout the day, alternating primarily between American-inspired Christian hymns and one or another of the numerous splinter groups that resulted from the latest series of internal band conflicts. The nonstop sounds, which are fine coming out of public address systems with cracked speakers, also have a visual effect. They

Figure 5. Welo Wasenga pictured in front of his hair salon, which features a portrait of Lutumba Simaro and other members of the group Bana O.K. PHOTO: BOB W. WHITE.

bring to life the posters and commercial paintings of famous musicians that decorate places of business across the city. The quick and dirty music videos that accompany virtually every album produced in Kinshasa keep the private television stations afloat since the advertisements that separate them also reference the musical idiom of *ambiance* so often evoked but almost never properly defined.[9]

As state structures and market mechanisms of the 1990s fell into further decay, Kinshasa increasingly came to be known as a place of violence and crisis (Biaya 1997; De Boeck 2005; De Boeck and Plissant 2005; Devisch 1995; Tsambu Bulu 2004; Yoka 1995, 2000).[10] People have become accustomed to the almost palpable mixture of exhaust, dirt, and dust that results from too many years of political neglect. With a state of generalized unemployment (at least in official terms), most people accept the fact that their earning potential is not enough to enable them to pay even for shared private taxis. So instead they wait, often for hours, to get a space in one of the large transport trucks known locally as *fulafula* (from the English *full*). As midnight approaches, those still waiting give in one by one and begin the long trek home on foot. People often say, "Mboka ekufi" (the country is dead), and for some time now "Kinshasa la Belle" has been known as "Kinshasa la Poubelle" (Kinshasa the Garbage Can). "This is not Kinshasa," explained Wendo Kolosoy, the doyen of modern Congolese rumba. "You should have been here before; it used to be a beautiful place, the most beautiful city in all of Africa! You could dance without working up a sweat. Now it's all dust and noise" (personal communication, June 1999). Throughout my research in Kinshasa, I heard a similar sentiment expressed often with the same frustration and bewilderment. How, I wondered, could one of the most beautiful cities in Africa come to be likened to a garbage can? And how could a garbage can produce something so full of power and beauty?[11]

As an ethnography of popular music at the end of the Mobutu regime, this book explores the links, both material and symbolic, between the performance of popular dance music and the emergence of a particular type of political culture in Mobutu's Zaire. To do this requires not only attending to the details of how popular music is produced and performed but also considering how music constitutes a privileged space for playing out certain scenarios with regard to what it means to be a "bon chef" (good leader). My central argument is that at each stage of its development since independence, popular music in Kinshasa has acted as a mediating force between the city's rapidly growing population of youths, who try to navigate their way through a complex political economy of clientage and authoritarian rule not of their making, and a state-based class of political elites who rely on music as a mechanism of political legitimacy since, as Mobutu was so fond of saying, "happy are those who sing and dance." Outside of politics and (to a lesser extent) education, popular music would become one of the few paths to upward social mobility for young people in Kinshasa, and this proved important as participation in political life became increasingly subject to the whims of those in power. Because of Mobutu's particular style of political leadership, one that attempted to create an image of him as an *homme fort* (military strongman) but also as an *homme du peuple* (man of the people), popular musicians (themselves mostly from modest backgrounds) were instrumental in shoring up support for the regime. The problem with this arrangement, however, was that it gave musicians little or no room for artistic or political freedom, and that the musicians successful under these conditions ended up unwittingly reproducing the organizational and symbolic mechanisms that would make Mobutu one of the most hated and feared political leaders in modern African history.

Chapter 1 (the current chapter) introduces several theoretical concepts important for the critical study of popular music in an African context, most notably popular culture and political culture, but it also takes a preliminary look at the context that gave rise to the uniquely urban cultural phenomenon of popular music in Kinshasa. In chapter 2 I present a brief overview of the primary genres of popular music in Kinshasa (religious, traditional, and modern). This is followed by a more in-depth look at my principal object of study, la musique moderne, and a consideration of how it evolved over several generations through various types of accommodation and aesthetic borrowing, especially from urban traditional music. Chapter 3 considers the political economy in which Zairian popular music emerged: first, it examines the ideological aspects and political consequences of Mobutu's cultural policy (especially the impact of the regime's authenticité campaign); second, it asks how the decline of the music industry caused musicians to become almost entirely dependent on the informal sector for the promotion and distribution of their music. These initial chapters provide important musical and historical information that serve as the backdrop from which to understand the larger question of how popular music is related to the emerging political culture of the postcolonial era.

The following three chapters give some sense of the ethnographic present that constitutes the core of this study: the social organization and public meanings associated with the performance of popular dance music in the final years of the Mobutu regime (1990–96). In chapter 4, I give a detailed description of the live concert atmosphere in Kinshasa during this period, focusing primarily on the dynamics of live performance and the various types of interaction among musicians and members of the audience. Chapter 5 considers the trajectories of a number of different musicians as they aspired toward upward social mobility through a career in popular music. A good part of this chapter examines my own experience as a member of a moderately successful local dance band, a story that provides some insight into the inner workings of the music scene in Kinshasa, but also provides important information about my field research. The material in chapter 6 is primarily concerned with the way in which popular song texts play into different aspects of oral culture and sociability outside the confines of the local music scene. More specifically, it considers the role that lyrics play in expressing a central motif in Congolese political culture in the 1990s—the fear of abandonment—and how this dynamic is played out through the relatively recent phenomenon of citing or "throwing" the names of people who can provide financial or political protection.

The final two chapters, which combine elements of description with more critical analysis, revolve around the question of what exactly links the performance of popular music to the world of politics. Chapter 7 describes the social organization of musical groups in Kinshasa during the period under consideration, with special attention paid to the way that hierarchies are organized and held in place. The second part of this chapter looks at how an ethos of charismatic authoritarian leadership is reinforced through the dynamic of "dislocation" or organizational splintering. The final chapter (chapter 8) is an extended reflection on Mobutu's political legacy and on how in many ways it represents a skewed version of local ideas about musical and political leadership. Applied to the context of popular music, this chapter attempts to work through certain social and political ideals that in some sense emanate from "tradition," especially the idea of political leadership as a form of reciprocity, or what one musician referred to as an "agreement." But it also tries to come to terms with the fact that one style of political leadership—that of the witch and not the chief—came to dominate political and social life during the postcolonial era and asks exactly what role popular music played in making this political culture the only game in town.

THE ZAIRIAN SOUND

TO UNDERSTAND THE POLITICAL CULTURE OF
popular music during the Mobutu era, it is necessary to examine the musical entanglements that occurred between
musique moderne and various types of state-sponsored traditional music, or *folklore*. In some cases these entanglements turned out to be defining characteristics of the
popular music genre, such as the fast-paced dance sequence at the end of each song or the role of the *atalaku*,
both of which will be described in some detail at the end
of this chapter. Of course there is nothing unique about
modern music borrowing ideas from traditional music,
especially in the context of African popular music. What
does deserve special attention is the way in which this
borrowing occurred, namely, through the highly mediated state-sponsored political rallies that used *folklore* as
part of Mobutu's cultural politics of *authenticité*, a topic I
will discuss in greater detail in chapter 3. Some information about the history of Congolese popular music has
been included here, but this chapter is not intended as
a chronology of the musical style, a project that is well
under way elsewhere. Instead, I attempt to identify important trends in the musical style over time and complement these observations with individual stories or cases.

Before discussing the genres of popular music in the Congo, it is important to comment on the genres of writing that have taken Congolese popular music as their object of study. A number of full-length monographs combine popular history and biography to provide the reader with a general overview of popular dance music in Congo-Zaire. The first book in this category is Michel Lonoh's *Essai de commentaire de la musique Congolaise moderne* (1969), in many ways the first text to attempt a serious sociological reading of the phenomenon of popular dance music. Emerging from the long wake of silence that followed Lonoh's work, Sylvain Bemba's *Cinquante ans de musique du Congo-Zaïre* (1984) offers a wealth of detail about many of the most important figures in the music scene and presents an original literary reading of the music's social significance. Unfortunately, it suffers from what seems to be the need to reclaim the musical style for Brazzaville Congolese.[1] More recently, two monographs stand out as comprehensive and original: Manda Tchebwa's *La terre de la chanson* (1996) and Gary Stewart's *Rumba on the River* (2000). Tchebwa's book has a sociological feel and shows wide coverage of music-related issues from a distinctly *kinois* point of view. Stewart's book — no less interesting, though for different reasons — is richly documented, rigorous in its attention to detail, and unsurpassed in terms of its coverage of musical biographies, though it is much stronger on the first and second generations than the third generation, and the music of the fourth generation is almost completely absent from his analysis. Perhaps for this reason he refers to the 1990s as "grey."

Over the past thirty years, a huge amount of information has been published within the Congo in the form of music journalism (*chronique de la musique*). The widely read early music magazines that began to be popular in the 1970s (*Disco Hit, L'as des as, Super Star*) and the newspapers with a cultural bent (*Salongo* and *Elima*) were mostly concerned with providing a hungry public with information about the private lives of the stars, their social comings and goings, and various types of inter- and intraband conflict. Outside of the Congo, serious music journalists like Martin Sinnock (of the *Beat*) have worked with specialized music magazines in Europe and North America and are primarily concerned with providing various audiences with information about new trends in various types of exotic or "roots" music. In a similar vein there exist a number of well-researched books giving general information about African music and artists by region (Barlow and Eyre 1995; Bender

1991; Ewens 1991) and about Congolese artists in particular (Ewens 1994; Lokole 1985).

Much of the academic literature on popular music has been concerned with themes in song lyrics (Luzibu 1973; Mwissa 1993; Tshonga various; Walu 1999); for obvious reasons it is more focused on the social significance of texts than on aesthetic or political aspects of the music. Several accounts of Congolese popular music have attempted to discuss the style in historical terms. The most well-known examples are discussions about the origins of the music (Kazadi 1979; Lonoh 1969), which seem primarily concerned with showing that this genre of music results from the intersection of various local and foreign musical forms in the context of the colonial city. Some historical scholarship has also attempted to look at the relationship between music and the development of an African urban consciousness during the colonial period (Gondola 1992; White 2002). For the postcolonial period, Debhonvapi Olema (1998) explores social critique and expressions of satire in the musical rhetoric of the Zairian singer Luambo Makiadi (also known as "Franco"), while P. Ngandu Nkashama (1979, 1992) focuses on the theme of rupture to examine how the performance of popular music interacts with various states of postcolonial consciousness and alienation.

Popular Music and Genre

Anthropology is no different from the rest of the human sciences in the sense that it begins with the impulse to categorize: Boasian cultural philology, classificatory kinship systems, comparative mythology, and comparative political systems. This taxonomic impulse has a life and a history of its own, and it has remained a central concern to the discipline, but it must be seen as part and parcel of long-standing Western discourses about science and knowledge (Fabian 1983). Not so distant cousins of anthropology such as folklore studies and ethnomusicology have been able to reproduce themselves through their commitment to collecting, the necessary precondition for classification. Literary studies and art history have put genre at the center of their intellectual agenda, but as Charles Briggs and Richard Bauman have argued, "the use of genre as a classificatory concept does not necessarily imply self-conscious attention to classification itself as an intellectual problem" (1992, 144). For these reasons, I am interested in the potential of ethnographic analysis to show how genre is embedded in various moments of cultural practice and performance.[2] As Johannes Fabian has shown, the process of the differentiation of genres shows concern with classification and thus with normativity: "Genre—much like value, norm, standard—embodies cultural injunctions to know what belongs and what doesn't, what is proper and what isn't, what is well crafted and what is *bricolage*" (1998, 41).

Genre often expresses itself as a marker of social distinction (Bourdieu 1984), but this stands as only one example of how genre works in society and how society works through genre. Peter Seitel's work on genre and epic tales among the Haya of Tanzania challenges us to see genre not as a set of rules, but as a way of working out the rules, since genre relies on speech, and "all speech answers and refers to other speech already spoken" (1999, 15). The Russian philosopher and literary critic Mikhail Bakhtin saw genres as repositories of social memory located in "the objective forms of culture itself," meaning that genres exist in relation to one another: "Thus, no new artistic genre nullifies or replaces old ones. But at the same time, every essential and significant new genre, once it has arrived on the scene, exerts an influence on the whole range of genres: a new genre heightens the consciousness of the old genres, so to speak; it causes them to better perceive their possibilities and their boundaries" (1986, 229). The fluidity of generic boundaries is of practical significance to the theoretical study of genre, and recent scholarship on the Congo provides some interesting examples of this phenomenon.[3]

If, as Robert Walser has claimed, "nowhere are genre boundaries more fluid than in popular music" (1993, 27), then what criteria should be used to define popular music genres? The identity of the artist? Stylistic features of the music? Musical structure? Instrumentation? Lyrical content? Audience-based perceptions? Marketing and sales categories? Simon Frith (1996) has shown how the generic categories of popular music result from various imperfect collusions between music makers, sellers, and listeners, with an end product that varies greatly from one record store to another. Despite the usefulness of this observation, we are still left with the sense that popular music genres are vague and fleeting. Walser, in what is one of the most intelligent analyses of popular music and genre to date, sets up his discussion of heavy metal music in opposition to more sociological approaches that are unable to go beyond lyrical analysis.[4] In the end, however, the answer to his question "what makes heavy metal heavy?" focuses almost exclusively on formal characteristics of the music (guitar distortion, volume, vocal timbre, mode and harmony, rhythm, and melody). Walser's analysis carefully situates these characteristics in a larger discursive field of heavy metal culture, but his focus on the music itself only swings the pendulum back on the same axis, a move that seems at odds with his emphasis on "how popular music circulates socially" (1993, 39).

Three basic genres of music exist in Kinshasa: modern, traditional, and religious.[5] Over the past fifty years, the three have coexisted and comingled, with the modern category taking up the most space—both sonically and symbolically—in urban centers and especially in Kinshasa. In fact, this music is so ubiquitous that many people do not have an obvious term for it apart from la musique zaïroise.[6] Some people referred to it as rumba, although in some situations this term refers specifically to Congolese popular music in its classical period (especially the 1950s and 1960s), when the majority of rumba-based rhythms were popularized.[7] Others referred to it as "young people's music" (la musique des jeunes), but this descriptor obviously failed to account for the various genres of popular music listened to by members of more than one generation. Throughout this chapter and for the rest of the book I will use the labels musique moderne and rumba, and the roughly equivalent English expression Congolese popular dance music, interchangeably.

In Kinshasa, popular dance music travels relatively freely across the social and cultural barriers of ethnicity, class, age, and religion. It is rare to meet people in Kinshasa with no knowledge or no opinions about la musique moderne. Nonetheless, some groups of people only listen to certain kinds of modern music, and some groups refuse to listen to any modern music whatsoever. For many practicing Christians, for example, musique moderne is not music at all but "the work of the devil" (une affaire de Satan). It is perceived as disrespectful, hedonistic, and immoral, blocking the various pathways between life on earth and the Kingdom of God. Beginning in the 1990s, a period of proliferating prayer groups and veillées spirituelles (lit. "spiritual late nights" or "vigils"), Christian piety has come to be defined in opposition to la musique profane and the world of ambiance (Biaya 1997). Listening practices also differ between generations, but they are less divisive. While older people view la musique des jeunes as a corrupt form of classical rumba, it is still considered a descendant of the latter tradition. From the perspective of seniors, young musicians are to be commended to the extent that they acknowledge their musical ancestors, but they will almost always be accused of straying too far from rumba's essence.

La Musique Moderne

The primary indicators of genre in popular discourse tend to be related to instrumentation and language. Thus *musique moderne* is defined by its use of Western instruments such as guitars and jazz-style drum kits (bass drum, snare, tom-tom, cymbals, etc.). With time these instruments have become increasingly mediated by electric or electronic technology (electric guitars, microphones with reverb, electronic keyboards, amplified percussion instruments such as congas and maracas). *La musique moderne* is sung primarily in Lingala, a local African language that for historical reasons stands as an icon of a cosmopolitan urban identity. When other Congolese languages (Swahili, Tshiluba, Kikongo) are used, their presence is conspicuous, though in the past twenty years Kikongo and Tshiluba have become more common during the animated dance sequences of many songs. In the rare cases in which Lingala is not used for the primary lyrics of the song, it is usually substituted with languages considered more cosmopolitan such as English, French, or Spanish.

The genre of *musique moderne* is also marked sonically, primarily by the strong presence of the electric guitar. Multiple guitar parts are carefully woven together to create a unique layered sound that bears some resemblance to the use of counterpoint in Western classical music. In much the same way as has been discussed for African percussion (see Chernoff 1979), guitars play off of each other, exploring combinations of harmonic and rhythmic complexity. Guitars themselves (especially bass guitars, but sometimes also rhythm guitars) are compared to drums because of the percussive ways in which they are played. The use of the guitar is likely the most promising area of future research on Congolese popular music, but will require the careful attention of specialists with training in musicology. Another important aspect of the sound is the use of parallel vocal harmonies. Singers, usually between three to five in number, will sing harmonies that begin at fixed intervals (thirds, fourths, fifths) up or down from the notes of the primary melody. This layering—together with the already layered multiple guitars—gives a thick, lush sound to the music, which is often described by non-native listeners as "rich" or "full" [audio].[8]

People in Kinshasa divide up the larger category of *musique moderne* in several ways. Some individual composers are known as poets or moralizers, but these skills are also considered markers of individual talent, thus it is unclear if they should serve as distinct categories within the larger family of modern music. There are also different types of band structures (sole founder, co-founder, nostalgia or cover bands, etc.), but these distinctions do not seem to correspond to any formal aspects of the music. Genre distinctions by generation and by aesthetic sensibility or "school" (traditional versus modern) probably stand as the most important ways of distinguishing different types of *musique moderne*. The characteristics of this music must be understood in the context of cultural politics during the Mobutu era, which promoted and sponsored certain types of supposedly traditional culture over others.

Le Folklore

In Kinshasa, traditional music (*le folklore*) is often heard at funeral mourning parties (*matanga*), which appear increasingly commonplace in recent years (see White 2005). It can also be heard at wedding ceremonies or in urban forms of traditional healing. Since this music usually accompanies important social events, it is often performed in a neighborhood or domestic setting. In the houses of wealthy families the group will play in a landscaped garden or on a patio. In middle-class or poorer families, the group is usually less well known and most likely composed of individuals from the neighborhood. In this setting, musicians play in the front courtyard of the house, sometimes acting as the primary attraction and sometimes serving as background entertainment.

When families cannot find a group of musicians specializing in the music from their home region or ethnic group, sometimes a prerecorded cassette is used.[9] Folklore groups use traditional instruments sometimes adapted for use in an urban setting (strings made from steel belting in tires, metal containers instead of gourds, modified electric thumb pianos, etc.); drums more often than not remain unaltered. The songs played by *folklore* groups are very often the same songs that can be heard at similar events in rural areas, but lyrics are frequently adapted to suit the occasion or to reflect daily situations associated with contemporary life in the city: economic hardship, memories of family and friends in the village, tension between members of the extended family, patron-client relations, accusations of witchcraft, among others. Singing in unison is more common than singing in harmony, but singing tends to accompany drumming, not the other way round. Rhythmic patterns are ethnically marked, and songs are generally continuous (not divided into verse, chorus, solo, etc.). The performance of one song lasts forty-five to fifty minutes and allows for a great deal of audience participation (hand clapping, call and response, spraying money, dancing, etc.). A typical *folklore* group will have eight to ten members, with at least four of them playing at any given time. Groups are usually organized around one senior musician, either the most senior or the most charismatic, but not necessarily the primary lead singer.

Playing *folklore* as a form of public entertainment was common practice in the early colonial period (Martin 1995), but beginning in the 1940s, the style increasingly found itself in competition with *musique moderne*. In the 1970s, partly due to the promotion of musical and cultural traditions through the Mobutu regime's elaborate state-sponsored political rallies, *folklore* began to enjoy a resurgence as an important form of urban popular entertainment. Consequently, a number of *folklore* groups found regular employment entertaining customers in bars and bistros. It was from urban traditional groups such as Bana Odeon (a group I will discuss later) and Kintweni National that the category of *tradi-moderne* was born. *Tradi-moderne* is a highly commercialized style whose song structure and language choice often resemble those of *musique moderne* but whose melody, thematic content, and percussion instruments are usually borrowed from *folklore*. The terms *urban traditional* and *tradi-moderne* refer to two different types of musical groups: in the case of the former, traditional music is performed with relatively few modifications, except that it occurs in an urban setting. In the case of the latter the structure and content of songs is modified considerably.[10]

As is the case with *musique moderne*, urban consumer tastes for *folklore* have changed over the years.[11] The most famous *tradi-moderne* group to emerge from this genre of music was Swede Swede Boketchu Premier, who at the end of the 1980s enjoyed huge success with their hit "Sundama" and were able to travel extensively and record two albums abroad. In Kinshasa in the mid-1990s the most common *folklore* to be heard was that of Eastern Kasai, which was played on a regular basis (four to five nights per week) as live entertainment in open-air bars in Matonge and Bandal (two Kinshasa neighborhoods) frequented by people of Kasai origin. Music from Bas-Zaire (Ba-

Figure 6. Dancers from the *tradi-moderne* group Les Bayouda in a neighborhood bar in Kinshasa. PHOTO: BOB W. WHITE.

yombe, Bantandu) could also be heard. The long tradition of *folklore* music in an urban setting is another topic that deserves future research, in particular the way in which *tradi-moderne* music objectifies certain ethnic groups or regional cultural traits, traits often only discernible in the sound of the music (figure 6). There is also the curious fact that so little of this music attempts to promote itself on the basis of a panethnic identity [audio].

La Musique Religieuse

After *musique moderne*, religious music is the most visible and the most commercially available form of popular music in Kinshasa. Indeed, in recent years *la musique religieuse* has exploded in the city, representing for many Congolese a source of comfort and hope in the wake of the political and economic crisis of the early 1990s (Devisch 1996; Ndaywel è Nziem 1993). Over the past five to ten years, religious music has become increasingly common in a wide variety of performative contexts, not only in a strictly religious settings but also at funeral parties, sporting events, holiday celebrations, and other public secular events, many of them broadcast on national television and radio. Apart from for its obvious spiritual and inspirational value, *musique religieuse* is appreciated by low-income families in part because it is inexpensive to acquire and reproduce. It is also sought out by middle- or upper-class Congolese who wish to distance themselves from the stereotypes of witchcraft associated with both *folklore* and *musique moderne* (White 2004).

I. Ndaywel è Nziem (1993) divides contemporary religious music into three categories: hymns or choral music (*cantiques*), prayer group music (*musique de prière*), and commercial religious music (*chansons religieuses mondaines*).[12] The first category has a history as long as the presence of European missionaries in the region. This music remained primarily imitative in nature until after independence, when reforms in the Catholic Church and the increasing presence of local charismatic churches enabled more experimentation with music that strayed from the European ecclesiastical canon. Prayer group music is almost always performed at prayer group meetings (an increasingly common phenomenon in Kinshasa), which can vary in size (usually between five to twenty-five people) and which generally take place in the house of the prayer group leader. This music requires very little in the way of special instruments or equipment: straw maracas filled with bottle caps or a handheld open-face drum. Songs have catchy melodies and simple lyrics and are mostly sung in unison, with some more musically inclined participants improvising simple harmonies and most members clapping along. Songs of this type are usually interspersed between readings of passages from the Bible and informal sermons pronounced by the prayer group leader. Some songs come from local hymnals, while others are composed by prayer group members and circulate from one group to another. Certain churches or religious presses publish prayer group songbooks for purchase by their members.

Commercial religious music is, in many Christians' view, the least religious of religious musics, not only because it is highly integrated into local networks of commercial distribution but also because of its structural resemblances to popular dance music, what Christians refer to as *musique mondaine*, or "thisworldly music." Commercial religious music is intended for meditation as well as dancing (Ndaywel è Nziem 1993), a combination that is less problematic for younger Christians, who make up the majority of its listeners. Commercial church music usually takes two forms, Congolese *moderne* and American evangelical. Religious dance music borrows directly from the aesthetic and song structure of *musique moderne*, in some cases integrating religiously based shouts and dances into the recording and performance of the music.[13] The lead singer—who is female as often as male—is usually upfront musically, but choir-style backup vocals are also important to this type of religious music. The preferred performance context is a relatively recent phenomenon called *veillée spirituelle*, an extended evening of prayers, witnessing, and sermons that begins and ends with commercial religious music (Pype 2006). Events such as these can easily last until daylight, and partially because of their association with the newly emerging charismatic churches, they often involve acts of heightened ritual activity (trance, speaking in tongues, laying on hands, healing, etc).

Songs resembling American evangelical music are also widely popular, and since they are generally not intended for dancing, they are played heavily on local religious radio stations and on private cassette decks and car stereos. Songs in this subgenre use American chord and melodic patterns, but harmonies resemble local church chorales and lyrics are most often sung in Lingala. During my fieldwork in 1995–96, Kinshasa boasted three privately run religious radio stations. The best-known, Sangu Malamu (Good News radio), was owned and operated by an American Protestant missionary who was also an accomplished musician and studio engineer. In the mid-1990s he was responsible for producing and promoting some of the religious music scene's most popular musicians. Cassettes of both the modern and the religious genre are among the easiest types of music to find in Kinshasa. *Musique moderne* is now only available at certain key distribution points throughout the city (Matonge, Kintambo Magasin, the main market, etc.), but religious music is available in stores and kiosks all over the city (figure 7), and the number of religious radio and television stations has increased considerably since the end of the 1990s. Religious music has also begun to compete with modern music for a position as the music of preference among Congolese communities living abroad [audio].

Three Generations?

The term *generation* in Congolese popular dance music does not correspond cleanly with biological generations; instead, popular discourse (especially that of musicians) relates the various generations to each other through an idiom of seniority (*bankolo* or *bavieux* for elders and *petits* for juniors). The first generation is usually associated with the wandering guitar minstrels who entertained in popular neighborhoods throughout Leopoldville (as Kinshasa was previously known) primarily in the 1940s; it is generally seen as a rela-

Figure 7. Promotional poster for *la musique religieuse*: the singer Samuel Matou.

tively homogeneous category of musical production. Only with the second generation of musicians did particular styles begin to develop within the larger category of Congolese rumba, and by the third generation the music had become fully diversified and commercialized, a process reinforced by the music's presence in markets elsewhere in Africa. At the end of this section, I will briefly address the complex debate about the existence of a fourth generation. This debate usually takes the form of generation-based social posturing that sets out to make a case for or against a qualitative break in the musical style.[14]

The exact origins of *musique moderne* are difficult to trace, but most historical accounts explain that the music has drawn inspiration from many sources since its emergence during or after World War I. People in Kinshasa have often brought to my attention that one of popular music's primary strengths is its ability to draw from various types of imported popular music. Fans of Congolese popular music, whether or not it has borrowed directly from foreign musical styles, have undoubtedly held certain international figures in high esteem: Jimmie Rodgers, Tino Rossi, James Brown, and Michael Jackson, to name only a few. The earliest forms of popular music in the region are thought to owe their origins to the colonial labor settlements of the Belgian Congo. Wa Munkuna Kazadi (1979) has raised the question of whether the style emerged only in the Kinshasa-Brazzaville region and then spread to other urban centers, or whether it sprang up in a number of different places at the same time.[15] What is certain is that Congolese popular music has been, from its inception, an urban phenomenon.

The transport industries of Leopoldville and the mining interests in Katanga brought together male laborers and musical traditions from various parts of Africa, but it is not exactly clear what kind of music was heard or played in these settlements. In Leopoldville, most African immigrants came from West Africa (Dahomey, Cameroun, Togo, and Senegal) either as administrative clerks educated in the French colonial system or as crewmen (*Krouboys*) employed on regional maritime transport.[16] Musicians from this period often reminisce about how they used to marvel at the palm wine guitar style of the West African "Coastmen" (or *Popos*) who came to work in Leopoldville and the Lower Congo in the 1920s and 1930s. Another important influence in modern Congolese music is a series of early Afro-Cuban recordings marketed in Central Africa by the HMV record company in the 1930s. The company's GV series was actually a set of reissues of Cuban *son* titles recorded in Havana and New York beginning in the 1920s and featuring groups such as Sexteto Habanero, Sexteto Nacional, and Trio Matamoros. This music had a profound influence on music elsewhere in Africa (Shain 2002), but it seems to have had its most lasting impact in the Congo (White 2002).

Obviously the influence of music from the outside did not occur in a musical vacuum. Local musical traditions had already been transformed through the emergence of new urban dance styles such as the *agbaya* ring dance, which was performed in various settings, but like other urban-traditional airs was most often seen in public squares on Sunday afternoons. The *maringa*, an early form of partnered dancing in the region, was especially popular in the semiprivate public spaces that were beginning to appear all over Brazzaville and Leopoldville. *Maringa* bands used a *likembe* (thumb piano), a bottle struck with a metal rod or bottle opener, and a *patenge* (a small square frame drum), which was held between the legs and played sitting down. Musicians from this period who are still alive clearly remember these musical styles and the context of their performance, but they are much more interested in reminiscing about their status as modern musicians or telling stories about their contact with the various foreign promoters that gave the early Congolese music industry its first push toward professionalization.

Tango ya Ba Wendo (1940s–1950s)

In its earliest form, musique moderne was a guitar-based popular music performed by roving solo musicians who wandered the newly formed urban labor settlements of the French and Belgian colonies. Often with nothing more than a guitar, urban chansonniers such as Wendo Kolosoy, Adou Elenga, and Paul Kamba animated popular neighborhoods in Leopoldville and Brazzaville, playing music in the bars and open-air cafes that became such an important part of the city's charm and urban culture. Beginning in the early 1940s, when expatriate entrepreneurs opened the first recording houses, this group of roving musicians became the first to make a living from their musical talents, signing contracts as individuals (Wendo Kolosoy, Leon Bukasa, Lucie Eyenga) and sometimes being billed as groups (Beguen Band, Le Trio Bow, San Salvador). These were the musicians who would come to be known as the first generation of professional musicians in the Congo, during the "Tango ya ba-Wendo" (figure 8).[17] More research needs to be done on the emergence of popular music elsewhere in the Belgian Congo. What seems clear is that certain musicians outside of Leopoldville (e.g., Jean-Bosco Mwenda or Edouard Masengo) were able to achieve a degree of success in regional music markets, despite the concentration of the early music industry infrastructure in the colonial capital.[18]

The first recordings in Leopoldville were rudimentary, usually not more than a singer and his guitar, though sometimes a clave instrument was included in the recording [audio]. As musicians became increasingly comfortable with their instruments and with work in the studio, instrumentation became more complex (traditional drums, acoustic basses, thumb pianos, accordions, and wind instruments such as clarinets and trumpets), and the musical arrangements became more adventurous. Many musicians from this period tell stories about how they simply copied melodies and chord progressions from the readily available GV recordings, and how this strategy

Figure 8. Wendo Kolosoy, whose name inspired the term used to designate the first generation of musicians, *tango ya bawendo*. SOURCE: BUREAU DU PRÉSIDENT DE LA RÉPUBLIQUE DU ZAÏRE, 1974.

enabled them to integrate new ideas into their music. But musicians also came into contact with European musicians, some of whom were hired by the studios as artistic directors and arrangers (see Stewart 2000). According to Congolese musicians this type of informal contact with Europeans was rare given the nature of race relations in the Belgian Congo, but it permitted an exchange of musical ideas that would prove to be defining moments in the history of the genre.

It was during this period that the local music industry began to show first signs of artistic individualization. Popular music was increasingly sung by solo artists rather than by a group of people singing in unison, as had often been the case in urban traditional music prior to the studios. A number of studios published record catalogues with a full page of information about each of the artists in the studio's repertoire [image], including the artist's picture, a brief biography, and a sampling of his hit songs: Camille Feruzi, Manuel D'Oliveira, Henri Bowane, to name only a few; these were the first true stars of popular music in the Belgian Congo. Certain studios even pressed their records with the name of the studio and a picture of the singer directly on the label. These practices marked an early phase of professionalization relative to many parts of Africa, and they reflected the implantation of a management model built around pop stars and hit songs. In a matter of only a few years, 78 rpm records were recorded in Leopoldville and mass-produced in Belgium to provide relatively inexpensive, decent-quality recordings to large numbers of urban consumers in the Congo. Improvements in recording technology (such as the introduction of magnetic tape) and the increasing availability of record players throughout the colonies in Africa meant that many of these early stars became known outside the borders of Leopoldville and beyond the Belgian Congo.[19]

The Big Rumba Period (1950s-1970s)

Advances in technology were not the only reason for Congolese music's popularity in many parts of sub-Saharan Africa. With the basic infrastructure of the industry in place, a new generation of musicians began emerging whose musical talent and star quality would surpass that of its elders and before long would colonize the rest of the continent. This was the golden age of rumba, the era of big band–style orchestras, led by the undisputed patriarch of the genre, Grand Kallé (Joseph Kabasele; figure 9), and his group African Jazz. Under Kallé's supervision, African Jazz would later provide Congolese music with some of its biggest names, among them Tabu Ley (Rochereau; figure 10) and Nicolas Kasanda (Dr. Nico; figure 11). This was also the generation of the "Grand Maître" François Luambo Makiadi, known as well as "Franco," the cofounder and leader of the country's most well-known band, l'Orchestre O.K. Jazz (figure 12). The rivalry between O.K. Jazz and African Jazz corresponded to the emergence of two distinct styles or schools of music [audio].

In the early music of this generation, it is difficult to distinguish stylistically between the different groups, many of which followed the lead of their predecessors and were busily integrating Afro-Cuban rhythms and dance steps (cha-cha-cha, bolero, beguine, etc.) into their recording repertoire. As the music evolved, however, a certain stylistic divergence occurred that became audible in the music by the end of the 1960s, with one group developing a clean, cosmopolitan, modernist sound (African Jazz and its offshoots), and the other a more rootsy traditionalist sound (O.K. Jazz). This proved an important development in the music, not only because it signaled a more

KABASELE JOSEPH,
chanteur du groupe DOULA GEORGES

Figure 9. Joseph Kabasele, "Grand Kallé," in a promotional photo for Opika Records. SOURCE: *HOMMAGE À GRAND KALLÉ* (KINSHASA: LOKOLE, KINSHASA 1985).

diverse field of musical creativity but also because the question of tradition would prove very productive in the context of Mobutu's postindependence cultural policy (see chapter 3). This period also saw important changes in instrumentation, with the widespread adoption of the electric guitar and electric bass and later the introduction of jazz drum kits and elaborate horn sections. If the music of this period was becoming increasingly amplified, it was not only because of the greater availability of electric instruments and PA systems but also because musical groups (and the venues at which they played) had considerably increased in size since Wendo's day [video].

One of the most important changes in the music of this generation occurred at the level of labor organization. Prior to this period, musical groups could not exist outside the local network of recording studios and record companies. Musicians were generally hired on an individual contract basis, and while they often recorded as members of an ensemble or group, their

Figure 10. Tabu Ley Rochereau, the most influential singer of his generation (*Le Seigneur*, Sonodisc, 1992).

only link to each other remained their relationship to the owner of the studio that employed them. This began to change in the middle of the 1950s when certain groups of musicians decided to venture outside of the studio houses and form independent orchestras. The most well-known example is O.K. Jazz, which formed in 1956 after having signed a contract to perform on a regular basis at a popular local bar, whose owner (Omar Kashama) is said to have inspired the name of the group. In the context of the Congo, then still a Belgian colony, this was certainly a bold move, but to many it was inevitable given the fact that increased competition had already begun to negatively affect the original studio houses.

The conflicts leading to Congolese independence and the political turmoil that followed caused a large number of expatriates to flee the Congo. This situation, while not necessarily good for the music industry, proved beneficial for Congolese musicians, who gradually found themselves filling positions of authority in various aspects of the music business. Their newfound authority as cultural operators reinforced their authority as band-

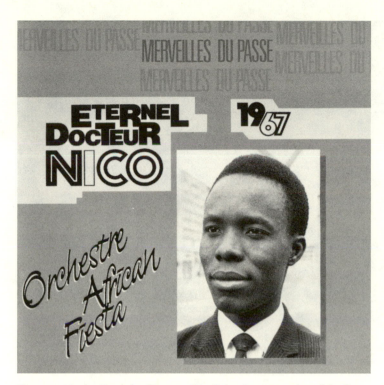

Figure 11. Nicolas Kasanda, "Docteur Nico," the signature guitar of the *fiesta* school (*Merveilles du passé*, Sonodisc, 1992).

leaders. As I will discuss in chapter 7, models of charismatic authoritarian leadership in popular dance bands took on a new meaning in the context of Mobutu's increasingly authoritarian regime. During the nationalization campaigns of the 1970s, the management of the large recording studios and record-pressing factories was handed over to Zairian nationals, and in some cases to Zairian musicians. The artists who benefited most from these programs were those who had already allied themselves with Franco and Tabu Ley, who (together with the producer-musician Kiamanguana Verckys) by this time had formed a loosely organized "cartel" in Kinshasa, making and breaking careers and exerting control over local networks of production and distribution.

La Nouvelle Vague (1970s–1990s)

The Belgian-based student orchestras of the late 1960s (Belguide, Los Nickelos, Yeye National)—also known as *les belgicains*—were extremely influential in the directions that popular dance music would take in the years

Figure 12. Luambo Makiadi, "Franco," the leader of the legendary O.K. Jazz. SOURCE: MICHEL LONOH, *ESSAI DE COMMENTAIRE DE LA MUSIQUE CONGOLAISE MODERNE*, 1969.

to come. Because of their privileged status in Europe, they were exposed to various styles of European music (French, British, Belgian), but their primary influence came from American music of the time, especially African American soul music such as that of James Brown, Aretha Franklin, Wilson Pickett, and Otis Redding. One of the remarkable aspects of their lives as musicians was the fact that they rarely had a single figurehead or musical patriarch in the organization of their groups. In most cases they were groups of young student musicians organized around the idea of cofounders (*système co-fondateur*), an organizational structure that would set the tone for many young groups of the Zairian new wave, or *nouvelle vague*. The music of these groups circulated freely among members of the Congolese community in Brussels and between Brussels and Kinshasa. When the musicians returned to Kinshasa during summer vacation, their presence caused a great deal of commotion, especially among the young people in the capital who had become their devoted fans.

But the strength of the musical empires that emerged during the second generation would not face serious challenges until the early 1970s, when

Figure 13. Zaiko Langa Langa, the flagship group of the *nouvelle vague*. Featured in this picture: Evoloko, Bimi Ombale, Nyoka Longo, and Sheke Dan. SOURCE: *ZAIKO MAGAZINE*, SPECIAL EDITION, N.D.

a new generation of musicians began to emerge with a markedly different style. Taking certain cues from African American soul music as well as from the *belgicains*, this new wave of music made a huge impact on the local music industry in part because its sped-up tempos and lively stage shows appealed widely to a growing number of urban youth (Nkashama 1979). During this period, especially after the formation of the youth supergroup Zaiko Langa Langa in 1969 (figure 13), a number of important stylistic innovations were introduced into the music, among them choreographed dancing and the distinct two-part song structure.[20] Many of the groups that followed (Viva La Musica, Langa Langa Stars, Choc Stars, Anti-Choc, Victoria Eleison, Quartier Latin) would claim ties to Zaiko Langa Langa, and those with no direct links to the Zaiko family—Lipua Lipua, Bella Bella, and Empire Bakuba, all groups mentored by the local media mogul Kiamanguana Mateta, also known as "Verckys"—considered themselves in competition with Zaiko [video].

A Fourth Generation (1990s–present)?

During my fieldwork in Kinshasa, the question of musical generations generally appeared unproblematic, except in the context of discussions about popular music released in the second half of the 1990s. This debate, which can easily develop into a heated argument, revolves around the question of whether or not the music of the 1990s constitutes a break with the third

Figure 14. Papa Wemba, the best-known solo artist of the Zaiko family.
PHOTO: SETH CASHMAN.

generation or simply a continuation of what came before. While Zaiko Langa Langa and its offshoots are clearly members of the third generation, a number of its members continue to compete for young audiences in Kinshasa (Papa Wemba makes for a particularly good example of this phenomenon; figure 14). In some cases their interest in mentoring young musicians and their attention to fashion have built an important fan base among young people. In general, however, the musicians of the Zaiko generation are catering to fans from the Zaiko generation (people coming of age in the 1970s).

The first real attempts to break with the Zaiko generation came in the early to mid-1980s, when two protégés of Papa Wemba started to become known as artists in their own right. Koffi Olomide emerged at a very young age as a songwriter (*parolier*) for Wemba, following a series of joint recordings in 1978. Olomide's first solo releases were extremely popular and highlighted his talent as a singer-songwriter, and also as a crooner. Breaking from the Zaiko generation's emphasis on fast-paced dancing and high fashion, Olomide quickly created a niche for himself in the local music scene. In the early 1990s, when he decided to integrate choreography and fast-paced dancing into his act, he rose to a level of commercial success that has remained constant even beyond the 1990s (figure 15). In some sense, the Koffi

Figure 15. Koffi Olomide during a concert in Kinshasa, June 1998. PHOTO: JOHN GRINLING.

Olomide formula (a combination of sentimental text-based ballads and slickly produced high-energy dance music) raised the bar in terms of compositional quality and sound-recording technology. These factors, together with a series of international record contracts, made him extremely popular in the Kinshasa music scene of the 1990s, and he remains a dominant figure today.

The other Wemba protégé who figures prominently in the debate about a fourth generation is King Kester Emeneya, who broke away from Viva La Musica in 1982 to form the hugely successful group Victoria Eleison. For a number of years Wemba and Emeneya were in direct competition for fans in Kinshasa (figure 16). Emeneya seemed to peak in the mid-1980s, but an extended stay in Europe following this success considerably diminished his sway over local audiences. When the previously unknown group of young musicians named Wenge Musica broke onto the scene in 1988 with a sound

Figure 16. Kester Emeneya at his home in Kinshasa. PHOTO: SERGE MAKOBO.

heavily influenced by Victoria, it seemed as if Emeneya's artistic career had
new hopes, but it was not long before Wenge began to eclipse all of its spiritual ancestors (figure 17). Wenge Musica enjoyed increasing success and visibility throughout the 1990s and is still going strong. Indeed, when people
in Kinshasa talk about the question of a fourth generation, they are referring primarily to Wenge, which since its debut has splintered into no less
than six offshoot groups. Since the unexpected separation of singers J. B.
M'piana and Werra Son in 1997, Wenge has completely dominated the music
scene in Kinshasa, at least in part because of the excitement surrounding
this rivalry.

Thus the question of a fourth generation revolves around whether groups
like Wenge Musica actually constitute a break from what came before. Wenge
has certainly enjoyed a degree of success comparable to that of the best of
the third generation, but opponents to the fourth-generation thesis claim
that musically the group has not contributed anything new to the music,
whether in terms of vocal style, song structure, or sound. Proponents of the
fourth generation argue that Wenge is different because of its accomplishments (filling concert halls in Europe, winning international music awards,
etc.), and its strong presence in the national media. They might also argue
that Wenge constitutes a fourth generation in musical terms (e.g., the guitar

CHAPTER TWO

Figure 17. Wenge Musica, B.C.B.G., in one of the group's first promotional shots.
PHOTO COURTESY OF GABY PHOTO.

playing and compositional skills of the Wenge cofounder Alain Makaba), but in my opinion Wenge's contribution has to do with the development of a particular style of dance sequence and with the transition from a shouting to a singing *atalaku*, which I will discuss in greater detail at the end of this chapter.

Two Schools?

It was during the second generation of Congolese popular music that the music industry witnessed a considerable expansion in the local demand for music. During this period popular discourse about the music began to reveal a process of differentiation, a process fueled by ongoing competition between the two giants of classical rumba, Grand Kallé and Franco. This evolution was marked by the differences in their style of music: one was considered sophisticated (Kallé), the other as emanating from the gut (Franco); one refined, one *sauvage* (wild); one soft, one noisy; one clean, one dirty; one romantic, one erotic; one for listening, one for dancing; one melodious, one rhythmic; one modernist, one traditionalist; one *fiesta*, one *ondemba*.[21] But this difference was also marked in their personal style. Kallé was clean-cut, sharply dressed, and known to speak "proper" French. Franco, on the other hand, had a reputation for being misbehaved, poorly educated, and close to his roots in the village (Ewens 1994). Popular stories about Kallé usually talk about how strict he was with his musicians, and about the fact that he learned to sing in the church. Franco, it is often said, came from a poor family and grew up on the lap of his mother, who was forced to sell donuts in the nail market to make ends meet.

Even after several months of regular listening it is difficult to distinguish between the *fiesta* and *ondemba* schools. Most experienced listeners will explain that the difference rests most clearly on the lead guitars [audio]. The African Jazz (*fiesta*) guitar of Dr. Nico is light, upbeat, measured, and refined. The melody lines he plays are sweet and well rehearsed; they rarely repeat and they always resolve. "It makes you want to hold your partner tight," people often say. The O.K. Jazz (*ondemba*) guitar of Franco is heavier in nature. His touch is more aggressive, more repetitive, seems improvised, and sounds raw. "It makes you want to move your hips," people often say.[22] The association of *ondemba* with dancing is often expressed in terms of a physical release into the rhythm: "Franco was the one who started playing the *seben* [animated guitar solos]. He wanted to play extended solos all the time. When we listened to his *seben*, all we wanted to do was dance" (interview with Achille Ngoy, June 28, 1995).

According to most people I spoke with about the two schools, the majority of today's musicians form part of the *fiesta* school: Koffi Olomide, Papa Wemba, Tabu Ley, General Defao, Wenge Musica, Reddy Amisi, and Kester Emeneya. The only musicians still remaining wholly in the *ondemba* school are the former musicians of O.K. Jazz, a group that has been considered somewhat of an endangered species or a progenitor with no progeny since the death of its leader Franco in 1989. The *fiesta* school, on the other hand, has shown the ability to regenerate itself, I was told, as evidenced by the large number of young musicians wanting to continue in the *fiesta* tradition. Given the number of people who expressed a clear preference for *fiesta* over *ondemba*, I think that there might be a tendency to favor *fiesta* for its air of cosmopolitanism that *ondemba* did not carry.

Bholen, one of the guitarists and founding members of the group Negro Succès, told me a story with a similar dynamic. In the late 1950s, Franco was known as the leader of O.K. Jazz. But he was also known as a showman and a lead guitarist. After having been jailed for driving without a license, he instructed one of his band members to call on Bholen as a replacement. At that time Bholen was playing guitar in an O.K. Jazz amateur group called Vedette Jazz.[23] On his release from jail, Franco was impressed enough with Bholen that he asked him to remain with the group. Franco's idea was to have two different lead guitars playing different solo styles at different points in the song. This plan was never fulfilled, but Bholen took the idea with him, and some years later when he approached Franco for assistance in forming his own group, he saw his chance to make it happen:

> When I came back there was some equipment [musical instruments] that Franco had available. I always had the desire to start up my group again. I went to Franco and said I was interested in the equipment. Franco said, "OK, but under one condition, you have to take in my little brother. He's a good guitarist, he's been training with Papa Noel, but Noel never lets him play. He is a musician after all; he should be able to play." I accepted. "Your protégé is my protégé," I said. I was born in 1936, Bavon [Franco's brother] in 1942 or 1943. I took him in and started showing him what to do. I told him not to play like his brother, but to develop his own style. And this was what I always wanted to do. I wanted to do something new. In music there is no age; even the young musicians can show something to the elders because in music you have to do new things to hold on to success, if you just imitate you won't have success.
>
> So we wanted to do something new. I wanted to bring together African Jazz and O.K. Jazz, a fusion of the two styles. You have to understand that Kallé's music was based on romantic love. It was extremely romantic. O.K. Jazz was considered for people of the lower classes, but African Jazz was for the evolués, it was kind of academic, for the intellectuals. O.K. Jazz was a bit . . . savage [he hesitated as if he did not want to use that word]; it was barbaric. It was all in the guitar: Franco's guitar was barbaric and Nico's was sentimental. I remember a contest between O.K. Jazz and African Jazz at the Place des Anciens Combattants. They went to see who was the best, and the jury gave the prize to Kallé, and I was very happy. I was pulling for them. But I always wanted to do something new. (interview with Léon Bholen, March 9, 1996)

The group that Bholen formed with Franco's brother, Negro Succès, enjoyed a great deal of success until Bavon's untimely death in a car accident in

1970. To this day they have a small number of devoted fans whose interest in the group is related to their ability to draw from both the *fiesta* and *ondemba* schools. Today, while the distinction between the two schools is still recognized, it has been rendered more complex by the intermingling of musical personnel (see Rumba Family Tree, www.atalaku.net) and by the fact that the terms are no longer used in relation to the controversial fourth generation.

Kinshasa's Secret Formula: *L'animation*

> *The first shout was "good gold, I get soul!" [sic] This shout gave us a feeling of decision and competition. It was like a stimulant!*[24]

The term *animation* refers to three different aspects of the music: (1) the fast-paced dance sequence of each song; (2) the action of encouraging people to dance and have a good time (this is the work of the *atalaku*; see below); and (3) the emotional state that results from this action, a kind of liveliness or excitement often described as joy or ecstasy. These particular musical uses of the term must be teased out from the more general use of the term as a verb in French (meaning "to lead" or "to conduct") and the Mobutu regime's very particular use of the term for political propaganda. For the purposes of this discussion I am most interested in the first usage. A detailed analysis of *animation* is crucial to explaining the sound of Congolese popular dance music, but it also provides valuable information about the evolution of the music over time and how this evolution has been influenced by the music's relationship to *folklore* in the context of cultural policy during the Mobutu era (see chapter 3).

To grasp the meaning of *animation* in the context of *musique moderne*, it is necessary to first understand the structure of a typical Congolese song. Song structure obviously varies somewhat from artist to artist and from song to song, but commercial dance music produced in Kinshasa has followed certain identifiable patterns. The majority of commercial dance music before 1970 bore some resemblance to the standard Euro-American popular song format:

verse
chorus
verse
chorus

solo (with *seben* or guitar solo)
chorus
chorus

Verses and choruses would alternate, and during solo sections the intensity of the improvising instruments (especially the guitar) would lead to a heightened sensibility or feeling of excitement, something similar to what Charles Keil and Steven Feld refer to as "groove" (1994). In early Congolese music this solo section, usually referred to as *seben*, would be extended and elaborated to encourage people in the audience to dance. In the early 1970s musicians began to experiment with a new song structure. This structure, instead of alternating between verses, choruses, and *seben*, eventually placed the three elements one after the other and lengthened the *seben* considerably, resulting in a song format that looks like this:

verse
verse
chorus
chorus
transition
seben

A brief introduction is followed by several verses usually sung by the lead singer, and the theme of the song (both musical and lyrical) is first stated. This section of the song, focusing on the words and the melody, usually sounds soft or slow; the word *sentimental* is often used. At the end of each verse comes a small vocal break, and the guitar fills in with improvised riffs until the beginning of the next verse cycles around. After several verses (anywhere from two to five), the front line of singers joins together to sing the chorus, which is often more upbeat and lively than the verse. Near the end of a series of choruses, the snare drum and the lead guitar signal a transition that announces the change to the *seben* (or *animation*), which will be filled with shouts—with some words spoken and others sung—and choreographed dancing that will continue until the end of the song [audio].

The musicians of the new wave did not invent the *seben*. They did, however, make it longer than in the past, and they gave it a fixed position at the very end of the song (with no return to the chorus)—both factors that led to a clearer separation between words and dance. The majority of music produced since the new wave period has adapted this new two-part song structure: a slow lyrical section filled with words (verse and chorus) and a fast-paced dance sequence (*seben*) filled with choreographed dance moves and *cris d'extase* (shouts of joy). Obviously there are examples of songs from this period that do not follow the two-part format, especially ballads (like some of the early music by Koffi Olomide), music of the older generations that sees itself as "protecting the rumba" (e.g., Bana O.K.), and some cross-over projects (e.g., Lokua Kanza and the album *Emotion* by Papa Wemba). The two-part song structure became important enough that many of the recordings during the new wave period included the first part of the song on the A-side of records and the *seben* on the B-side. Since the second half of the 1990s it has become common practice to begin albums with a *seben* that is also the title track of the album (locally referred to as "générique").

According to most Congolese musicians, the term *seben* was adapted from the English *seven*. Though this is most likely a folk etymology, it is believed that Congolese musicians picked up the term by observing the palm-wine guitar style of the West Africans who had migrated to Leopoldville for work in the early part of the twentieth century and whose music was interspersed with seventh chords ("seventh" → "seben"), said to have a sense of suspense that makes people want to dance. Other descriptive terms are used to designate this section of the song (*chauffée, saccadée, animation, partie dansante, ambiance*), but of these, *seben* seems to be the oldest and the most common. It is also the only non-French term, and the term most used by musicians. Franco is often given credit for inventing the Congolese *seben*, but given that word appears before he began playing professionally in 1956, it was most likely a musical term that drew from various sources (Afro-Cuban, local African, West African, etc.). What seems clear is that Franco was responsible for perfecting and popularizing a *seben* that was primarily guitar-based and that explicitly associated guitar music with physical release (*défoulement*).

Three necessary elements are brought together to make a good *seben*: the *cavacha* rhythm, a particular style of lead guitar, and the shouts of the *atalaku*. Although the word sections of songs can (and often do) display a wide variety of rhythms and tempos, the rhythm used for the *seben* is remarkably standard across groups and over time. *Cavacha*, the name of the rhythm, is an onomatopoeic term whose origin is explained with two conflicting stories collected in Kinshasa. The first is told by the lead members of Zaiko Langa Langa, the band usually given credit for introducing the rhythm. They contend that while on tour to Pointe Noire from Brazzaville, they traveled via train overnight and after many hours of hearing the churning, rhythmic sound of the run-down railroad engine, they had the idea to create this rhythm: *ca va cha, ca va cha, ca va cha*. The next morning they woke up and decided that this would be their new musical signature [audio].[25] The other version of the story comes from Zaiko Langa Langa's drummer, Meridjo, who is the individual most often credited with popularizing the *cavacha* rhythm. According to Meridjo, he not only popularized the rhythm but also discovered it. He explained to me that he first heard the rhythm while sitting having a beer and listening to one of Kinshasa's many urban traditional musical ensembles: "It was the rhythm being played on the big drum [*mbonda mama*], but just with one stick. I memorized it, took it home and adapted it to the music we were playing in Zaiko, and that's how it was born" (May 14, 1996).

Those with musical training will hear the distinctive clave in this rhythm, an instrument important in early Congolese popular music, especially in that of the first generation.[26] Regardless of the rhythm's exact origin, *cavacha* is the undisputed mother rhythm of contemporary Congolese dance music, and Meridjo is the undisputed doyen of *cavacha*. The primary phrase of the rhythm is played on the snare drum. The bass drum plays on every beat, giving a solid, driving feel to the rhythm. Except for fills or scattered crashes and hits, *cavacha* only makes use of the snare and bass drums, but there are obviously many variations [audio]. What is remarkable about these variations is not their number or frequency, but the way in which they implicitly refer back to the original *cavacha* theme. The only songs that escape this rhythm are those that do not play any *seben* at all. Some groups have signature variations on the *cavacha* rhythm, but there is more variation among songs than among groups. Individual or group style is more clearly identifiable through the other key elements of *seben*, namely, the electric guitar and the use of shouts or *animation*.

Most accounts of the musical style attest to the importance of the guitar's role in creating a sound that is both warm and rich, but the guitar is particularly important during the *seben*. Bands in Kinshasa perform with three guitars (bass, rhythm, and lead), but as in many popular styles, the lead guitar is the most prominent.[27] The lead guitar carries the melody in the absence of vocals, and during the *seben* it occupies the highest registers of the three guitars. Short, melodic phrases are tied together in flowing, rhythmic combinations that alternate at key points in the *seben* in an attempt to maintain or increase intensity. While lead guitarists invariably enjoy the most attention from fans, many musicians will admit that the foundation of Congolese dance rhythms rests with the guitars of the rhythm section. The bass guitar plays heavily on the octave and fifth of the tonic and is often compared to a conga drum (*mbonda*) because of the percussive way in which certain notes are struck [audio]. The rhythm guitar is the most constant of the three guitars, and although the chord structure of songs is relatively simple (usually I–IV–V or I–IV–I–V), chord positioning and rhythmic complexity make this instrument the most difficult to master. The simultaneity of three or more guitars with distinct but highly complementary partitions gives Congolese dance music a distinct layered sound, simultaneously raw and mediated.

The third ingredient required for a good *seben* is the *atalaku*, the musician who creates and strings together the seemingly random series of short percussive phrases known as "shouts." The few written references to the *atalaku* all in one way or another capture the contradictory nature of his persona (White 1999). The *atalaku* rarely appears in music videos, and despite the fact that most people are familiar with his voice, he does not classify as a singer. He shares the spotlight with some of the biggest names in the Kinshasa music scene, but he leads a stigmatized existence relative to his fellow band members. People criticize him for his crass behavior on stage and for his uglification of the fluid sentimentality of old-school rumba, but he has somehow become *the* necessary ingredient to every Kinshasa dance sequence. The term *atalaku* supposedly derives from the Kikongo expression for "look here, look at me" and first appears in common parlance in Kinshasa in the early 1980s. The *atalaku* (also referred to by the French word *animateur*) creates an atmosphere of excitement for the audience by improvising a careful combination of shouts, melodies, and various other vocal pyrotechnics intended to drive those in the audience and onstage to dance and lose themselves in the music: "The shouts that are heard in almost all of the youth music produced throughout the 1980s and to the present day . . . are indispensable, if not unavoidable, in today's music, hysterical shouts without which there would be no true *ambiance* in a song, on the dance floor . . . in our hearts" (Tchebwa 1996, 208).

The Emergence of the *Atalaku*

Although shouts have always existed in Congolese popular music, it was not until the emergence of the *atalaku* that they became used in any systematic way. Before the *atalaku*, musicians commonly shouted out the names of fellow musicians (as in the early recordings of the 1940s and 1950s) or the names of new dances as they were being performed (a practice that became common in the 1960s and 1970s). However, these shouts were much less complex than those of today, and they did not constitute a structural aspect of the music (see Kenis 1995). Since the early 1980s, shouts have evolved from being merely shouted [audio] to being both shouted and sung [audio], to being completely sung [audio], finally culminating in the practice of some lead singers (Koffi Olomide, General Defao, J. P. Busé) to croon shouts with "care" (*atalaku ya soin*) or "charm" (*atalaku ya charme*). The artistry of *animation* is constantly changing. Since the late 1990s, Kinshasa has witnessed at least two innovations in this area: a wave of junior *atalakus* (one of whom was eleven years old) and a series of shouts that appeared in languages other than Lingala and Kikongo, especially Tshiluba.

Today, very few bands in Kinshasa perform without the presence of at least one *atalaku*. Given the music's emphasis on a lively stage show, the *atalaku* has become an integral part of the modern dance band phenomenon, since he is an instrumentalist (he plays the maracas), a vocalist, and a dancer (figure 18). The *atalaku* is interesting not only for his shouts and stage antics that make him a sort of live-time trickster but also because the material he uses very often comes from traditional or urban-traditional music forms. Unfortunately the *atalaku*'s association with traditional music constitutes somewhat of a stigma, and this limits his position within the band hierarchy, as well as within society. Following the first *atalakus*, Nono and Bébé Atalaku, only a handful of musicians have been able to make a name for themselves in this musical role: Djuna Mumbafu (Empire Bakuba), Ditutala (Choc Stars), Beevans (Quartier Latin), Robert Ekokota and Tutu Kaludji (Wenge Musica BCBG), and more recently Bill Clinton (Wenge de Werra Son). In recent years a number of *atalaku* have branched out to form groups of their own (Djuna Mumbafu and Bill Clinton), something that would have been unimaginable even ten years ago (figures 19 and 20).

Kintambo is an urban zone located on the west end of Kinshasa and is

Figure 18. Zaiko *atalaku* Nono playing the maracas. PHOTO COURTESY OF NONO.

one of the areas of earliest settlement in the Pool region. Kintambo still carries with it the image of a village within the city and is often referred to as the cradle of urban traditional music and the birthplace of the *atalaku*.[28] Under the supervision of Kumaye, a Kintambo-based businessman and local community figure, Bana Odeon was one of the first neighborhood *folklore* groups to manage an administrative office and personnel for its activities. Taking inspiration from the elder (predominantly Baumbu) musicians of Kintambo, but also from the state-sponsored *folklore* performances that became increasingly visible in the 1970s, Kumaye and his assistants brought together a large number of unemployed local youth and began training them in the arts of traditional music and dance. In 1978 the music section of Bana Odeon began playing in local bars, attracting the attention of modern music fans with *folklore*-inspired dance steps and shouts. In 1980 they were named "best new group of the year" (*révélation de l'année*), and in the same year they received the award for the year's best dance, *zekete*.

It was perhaps this exposure to Bana Odeon's particular brand of modernized *folklore* that led a member of Zaiko to approach one of the group's percussionist-singers with a proposition in 1982. From my notes: "The day that Sonnerie came to my house," remembers Bébé, "he said to me: 'Bébé, you have to come play with Zaiko. Dress nice and bring that maracas of

Figure 19. *Atalaku* bandleaders: Djuna Mumbafu (*Tonnerre de Brest*, Avantages Plus, 2004).

yours.' I remember that day. They came to get Nono too; we started just playing maracas. We had our own microphones, and I was so proud to play with such a big group. It was the biggest day of my life" (interview with Bébé Atalaku, February 3, 1996). Bébé and his Bana Odeon colleague Nono (along with a third Bana Odeon musician named Manjeku) soon became permanent members of Zaiko Langa Langa and their *folklore*-inspired shouts and dances soon became Zaiko trademarks (figure 21). The first shout they popularized in 1982 was the same one that would inspire the name for this new musical role:

Atalaku! Tala!	Look at me! Look!
Atalaku mama! Zekete!	Look at me, mama! Zekete!
Zebola ka zebola, na	Zebola, zebola and
Zebola dance!	The zebola dance!

Reaction to Zaiko's innovation was mixed at first. Some musicians and fans, perhaps purists, believed that the introduction of *folklore* constituted a

Figure 20. *Atalaku* bandleaders: Bill Clinton (left) with Hiroshima, one of the singers in his group. PHOTO: SERGE MAKOBO.

compromise to the rich tradition of modern rumba for which Kinshasa had become known. They viewed *folklore* as music that was appropriate in certain contexts, but not as worthy of sharing the stage with Zaire's *musique moderne*. Some fans claimed that Zaiko had gone too far and had become the laughing stock of the capital. Others, however, especially younger fans, saw the arrival of the *atalaku* in a more positive light, since at some level it challenged the hegemony of the musical elders: "Zaiko had been playing pretty much the same music for ten years. We brought a breath of fresh air to the music. At first they said all we did was scream and shout, but now they respect us. We were proof that the older generation was dead and buried" (Bébé Atalaku, February 3, 1996).

Bébé remembers with pride the series of shouts that he and Nono made famous during their early years working side by side in Zaiko: "The shouts we came up with were the rage in Kinshasa." Seeing the effect that this innovation had on Zaiko's record sales and concert attendance, many music groups began to follow Zaiko's lead, and today numerous bands in Kinshasa have three or more *atalaku* at any given time. If the *atalaku* has become central

Figure 21. The original four *atalaku* on tour in Europe: Ditutala, Manjeku, Bébé, Nono.
PHOTO COURTESY OF NONO.

to the sound of music in Kinshasa, it is partly because of how his role has reinforced and amplified the phenomenon of *animation*.[29]

According to Manda Tchebwa (1996), *animation* (the primary work of the *atalaku*) forms an integral aspect of Congolese music, but one ignored by most commentators and critics. A small number of Congolese scholars have devoted themselves to analyzing song lyrics, and a handful of aficionados and music journalists have documented the comings and goings of the music's most well-known personalities. Curiously, no one has written about *animation*. As a foreigner and a newcomer to the music, I found *animation* and the two-part song structure the most striking thing about Congolese popular dance music, and this certainly influenced the direction of my research. But when I tried to discuss the phenomenon with people in Kinshasa, even people with extensive knowledge of popular music, they most often reacted with curiosity or surprise. Congolese know that their music is unique and that it is extremely popular in other parts of Africa, but it rarely occurs to them that this special position might be due in part to the music's unique two-part song structure, or that the two-part song structure is in fact unique at all.[30] Nor has anyone remarked on the fact that *animation*, the term used to describe this relatively recent structural innovation, is the same term formerly used to mobilize support for a government seeking new ways to re-assert its political legitimacy.

Chapter 3 will discuss how the Mobutu government organized popular performers in an elaborate system of praise-based performance to mobilize support for the regime: *animation politique et culturelle*. The Zairian state's conspicuous use of *folklore* undoubtedly influenced the emergence of the *atalaku* in popular dance music, but the connection between these two spheres of performance is one that needs to be explained. Some popular musicians were directly involved in *animation politique*, while others became involved in popular music after their experience as *animateurs*, but everyone in Kinshasa was aware of *animation politique*. These larger impersonal connections, however, did not prove as significant as the role played by local *folklore* groups or cultural associations such as Bana Odeon. This group, which will always be remembered for having trained the first group of professional *atalaku*, was one of hundreds of neighborhood cultural associations attempting to create a space for themselves within Mobutu's cultural policy, which began to place increasing emphasis on so-called authentic cultural traditions.

As with most associations of this type, Bana Odeon originally served the needs of a particular ethnic community in a specific part of Kinshasa. Unlike most associations, it was able to cross over from *folklore* to *musique de bars*, and Bana Odeon's success in this latter domain made its members attractive to a group of popular musicians looking for the "next big thing." But the idea that *folklore* could prove of interest to larger audiences was not one entirely of their making. Mobutu's authenticity politics had already created a political climate that encouraged people to think in terms of how they could mobilize their culture, if not for the benefit of the nation then at least to benefit themselves. In this sense, the *atalaku* is essential to understanding the dynamic between popular music and the larger political context, a topic to which I turn in chapter 3.

3

MADE IN ZAIRE

FOLLOWING A SERIES OF FAILED NATIONALIZA-
tion measures in the first part of the 1970s and increasing evidence of political corruption, popular support for
Mobutu reached an all-time low by the end of the decade.
Not coincidentally, it was also during the first half of the
1970s that the Mobutu government began to articulate a
series of cultural-policy measures built around the notion
of *authenticité*. According to the philosophy of *authenticité*,
real progress and economic development could only be
achieved by mobilizing a vast repertoire of traditional
cultural practices and knowledge. In order to ensure
the transmission of this message to the largest possible
number of people, the Zairian state began committing resources to various types of authentic theater, music, and
visual arts. A cultural policy privileging folklore and traditional arts and performance had a real impact on the local
music industry, which for many years was considered the
center of the African musical universe (Ewens 1991). But
by the mid-1990s the music industry was in such bad
shape that it was not uncommon to hear, as one prominent observer of the region suggested, that "the creative
center at this moment is no longer in Kinshasa, but in

Paris, Brussels, London, and other places where exiled Zairians congregate" (Fabian 1998, 77). As the following chapters will show, this was far from being the case.

In April 1996 I played host to two Europeans visiting Kinshasa on vacation from Rwanda, where they were based as employees of an international NGO. As longtime fans of la musique zaïroise, they were very excited to be in Kinshasa and asked me to give them a musical tour of the city. I started by taking them to the capital's crowded popular center, Matonge, an important site in the historical imaginary of popular music in Kinshasa, primarily because during the heyday of the music industry Matonge was home to an important number of bars, concert venues, and record stores. As we were crossing the street I told them about all of the people who had advised against doing fieldwork on the music industry in Zaire since "all the musicians had left" or because "the music industry was finished." This turned out to be bad advice, not only because the music scene was still very much alive in the mid-1990s but also because following in the wake of cultural policy in the 1970s, the music industry (which is not the same thing as the music scene) had not disappeared: it had simply gone underground, becoming a part of the country's mythic informal sector, what Janet MacGaffey and her collaborators have referred to as Zaire's "real economy" (1991).

"This part of the city used to be full of record stores," I explained, "but now there are basically two." The store I took them to see was so small that the three of us filled about one-third of the store's floor space. "This is the second store," I told them, and they seemed completely perplexed. For these visitors, the high visibility of Congolese popular music elsewhere in Africa was difficult to reconcile with the image of this one-room music shack, which served both as a central meeting place and a central point of commercial distribution (figure 22). Their reaction surprised me because I had become accustomed to what is effectively a central paradox in the history of Congolese popular dance music, namely, the possibility of a thriving music scene and a simultaneously declining music business. To understand this paradox we have to look at what was going on both politically and economically when the Zairian music industry of the 1970s, then one of the most influential on the continent, began to lose ground.

My analysis of cultural policy under Mobutu is intended to convey a sense of the political climate when the music industry was at its peak in the 1970s, but also to show how changes in the economy came to bear on the evolution

Figure 22. One of the main music stores in Kinshasa, Chez Socrates.
PHOTO: BOB W. WHITE.

of the music in the long term. Zairian music's popularity in other parts of Africa was initially due to the infrastructure of the music industry, which proved profitable for long enough to enable the development of a uniquely Zairian sound, one that was modern yet still clearly "made in Zaire." Unfortunately, the formal infrastructure of the music industry would not prove sustainable. By looking at changes in the Congolese music industry over time, I hope to show how the political economy of Mobutu's Zaire—one marked by a disastrous series of nationalization measures, chronic inattention to local culture industries, and a bloated informal sector that would eventually take over the economy—had an impact not only on the music's distribution but also on its sound. According to more than one musician in Kinshasa, the government's mismanagement of the music industry under Mobutu was proof that he intended to keep popular musicians poor and dependent. This political neglect, which became an integral part of the local cultural economy, was reproduced in the organization, distribution, and performance of popular music well into the 1990s.

Cultural Policy in Mobutu's Zaire

In recent years, the literature on popular music has witnessed an explosion of interest in the questions of national politics and identity, especially in non-Western settings.[1] This emerging literature shows a real concern with the structures and institutions of state power, but it is limited by the long shadow of literature on nationalism, which in many ways has dominated critical thinking about politics since the 1980s. This is perhaps why Thomas Turino (2000), in his recent monograph on popular music and nationalist movements in Zimbabwe, observes a certain fatigue with the nationalism question. Indeed, what is so interesting about recent writing on popular music and nationalism is its ability to go beyond the well-rehearsed formulations of Ernest Gellner and Benedict Anderson, both of whom have been criticized for assuming a certain degree of homogeneity in their analysis.[2] Scholars of popular music in non-Western countries, where mass media are more often than not controlled by the state and where censorship is the rule instead of the exception, are faced with a set of institutional realities that make it difficult to separate popular culture from politics. The analysis of particular cultural policies enables us to consider the relationship between these elements and the impact that they may have on what Kelly Askew has referred to as "national imaginaries" (2002, 272).

I use the term *cultural policy* to refer to two types of official or governmental practices. The first pertains to legislation or initiatives that affect culture industries, popular forms of entertainment, or associational activity (bars, bands, dance and theater troupes, sports clubs, special interest groups, cultural associations, art schools and galleries, radio programs, local newspapers and magazines, etc.).[3] The second is focused on the promotion or protection of culture in the anthropological sense (magico-religious beliefs, traditional art, dance, ritual, language, proverbs, etc.) with an eye toward making more explicit the link between cultural and national identity. One of the most striking aspects of the now well-established literature on cultural policy (with the important exception of a series of publications sponsored by UNESCO; see, e.g., Botombele 1975) is the relative absence of research on cultural policy in developing economies. The case of sub-Saharan Africa is particularly relevant because of the relatively short period of independent state formation and the centralized nature of colonial government in most parts of the continent.

Like the notion of culture itself, cultural policy and the way it is implemented varies over time and space.[4] In the Belgian colonial context, culture was not something that Africans possessed but something to which they were given access. This does not mean that administrators in the Belgian Congo had no understanding of culture in a strictly anthropological sense, since much of the information they used to formulate policy came from missionaries and other amateur ethnologists who clearly viewed culture as a set of beliefs and practices. It does mean, however, that culture in the anthropological sense was only relevant to colonial authorities to the extent that it facilitated the administration of the colony and its subjects.[5] Johannes Fabian reports an increase in cultural activities in the mining regions of the southeast during the mid-1950s, perhaps as part of a "last-ditch effort" on the part of Belgians of various persuasions to save the colony from what must have seemed like an inevitable (and potentially bloody) move toward independence (1990, 49). To the extent that there was a cultural policy to speak of during the colonial period, it was far from coherent.[6] Despite certain advances in the areas of film (Diawara 1992) and sports (Martin 1995), the Belgian colonial administration was less concerned with cultural policy than with a set of issues about how to govern, how to systematize colonial interventions, and how to keep the public order. If, as Didier Gondola (1992) has suggested, popular music remained a blind spot for the colonial administration, it certainly was not for the governments that would follow. Indeed, song and dance would become an integral part of Mobutu's elaborate propaganda machine, one that relied on the power of public spectacle as a means of mobilizing support for the state.

Recours à l'Authenticité

Mobutu's particular brand of cultural nationalism was an inspired expression of high modernity that in late 1971 placed authentic African values at the center of its political ideology.[7] At the same time that he constructed an image of Zaire as a modern nation made up of one people (les Zaïrois) and more than three hundred distinct ethnic groups, Mobutu also imposed non-Western traditional dress and authentic political models that used the metaphors of kinship and traditional chiefly authority to legitimate a centralized form of authoritarian rule (Schatzberg 1993). The Janus-faced nature of such a gesture was most clearly expressed in the recurring phrase "nous les Zaïrois authentiques" (We the authentic Zairians), which indexes the past (cultural authenticity) and an imagined present-future (national identity) at the same time (figure 23). This amazing machine of authenticity used staged

Figure 23. "President Mobutu sees his new role as chief of state consecrated by traditional chiefs." SOURCE: BUREAU DU PRÉSIDENT DE LA RÉPUBLIQUE DU ZAÏRE, N.D.

images of traditional culture that tended to obscure a complex history of contact with foreign ideas about governance.[8]

The architects of Zairian *authenticité* (see for example Kalanda Mabika's 1967 text *La remise en question*) were most likely influenced by Placide Tempels's *La philosophie bantoue* (1949), which in turn echoed a long tradition of Western thinking about the relationship between culture and the self (especially J. H. Herder's romantic nationalism and Martin Heidegger's phenomenology).[9] The intellectual history of *authenticité* as it pertains to African philosophy and politics has yet to be written, but it is clear that this history must be cast in comparative terms.[10] The study of authenticity in contemporary political philosophy is concerned with the emergence of Western notions of the self as they relate to alienation in postindustrial capitalist societies (Taylor 1991; Berman 1988; Giddens 1991). Read through the eyes of Theodor Adorno (1973), however, Mobutu's Zaire offers a perfect example of how essentialist discourses about an authentic self are capable of covering up the alienation they ostensibly set out to criticize. The Mobutu regime began, just after taking power for the second time in 1965, with a model of government based on economic nationalism, but it then quickly and decisively moved toward a stirring rhetoric focused on the concept of *authenticité*.

A close reading of official policy statements from the Mobutu years shows that the authenticity motif went through several stages or phases. These stages are not discreet or self-contained, but they represent subtle shifts in the content of political discourse during the period between 1965 and 1985. During the early years of Mobutu's rule (1965–69), speeches and party documents drew heavily on a discourse of economic nationalism (*indépendence économique* or *nationalisme authentique*), which criticized the foreign exploitation of national (especially mineral) resources while at the same time denouncing the abuses of the Congolese politicians who had inherited control of the economy from the Belgians immediately following independence. During the period from 1970 to 1974 — in many ways the most critical in terms of understanding Mobutu's cultural policy — a much greater emphasis was placed on culture, both as a source of national pride and as a motor of economic development. While these years corresponded with the beginning of the nationalization measures, political discourse during this period was dominated by discussions of traditional African values, the cultural alienation caused by colonial rule, and Mobutu's recourse to authenticity. The official introduction of *mobutisme* in late 1974 marked a third and final phase of political discourse. *Mobutisme*, defined very generally by the MPR as the philosophy and teachings of Mobutu, came under increasing criticism for its lack of clarity as policy, but also because of its association with widespread corruption and the abuse of political privilege.[11]

Mobutu himself realized that these shifts in policy were leading to a great deal of confusion, and not only with everyday citizens (see Schatzberg 1978; figure 24).[12] But if any aspect of the new regime's rhetoric had the potential to focus people's thinking and mobilize their imagination, it was probably the concept of *authenticité*. To most Zairians *authenticité* meant that the name of their country, its principal body of water (the Congo River), and its national currency had all been changed to "Zaire" and that on every October 27 (beginning in 1971) they were expected to celebrate this occasion, which became known as the Day of the Three Zs (La Journée des Trois Z). It meant that they were forced to substitute their Christian names with authentic African names (1972) and that men wishing to stay in the good graces of the regime (especially civil servants) were expected to wear an *abacost* (a specially designed suit with a modified collar and no necktie, introduced in 1973) and to address their compatriots not as "Monsieur" or "Madame," but as

Figure 24. Mobutu during a press conference in 1978. SOURCE: BUREAU DU PRÉSIDENT DE LA RÉPUBLIQUE DU ZAÏRE, N.D.

"Citoyen" and "Citoyenne" (1974).[13] For women, African-style three-piece dresses were required and pants strictly forbidden. Because these measures were often carried out with considerable zeal, most Congolese viewed them as profoundly political.

With some hindsight, the signposts of political discourse under the Second Republic—authentic Zairian nationalism, *le recours à l'authenticité*, and *mobutisme*—are probably best seen as rhetorical strategies used to justify the coup d'état of 1965, the nationalization measures of the 1970s, and the institutionalization of one-man rule. Zairians watched as each successive pronouncement, somehow more revolutionary and more authentic than the last, was accompanied by a more elaborate deployment of human and financial resources and an increasing gap between those with access to the resources of the state and those without it (Ngoye 1993).[14] As a state ideology, *authenticité* was only able to sustain itself in fits and starts until the demands of hegemony began to require the more draconian (and less transparent) methods of detainment, deportation, and disappearance (Braeckman 1992; Schatzberg 1988). Mobutu's cultural policy should not be criticized because it lacked coherence or depth (Badibanga 1992; Longa 1992) or even because it failed to provide for the needs of cultural producers (Liyolo 1992), though both of these criticisms hold, but primarily for the blatantly opportunistic way that it used culture as a tool for the consolidation of power.

CHAPTER THREE

The most visible manifestation of cultural policy under Mobutu was *l'animation politique et culturelle*, the system of state-sponsored singing and dancing that came to be synonymous with the image of the regime and the idea of one-party rule. Much more than other forms of political mobilization, this practice (often referred to simply as *animation politique*) captivated local audiences and dominated state-run media [video]. The wide diffusion of *animation politique* was facilitated by a particular kind of performance combining the aesthetics of folklore with the spectacle of popular dance music whose lyrics sang the unconditional praises of the one-party state and its leader (figure 25). Gazungil Sang'Amin Kapalanga, in the only published monograph, to my knowledge, devoted specifically to this subject, explains how *animation politique* found its way into the everyday lives of people living in Zaire:

> *Animation politique* penetrated the rhythm of parties, work, and leisure . . . [and] located in the subconscious of the [Zairian] people, it ultimately created certain reflexes and attitudes in relation to situations that people experience every day: we hum the melody of an *animation politique* song while working, we go to parties with the songs and dances of *animation politique*, in front of a radio or television, the whole family sings and dances with the *animateur*, the funeral procession coming from or going to the cemetery shakes with the rhythm of *animation politique* in a hearse that becomes a space of play and a musical instrument that is played by any number of hands. (Kapalanga 1989, 20)[15]

From the policy's formal beginnings in the early 1970s until it began to fade in the late 1980s, tens of thousands of people were directly involved in the organization and execution of *animation politique*. When *animation politique* first became a part of national television programming on a daily basis, it occupied close to six hours per day, usually beginning at 4 P.M. for two hours, with a short break in between the news and sports and then returning to the airwaves until midnight. In 1976, only ten years after the introduction of television to the region, *animation politique* took up anywhere from ten to twelve hours of programming per day, occupying as much as one third of total broadcast time (Dieudonné Mbala Nkanga, personal communica-

Figure 25. "The rhythms coming from a rich cultural heritage are expressed through the wisdom of those who perform *animation politique.*" SOURCE: BUREAU DU PRÉSIDENT DE LA RÉPUBLIQUE DU ZAÏRE, N.D.

tion, May 2000).[16] Thomas Callaghy (1987) discusses four ways in which the Zairian state attempted to mobilize and maintain support for the regime: monuments and signs, political marches, mass meetings, and *animation politique*. Of these four, he argues that *animation politique* was the most common in the region of Bas-Zaire where he conducted research. Crawford Young and Thomas Turner agree with his assessment and estimate that around 10 percent of class days in schools were canceled "to make way for party ceremonials" in 1973 and 1974 (1985, 219).

The few scholarly references on this subject suggest some connection between *animation politique* and the CVR (Corps des Volontaries de la République), which much like *animation politique* operated as a means of rallying support for the regime. This connection obviously complicates the version of the story in which Mobutu had the idea for *animation politique* following a state visit in 1974 to China and North Korea, where he was charmed by large-scale political choreographies, especially those of Kim Il Sung.[17] Well before Mobutu's trip to Asia, the CVR was itself drawing on a tradition of cultural associations and cultural activities that emerged during the late colonial period in response to the rapidly growing number of youths in urban centers and in the context of increasing fears about decolonization.[18] As Kapalanga has observed, "The movements that were either Western-inspired or the creation of local white missionaries played a major role in the re-valorization of traditional culture" (1989, 69). Their activities—summer camps, survival training, hiking, marching, singing, dancing, and classes in morality— served as an important source of ideas, and many of the Congolese who held important leadership positions in these organizations were among those recruited to organize *animation politique* (Sampasa Kaweta Milombe, Momene Mo-Mikengo, and others; see Lonoh 1990). *Animation politique* also included certain popular musicians such as Nyboma (who sung as an *animateur* for a short time), Franco (who recorded a number of songs in praise of Mobutu's policies), and Papa Wemba (who sometimes integrated the accoutrements of *authenticité* into his stage performances) [audio, video].

The thematic content of *animation politique* is complex and merits further research, but several observations emerge from a preliminary analysis of slogans and song lyrics. The most obvious aspect of these texts, both song lyrics and political slogans, is the excessive praise expressed for Mobutu and his policies. While some texts focus specifically on the heroic qualities and patriotic deeds of Mobutu ("Mobutu the Savior"), others are less coherent, combining words of praise for Mobutu or the MPR with extracts from various official pronouncements (Kapalanga 1989, 155, 221). In fact, much of the content of *animation politique* came directly from Mobutu's speeches, which were widely distributed to the Zairian public and considered required reading for party members [audio].[19] Because the content of *animation politique* was directly linked to official statements of policy, the occurrence of particular themes varied over time and, like any form of political propaganda, was subject to ideological whims and political fashions.

Despite these variations, the content of *animation politique* generally conveyed three types of information. First and foremost it expressed devotion to Mobutu and unconditional support for his ideas and his government ("One Hundred Years for Mobutu," "We Believe in You Sese Seko"). Even texts with no direct reference to Mobutu or the MPR could be interpreted as expressions of support for the regime, since the performance of traditional songs or texts was vaguely consistent with the ideals of *authenticité* (Kapalanga 1989, 181). But *animation politique* also provided a means of disseminating information about national policy and ideology (Kapalanga 1989, 99–100). Keywords and phrases such as *authenticité, revolution, national unity, mobilization, vigilance,* and *salongo* were very common in song texts and slogans, and despite their clumsy deployment, they persisted, perhaps even increased, over time.[20] Finally, the texts of *animation politique* conveyed information about the diverse customs and practices of Zaire's many ethnic groups, information that certainly added to public interest in the phenomenon (MacDougall n.d.).

Many people in the Congo saw *animation politique* as a form of submission to a government that, even on its own terms, failed to fulfill its promises for social and political reform following colonial rule. An open letter to the regime stated it thus: "What have we not done during this time to be useful and pleasant for you? We have sung, we have danced, we have animated. We have been through all sorts of humiliations, all kinds of degradation that even foreign colonialism never subjected us to. All of this so that nothing would be missing in your fight to achieve, even halfway, the model of society that you have proposed. Have you succeeded? Alas no!"[21]

A report from the 1982 conference on authenticity and national development concluded that *animation politique* had been reduced to a series of "dances, slogans, and protocol," not least because of its "useless and at times pornographic exhibitionism" (Union des Écrivains Zaïrois 1982, 384–85). One former *animateur* explained to me that he was happy to sing the praises of Mobutu because "every time we played we got free drinks" (March 21, 1996).

By the mid- to late 1980s, *animation politique* had made its way into almost every aspect of public and private life in Zaire. It was during this period that *animation politique* became required for all companies and organizations in Zaire, regardless of their connection with the state.[22] This included schools, hospitals, associations, and companies in the private sector. *Animation politique* was performed at the beginning of the workday with employees and supervisors clapping their hands and singing patriotic songs, and it was mandatory practice during the arrival of political dignitaries (figure 26). Some companies hired teams of professional *animateurs* to outdo their competitors, but also to avoid being reported to the government for failing to

Figure 26. *Animation politique* in preparation for dignitaries' arrival.
SOURCE: BUREAU DU PRÉSIDENT DE LA RÉPUBLIQUE DU ZAÏRE, N.D.

properly fulfill their patriotic duty. And there was good reason for concern since a number of well-placed directors and CEOs were either replaced or sent to prison for neglecting this aspect of their organization's activities. In this way the Zairian state, faced with increasing debt and a looming financial crisis, gradually shifted the responsibility for state-based propaganda to the private sector (Nkanga, personal communication, May 15, 2000).

Of course *animation politique* constituted only one part of a larger campaign to link Mobutu with Zaire in the minds of Zairians. Mobutu's particular form of autocratic rule blurred the lines between traditional chiefly authority and African nationalism, arguing that a strong, unopposed leadership was necessary to ensure national cohesion and that "two or three heads on one body make a monster" (Mobutu n.d., vol. II:201).[23] Unsurprisingly it was Mobutu's head that descended from the clouds at the beginning and end of every national television newscast, and in 1974 it was decided that a series of shrines should be erected in his honor at various places across the country to commemorate his rise to power [video]. In the same year, public school courses in religion were replaced by courses on the doctrine of *mobutisme*, and for a period of several weeks in early 1975, official media were not allowed to mention by name anyone other than Mobutu Sese Seko,

Figure 27. One of many *pagne* (cloth wraps) depicting Mobutu. This *pagne* commemorates the First Ordinary Congress of the MPR (May 21, 1972), at which Mobutu first elaborated what he meant by *authenticité*. PHOTO COURTESY OF BERNARD COLLET, COLLECTIONS COLLET, PARIS.

since the average Zairian was supposedly unable to understand power in any disembodied, abstract way (figure 27).

The violence of authoritarian rule is taken to another level when citizens are compelled to move their bodies as an expression of loyalty to a corrupt regime, especially in a place in which singing and dancing make for an extremely important form of personal expression. Those opposed to singing and dancing could only take exception in private: "How could we maintain our dignity," a university professor in his late fifties explained to me, "when we were supposed to stand up and start shaking our rear ends?" Thus *animation politique* was more than political propaganda or even psychological manipulation; it was a way of mobilizing the masses literally, through their bodies. Many of the people with whom I spoke informally referred to the common practice of offering the sexual services of female singers and dancers to visiting politicians and dignitaries as a means of securing po-

　　　　　　　　　　　　　　　　　　　CHAPTER THREE

litical or financial favors. This "sexualization" of politics (Biaya n.d.) came to be symptomatic of the excesses of *authenticité*, and its prevalence as a practice explains the common association between *animation politique* and corruption (Nkanga, personal communication, May 15, 2000). Taken on its own, *animation politique* could be seen as relatively benign, but in the context of Mobutu's Zaire, it stood for a system of rule that required regular displays of submission and praise and ruled out the possibility of any form of opposition.

Popular Music and the State

Of those musicians who openly supported the Mobutu government during the 1970s, the most visible was Luambo Makiadi, "Franco."[24] Indeed, no one else in the history of Congolese popular music can be credited with more songs so directly related to the political life of the country, and Franco was generously rewarded for his loyalty.[25] There were several reasons for Franco's privileged status in the eyes of the regime. Apart from allegedly having served as an informant for Mobutu's notorious secret service, he also composed an important number of songs in praise of particular policies or political figures.[26] His songs ranged from anodyne praise pieces for various political personalities ("Kodo Yaya," "Colonel Bangala," "Docteur Tshombe," "Lumumba Héros National") to the more carefully constructed subjects based on political themes ("République du Zaïre," "Belela authenticité," "Salongo") and later on the unconditional support for the regime and its policies ("Cinq ans ekoki," "Votez vert," and "Mobutu candidat ya biso"). The high point of Franco's career as the "official griot" of the regime occurred when in 1975 he produced an album of songs honoring the tenth anniversary of the MPR. This album, made up mostly of reissues, is interesting to listen to in the context of Franco's own statements about his motivations for writing music in the name of authenticity. "When President Mobutu began his authenticity campaign, I wrote songs to help speed up the process so that people could understand what *authenticité* means" (qtd. in Ewens 1994, 142).

Franco was also important to the regime because of his reputation as a "man of the people," "chronicler of the times," and the "Congolese Balzac." Unlike most of his competitors in African Jazz, Franco came from a poor family with little education, and his particular combination of saucy lyrics and rough-hewn satire continuously commanded the attention of audiences, especially in the capital (see Walu 1999). At the same time that Franco composed songs in honor of important politicians, his repertoire also included songs understood as critiques of the system that kept these politicians in power. In a very careful analysis of political and social satire in Congolese popular music during the Mobutu years, Debhonvapi Olema (1998) has shown how Franco's lyrics constituted a critique of the socioeconomic inequality that came to characterize Zaire under Mobutu. There are specific songs in which Franco indirectly criticizes those in positions of power—for example his controversial "Luvumbu kindoki," inspired by a traditional Kikongo song about the abuse of chiefly power, or his recurring critiques of the *acquéreurs*—those benefiting from Mobutu's nationalization measures (as in the song "Lisolo ya adamo na nzambe"). But as Olema shows, it is the overwhelming presence of poor and struggling people in Franco's songs that creates a contradiction between claims about the good deeds of the regime and the everyday reality of suffering in Mobutu's Zaire.

If, as Olema argues, Mobutu "showed a particular interest in musicians at the critical points in his regime" (1998, 6), it is because he recognized that the participation of certain key figures from the world of music was necessary to sustain the appearance of legitimacy (figure 28). In the case of certain musicians, for example Franco, this participation in support of the regime was relatively frequent. Apparently it was common for Franco to warm up audiences before Mobutu's speeches, improvising lyrics about the high price of food or the abuses of people in positions of power. Before beginning his speech Mobutu would comment on what Franco had just sung, making jokes on the subject in passing and effectively diffusing any real criticism of the regime or its policies.[27] Thus the presence of musicians and music constituted an important part of constructing an illusion of consensus: "In the end, the best way to achieve happiness, is it not through one's culture? Isn't a happy man the one who sings and dances? For us here in Zaire, happiness is a lived experience, and we express it that way. It is when people are able to communicate what they feel deep inside, when they can sing and dance, that they are truly happy" (Mobutu n.d., vol. III:72).

The expression "heureux ceux qui chantent et dansent" (happy are those who sing and dance) would resonate for a long time in Zaire's political discourse and in the popular imaginary.[28] Even today Congolese of various

Figure 28. *Candidat na biso*, a government-sponsored album in support of Mobutu containing music composed by Franco (MOPAP 1982; PHOTO COURTESY OF NOSTALGIE YA MBOKA).

backgrounds refer to this unforgettable moment in the history of their country when the head of state used music to somehow link cultural traditions and national sentiment. But the irony was lost on no one: who was this "us" that Mobutu referred to? And what did they have to do to become "truly happy"? The ultimate irony of course is that the more Mobutu talked about cultural identity and authentic African values, the more acute the economic and political crisis became. According to many of the musicians I spoke with in Kinshasa, a strategic neglect of the music industry by the government kept musicians poor and silent. If the music business became increasingly fragile in the 1980s it was not only because of an increase in piracy but also because it was in the government's best interest to keep popular musicians dependent on the regime for financial support and political protection. A brief historical overview of the music industry, followed by a description of the networks of informal distribution, will show how cultural policy under

Mobutu came to bear on the music industry, and how these developments in turn led to changes in music's distribution and performance.

The Music Industry Goes Informal

Imported phonographs and sound recordings circulated through expatriate communities in the Belgian Congo since at least as early as the 1920s (White 2002), but the recording of local music did not begin until the establishment of several modest recording studios by expatriate entrepreneurs in the 1940s. These businesses, or studio houses (*maisons d'édition*), served the dual function of recording studios and record labels, producing local musicians but also providing them with full-time employment and some degree of professional training. The first of these houses (Olympia) opened in 1939, but it was not until the arrival of Ngoma in 1948 that musicians were able to work as full-time professionals. Under the supervision of Ngoma's owner Nicolas Jeronimidis, some of the music's early local personalities received employment contracts as in-house musicians—some as individuals, others as groups. Other houses would soon follow suit. In 1950 three major studios were producing and distributing records. By 1960, the number had increased to nearly twenty (Radio France International 1992, 6). With competition between studio houses, some studio owners attempted to offer better terms of employment, but many musicians preferred to strike out on their own and negotiate distribution agreements with European-based multinational record companies.

After independence in 1960 there was a steady increase in the number of Congolese involved in music production and promotion. Roger Izeidi, formerly of Kallé's African Jazz, was one of the first Congolese to act as a professional producer. As the director of several record labels (CEFA, Paka Siye, Flash, Vita), Izeidi's visible material gains encouraged other musicians to get involved in the commercial aspects of music: Kallé's Surboum label, Franco's Epanza Makita and Éditions Populaires, Vicky Longomba's Vicklong, Rochereau's Isa, Verckys's Éditions Verckys, and somewhat later the Soki brothers' Allez-y Frères Soki and Éditions Bella-Bella. In 1974, under Zairianization, Franco obtained control of the huge record-pressing factory MAZADIS. Like many of the industries handed to Zairian ownership during this period, MAZADIS enjoyed a short period of relative success, but quickly became plagued by inefficient management and widespread accusations of corruption (see Stewart 2000).

The heyday of record production in Congo-Zaire occurred in the years between 1970 and 1975 (Tchebwa 1996, 231), with estimates that yearly sales totaled as much as 5 million units for Kinshasa alone (interview with Mampala, January 9, 1996). In these years it was not uncommon for certain records to sell as many as five hundred thousand copies.[29] Producers from that period tell stories about how they could put recordings on the market in the space of three days (primarily because at that point Kinshasa was self-sufficient in terms of recording and pressing facilities). Most songs were pressed on 45 rpm records, approximately five minutes to a side. Side A contained the lyrical section of the song, and side B the *seben*. Filling both sides of a record with the same song (instead of with two different songs) was a strategy many producers used to increase record sales: "If the consumer buys a record with two songs, he's done well, but if I put only one song on the record, they have to buy more records. This was how we sold more records" (interview with Mampala, January 9, 1996).[30] Comments from producers active in the 1970s reflect the optimism that characterized the music industry during this period: "As record producers we were able to make good money, and at the same time musicians also saw improvements in their lifestyle. As producers we could even buy cars for our musicians from our general budgets, because during that time we had to fight over the best artists. In the end, we knew we would always make it back" (Kiamanguana Verckys qtd. in Tchebwa 1996, 231). Mampala stated the following: "With one song I went to Europe, bought a truck, came back with it, and it is [still] in Bas-Zaire moving merchandise. When I came back I had to buy a car for myself too; I think it was US$1,500. In those years it was hard to imagine a producer getting around on foot. We made a lot of money in those days because costs weren't high, and musicians never asked for a lot of money" (January 9, 1996). The musician and producer Ben Nyamabo claimed, "It used to be easy. When a new artist came on the scene, he only had to be a little good and he became a hit overnight. In the seventies and eighties it was easy to make money" (interview, May 21, 1996).

But the optimism thus expressed would prove short-lived. At some point in the late 1970s, record sales suffered a sharp decline, and it seemed that the bottom was beginning to fall out of the industry. Explanations for this phenomenon (from both producers and musicians) hint at state neglect of the infrastructure necessary to support the local music industry. Mampala described the situation in these terms: "Since 1986 there's no more infrastructure; it's hard to do business. In 1986 MAZADIS closes, and Franco goes to Europe. From then on you have to leave the country. You can still make music, but you can't 'materialize' it. [In Kinshasa] there is plenty of inspiration, but no materialization. Before 1973, we used to sell millions of records. In 1970 it was 1,500,000 per trimester. It's not like that anymore" (January 9, 1996).

These comments do not reflect the fact that the 1970s saw dramatic changes in the prices of copper, for which Zaire was a major exporter, and for the price of oil, for which Zaire was a net importer. They also ignore Mobutu's nationalization measures of the 1970s, which along with external economic factors had a devastating effect on local productivity and investors' confidence. These factors combined to cause a general decline in economic opportunity that by the middle of the 1980s had become increasingly acute. Meanwhile the infrastructure of the music industry consisted of poorly maintained recording and duplicating facilities, propaganda-heavy state-run media, a dysfunctional copyrights office, and increasingly difficult transport and communication among regional trading centers. The arrival of audiocassette technology to the region would prove the crucial last blow to the already declining vinyl-record industry, since audiocassettes could be easily duplicated and distributed through Zaire's infamous networks of informal exchange.[31] The introduction of cassettes and cassette players meant that locally produced music would continue to be listened to on a large scale—perhaps even more than before—but it also meant that producers and musicians found it increasingly difficult to make money from selling music. The new technology substantially changed the nature of relations among musicians and their fans by adding an entirely new layer of commercial activity that depended on the sale of cheaply manufactured, illegally produced cassettes.

Distributors and Redistributors

Compared to the production of popular music, distribution occurs in a much more decentralized fashion, with an initial distributor and a multitude of redistributors both local and global who make a living primarily from the sale of pirated audio- and videocassettes.[32] These redistributors, who range from large-scale (usually international) cassette counterfeiters to homemade cassette copiers and individual itinerant street vendors, can be seen as the key to the music's spread, but they are perceived by most people as profiteers since none of the money they earn actually returns to the artist: "The problem with Zairian music is that the artist makes his music and someone else sells it, so he never makes any money. He makes the music but doesn't benefit from the fruit of his labor" (interview with Bruno Kasonga, June 22, 1995).

Since the mid-1980s, when the business of pirating Congolese music was booming in many parts of sub-Saharan Africa, there have been efforts in the Pool region to crack down on the sale of illegally produced cassettes. But raids on commercial pirates, most of which occur outside of the music's country of origin, are difficult to orchestrate. Pressure from authorities has meant that large-scale commercial pirates either invest more money in the duplication procedure (to make the cassettes more closely resemble originals) or that they simply begin to sell their products elsewhere. It is also true, however, that some of the industry's most notorious cassette pirates went on to become important producers and distributors, and it is often these same individuals who speak out about the problem of piracy. One cassette distributor in Kinshasa was rumored to have lured other pirates into buying pirated products and then to have had them arrested for selling illegal goods.

In theory the government is responsible for protecting cultural products and their producers, and this was one of the reasons behind the creation of Zaire's SONECA (Société Nationale des Éditeurs, Compositeurs et Auteurs) in 1969.[33] As in copyright systems elsewhere in the world, in Zaire it is expected that artists should be compensated for the broadcast, performance, and duplication of their music. In practice, however, many Congolese musicians cede ownership of albums to the producer and content themselves with the flat fee paid at the time of recording. Furthermore, most royalty payments in Kinshasa come from foreign copyright agencies and are intended for a small number of Congolese musicians registered with agencies in Europe and North America. According to the SONECA agents with whom I spoke in 1999, a yearly royalties payment for an average artist amounts to about US$50. Top recording artists such as Koffi Olomide, who is registered with the French copyrights office, can earn approximately US$5,000 per year in royalties. Given this reality and given that because SONECA employees are paid irregularly their services are limited and sporadic, it should come as little surprise that most young musicians are either indifferent or skeptical when it comes to the collection and payment of royalties.

At the end of a long day shadowing Socrates, at that time the manager

Figure 29. Socrates: "I'll introduce you to a pirate."
PHOTO: BOB W. WHITE.

of Bondowe Records, I mentioned to him my desire to meet some cassette pirates. "You want to meet the pirates?" he asked eagerly. "I'll introduce you to a pirate. When do you want to go?" (figure 29). We arrived at the central market late the next afternoon and walked briskly to the center of a large section of vendors who sold nothing but audiocassettes. The person we came to see was the only one sitting down, by far the tallest and best-fed of the group. He was sharply dressed in an American-style polo shirt, khakis, several gold chains, and large Ray-Bans. Socrates introduced me: "Tito, this is Monsieur Bob. He's our friend. He wants to see how you work." Tito looked over the rim of his glasses and tilted down his head as we shook hands. Socrates left me on my own and we agreed to meet again in the days to come.

Tito's specialty, like that of the other twenty or so vendors that shared this section of Kinshasa's central market, was somewhat difficult to characterize. His cassette stand, one of the larger ones in the area, displayed not only recent issues and used original cassettes but also pirate cassettes, homemade cassettes, and used CDs. Some of his colleagues specialized in homemade cassettes or in used French and American pop music, but most of the vendors around him combined the sale of a variety of products to make a living from their trade. Tito not only had one of the stands with the highest visibility but he also had two assistants, a portable radio-cassette player for customers to listen before buying, and a small collection of homemade videocassettes (primarily imported commercial films). Not long after I arrived (just before 5:00 P.M.) several vendors began to pack up their cassettes in the carton boxes behind their stands and fold up the flour sack parasols that only partially protected them from the city sun. When I arrived the next morning, Tito's assistants were almost finished setting up his stand, and Tito gestured for me to take a seat on his stool. As the first few customers strolled by his stand, he began to turn on his charm: "Good morning, friend, how are you today? What would you like to hear?" In most cases the passersby seemed to be drawn in against their will. They were usually young men (aged eighteen to thirty-five) carrying a plastic bag with powdered milk or soap, and they stood in front of Tito's displays holding their neck, seeming overwhelmed by what he had to offer.

Tito's display usually included approximately one hundred original cassettes (placed facing the customer on a vertical backdrop), about fifty homemade cassettes (kept at the foot of the backdrop and arranged with the spine showing in their original cartons), and four to five cassettes of traditional music (folklore, usually arranged with the homemade cassettes). In this section of the market there were anywhere from fifteen to twenty cassette vendors with stands who had more or less similar displays, though among a variety of vendors Tito was one of the largest and most prominent. The two vendors that specialized in homemade cassettes were located directly beside Tito, and they offered three to four times the number of cassettes on display, all of which were laid flat on a table arranged alphabetically by artist and name of the album (figure 30). Cassette prices varied according to quality and type, but even taking into account price haggling, prices at the beginning of 1996 were relatively standard:

original cassettes:	a little less than US$4.00
used original cassettes:	about US$2.50
original pirate cassettes:	about US$2.00
homemade cassettes:	about US$1.25

On any given day, the number of cassettes sold at one stand came to about thirty. Tito's assistants were also responsible for selling cassettes, but Tito handled the majority of money transactions. Customers were allowed to listen to the cassettes before purchasing, but Tito would usually only play sections of songs in order to preserve the batteries as long as possible. His assis-

Figure 30. Cassette vendors: homemade pirate copies. PHOTO: BOB W. WHITE.

tants spent most of their time arranging, dusting, and manually rewinding (with a pencil) the cassettes that customers had listened to but did not buy. After a week or two of showing up at Tito's stand at different times during the day, I noticed a crowd of mobile vendors huddled around a man holding a calculator and a notepad, a wholesaler by the name of Noah. He was selling to the mobile vendors, and they all massed around him trying to get their orders filled. There was money going toward a person sitting in the middle of the huddle, but the transactions occurred at a very brisk pace, and it was not always easy to understand who was buying and who was selling.

After a few purchases, one vendor looked down at his money, first counting, then only leafing through it. "God, there's never enough money," he said, mumbling to himself. Noah continued, one cassette after another. Noah's brother was working with one vendor at a time, selecting the corresponding cassette sleeves that had been removed during taping to indicate the song titles. In some cases, there were more cassettes than sleeves, and Noah would write the song titles by memory on a spare cassette sleeve. He usually arrived in the morning at about 8:30 A.M. and had his entire box of cassettes sold by 10:00 A.M. The unsold ones were usually special orders that he would hold for particular vendors. Noah had a book for recording special orders and credit agreements with certain regular vendors whom he felt he could trust (usually not more than seven or eight people). He explained that he had four people who duplicated cassettes at home (mostly at night) and that he had relatively good cassette dubbing equipment (several tape-to-tape home stereo units hooked up in a series).

After returning to Tito's stand, I sat down and tried to figure how Noah made a living. A package of ten blank cassettes retailed for 140,000 NZ or 14,000 NZ per cassette. He could probably get the price down to 100,000 NZ (about US$4.00) since he purchased them in large quantities. He sold them for 16,000 NZ, making 6,000 NZ per unit and probably selling 200–250 cassettes every day. At this rate he would make between 1,200,000–1,500,000 NZ per day (about US$50–60). At $50 per day (excluding Sundays) he would make around $1,500 per month, and about $18,000 per year, with some expenses for his staff, transport, and equipment maintenance. This constituted a large sum of money considering that the GDP per capita for Zaire in 1992 was $380 (United Nations Development Program 1993). This informal calculation not only gives an idea of the salary of someone who can be considered, at least in local terms, a well-placed redistributor but it also gives a general idea about the number of homemade cassettes sold on a regular basis in Kinshasa. Noah was one of only about five major wholesalers in the capital.

Once they leave the *grand marché* (the central market), individual mobile vendors are completely on their own. The vendors who remain stationary in the market are more vulnerable because their inventory is both larger and more valuable per unit (since they sell not only original cassettes but also videocassettes and even some CDs). The vendors that specialize in homemade cassettes are the only true volume retailers. Since their activity is officially recognized as illegal, one would expect them to sell in smaller amounts in case they need to run from police or SONECA representatives. In practice, however, raids of this type rarely occur, and these vendors display their products like most others, taking up just as much space, if not more.[34] Mobile vendors (*ambulants*), however, face a very different professional situation. Their mobility, which gives them the advantage of bringing their product directly to the consumer, can also be seen as having a disadvantage. As mobile merchants, they are much more visible by a greater number of people, especially people in positions of authority such as unpaid soldiers or police officers. Moreover, most *ambulants* deal almost exclusively in homemade cassettes (for lack of resources), which results in a business both risky and unpredictable.[35]

Most mobile cassette vendors are young men between the ages of fifteen and twenty-five who, having some degree of secondary education, sell cassettes as a part-time means of generating an income. In fact, many of the mobile vendors I met were also students (some university) and were using cassette sales to pay for their school fees and materials. It is important to note that mobile vendors remain limited in their mobility. Most vendors work in a particular neighborhood only. This is necessary for them to establish contacts in the public places in which they solicit customers (bars, cafés, retail shops) and relate to local authorities. One vendor explained the importance of working the same territory in case the customer had a problem with the cassette and needed a refund or exchange. For obvious reasons, vendors usually focus on areas with a high concentration of commercial activity. In some sections of the city, vendors are organized into informal vendor associations (*associations d'ambulants*).[36] It is difficult to estimate the number of vendors working in Kinshasa, not only because vendors must remain discreet but also because selling cassettes on the street is a job many young men do intermittently or only when they are in need of additional cash. But judging from certain key sectors, I would estimate there to be two hundred to three hundred mobile vendors in Kinshasa at any given time.

Depending on the neighborhood and the vendor's luck and charm, vendors who sell homemade cassettes can hope to sell up to ten cassettes per day. In 1996, ten cassettes were considered a good day, and five to six about average. At four the vendor begins to get discouraged, and there are days on which he can sell but one, two, or no cassettes at all. Vendors with more experience remember selling thirty or more cassettes per day: "Before we didn't even have to move around. People would buy ten cassettes just like that. But that was before the [1991] riots" (interview with Agostino, March 12, 1996). The asking price for homemade cassettes was usually around 50,000 NZ (US$2, or about three times the amount actually paid), but most vendors would "let them go" for as low as 30,000–35,000 NZ. Original cassettes, which at that time could be purchased at the central market for 85–90,000 NZ, could be bargained down from the initial asking price of 120,000 NZ. For a good vendor it was possible to clear (after transport and food) about US$5 per day, earning him about US$100 a month.

Most vendors will carry about four or five cartons of cassettes (fifty units), and the majority of those (about 60 percent) will constitute recent releases (*nouveautés*). The rest will be primarily "golden oldies" (*vieilleries*) from either the classic rumba years or the early time of the third generation (Zaiko Langa Langa, Thu Zaina, Los Nickelos, etc.). A particularly good recent release will sell for about three to six months. A small handful of rarities will continue to sell over a period of years: "The record by Mayaula put food on our table," one vendor explained. Certain vendors developed strategies that enabled them to increase sales. Agostino, a student at the University of Kinshasa, gave credit to his customers. He handed out about thirty cassettes a day, selling only fifteen and giving away the rest on credit, while collecting payment on another fifteen previously given on credit. Agostino was also one of the few vendors to circulate with a portable cassette player, a tool that greatly facilitated sales. The mobile vendors I spoke with seemed very sensitive to differences in consumer buying habits. Several vendors were able to give clear explanations of what kind of people preferred what kind of music, and because their sales depended on an interactive relationship with customers, they often had a fine-tuned sense of popular tastes at any given time (figure 31).

Mobile vendors are obviously aware of the fact that many musicians and producers look down on their activities. Ilo Pablo, the founder of Zaiko Familia Dei and himself a producer, would occasionally summon a roving vendor to see what he was selling and to get an idea of what was popular at that time. Most vendors, however, immediately recognizing Ilo Pablo, would act as if they did not hear his call and would continue nervously in the opposite direction, usually speeding up their pace somewhat. When musicians are not around, redistributors are quick to defend their choice of income-generating activity: "We do a lot of advertising for musicians. If we weren't here, people wouldn't be able to afford this music." And in some cases, people would not even be able to find the music, since very often mobile vendors offer popular music from years past that is no longer available. As Tito told me, "We promote Zairian music much more than the stores do."[37]

Too Many Intermediaries

The role of brokers and other types of intermediaries, especially in the context of cultural industries, has received little attention in anthropology. In the context of this discussion, cultural brokers are of primary importance, for it is they who manage the material and symbolic resources that constitute notions of taste (and thus value) in a given society. Drawing from Steiner

Figure 31. Mobile vendors are an important part of the distribution chain.
PHOTO: BOB W. WHITE.

(1994), I see a cultural broker as someone who demystifies demand for the producer and communicates some form of authenticity or cultural identity to the consumer. In Arjun Appadurai's (1986) terms, the broker is that person who in effect makes taste through activities such as "enclaving" or "diverting." Bennetta Jules-Rosette (1984) refines the use of the term further by suggesting that brokers do not simply manufacture taste but that taste results from a sort of three-way dialogue among producers, brokers, and consumers. Robert Paine (1971) makes a crucial distinction between "broker" and "go-between," showing that some intermediaries influence consumer taste while others simply read it. In his groundbreaking ethnography of popular music in Nigeria, Chris Waterman (1990) argues that musicians act as brokers, especially in relation to the emergence of regional or national identities. Following these analyses, I see cultural brokers as those who engage in the management of social meaning and economic value.

Before arriving to the field I expected to find an important number of cultural brokers working in the area of music. Given the preliminary research I had done on cultural brokers and the production of meaning (White 2000), I was very interested in examining the ways in which expressive forms of culture are adapted to various markets. Surprisingly, however, I found very

CHAPTER THREE

few people in Kinshasa who would qualify as cultural brokers. In fact, it even proved difficult to find full-time producers or promoters working in the area of music. This lack of cultural brokers was highlighted by the large number of redistributors and by the almost complete absence of managers or agents.[38] Given the size and vitality of the local music scene, this absence seemed conspicuous, to say the least. With time, I realized that the absence of cultural brokers is interesting in and of itself. It points to the fact that cultural brokerage in a setting of political and economic crisis such as that of Congo-Zaire manifests itself in unexpected, constrained ways. One music producer in Brazzaville explained to me that producers in Kinshasa prefer "quick money" to long-term investments, which works against the emergence of a large pool of full-time professional producers. The amateurism of cultural operators in Kinshasa certainly constitutes a drain on musicians' time and energy, and it can be seen as a factor that affects the quality of musical production and performance in general. For example, most groups are forced to handle their own promotions through direct relations with members of the press and the strategic placement of so-called band boards outside and nearby the venues of upcoming concerts (figures 32 and 33). The poor performance of producers, however, cannot be considered in isolation from the larger political and economic context in which professionalism and entrepreneurial follow-through are unable to flourish, since in the words of the philosopher Paulin Hountondji, the very act of survival in this context requires a constant "pushing at the wheel"(1992:344).

Working It Out through the Music

Even the most committed fans of Congolese popular music acknowledge a certain degree of monotony in the musical production of the past twenty years. Because of the increase in pirated cassettes, the current market for music can only sustain a small number of producers and distributors, and this means that musicians are forced to scramble for financial backing and to accept substandard working conditions and compensation. Without the security of an ongoing commercial sponsor or long-term contract with a record company, musicians lack the concentration required to bring new ideas to their music, and they tend to take shortcuts in production. Fans confirm this observation when they say that "musicians are tired," "they're not creative anymore," or that "they don't work like they used to."

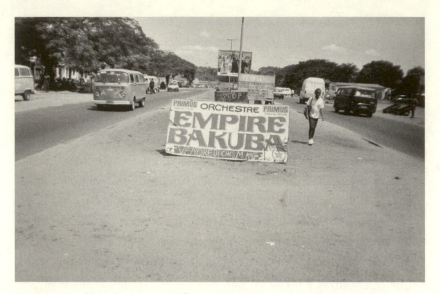

Figure 32. Band boards are one way for groups to manage their own promotions.
PHOTO: BOB W. WHITE.

In addition to the macroeconomic factors (nationalization measures, the oil and copper crises, etc.), problems also existed within local markets for music. For a good part of the 1970s, the national record-pressing factory in Limete (MAZADIS) was supplying domestic and international markets with locally produced 45 rpm singles. Since international markets brought a higher price for these exports, and because local audiences were captive, the record industry prospered during this period. Unfortunately, when musicians began making 33 rpm records outside of the country (primarily Belgium), consumer demand for longer recordings and the increased presence of audiocassettes in the region combined to seriously undercut local production. Wealthy consumers began to buy LPs, the majority of people in Kinshasa began to favor cassettes over forty-fives, and like some twenty years earlier, most popular music was produced abroad and imported back into the country. This pushed up the price of music for local consumers, making cassettes seem even more attractive than before and making it increasingly difficult for MAZADIS to remain economically viable.

In the first part of the 1990s, producers and distributors attempted to respond to the decline of the music industry by organizing under the auspices of a national association of producers, the Corporation Zaïroise des

Figure 33. Band boards are placed near the venues of upcoming concerts.
PHOTO: BOB W. WHITE.

Producteurs, Éditeurs et Distributeurs de la Musique (COZAPEDIM), and with very limited success they attempted to regenerate interest in local antipirate campaigns. Musicians have responded differently. Instead of becoming involved in the legal and political initiatives of the producers, they have attempted (perhaps unconsciously) to work out the problem through their music. On the one hand, they have become increasingly reliant on the practice of commercialized praise singing or *libanga*. This constitutes a relatively recent phenomenon in which musicians generate income by singing the names of potential sponsors or patrons both during live and prerecorded performances (see chapter 6). The phenomenon of *libanga* has become an integral part of contemporary popular music in Kinshasa, and it reflects not only musicians' urgent need for money but also the political culture of the Mobutu regime, which, through the mechanism of *animation politique*, customarily handed out financial and political resources in exchange for public displays of flattery and loyalty.

Beginning in the 1970s, the choreographed dance sequences in most popular music played an increasingly important role in creating and maintaining the atmosphere attracting large crowds in concert. The public's fascination with choreographed dancing and other visually dynamic forms of live spectacle were reinforced by the ubiquity of popular music on national television. Musicians sought the personal satisfaction of having a large following, but they also knew that large crowds increased their chances of earning additional income from fans, many of whom will "spray" artists with money during the *animation* to show their appreciation of the music. To keep the money flowing, musicians must fill concert venues, and to do this, they must have reputations as good performers. Dancing and shouting form part of a live performance dynamic that enables musicians to increase the pool of people from whom they can solicit financial and material support. If songs in concert last as long as forty-five or fifty minutes, this is in part because it gives musicians more time to cultivate the generosity of people in the audience.

By arguing that changes in the music (not only the length and structure of songs but also an increased emphasis on commercialized praise singing and live performance) in some sense constitute a response to cultural and economic policies during the Mobutu era, I do not want to give the impression that musicians are playing out a mechanical response to political economy, or that they are merely opportunistic. Musicians perform because they are compelled to do so (either for financial or for political reasons), but they also perform out of pleasure, and they are hopeful that their gift for musical entertainment will enable them to improve their lot in life. In the 1990s, however, it was difficult to ignore the fact that musicians could not make a living by selling the products of their labor; if musicians continue to produce records it is not to sell them but to symbolically assert their presence in the extremely competitive music scene. One of the primary ways in which musicians continue to make a living from music is by calling on the patron-client relations realized through the dynamics of live performance, a subject to which I turn in the following chapter.

LIVE TIME

MUSICIANS IN MOBUTU'S ZAIRE WERE FACED with a paradox: on the one hand, the state spent an enormous amount of time and energy promoting the notion of culture as a national resource (chapter 3), but at the same time popular dance music—undoubtedly the country's most valuable cultural export—was the object of systematic neglect. It is not cynical to explain this paradox in political terms. The Mobutu regime's cultural policy placed great emphasis on Zaire's rich cultural traditions, but it also transformed these traditions into an elaborate expression of state-based propaganda. Given this strategic use of traditional culture, the systematic neglect of popular culture seemed all the more remarkable. Apart from rewarding a handful of musicians who publicly supported its policies and leaders, the Mobutu regime relegated the music industry to a state of financial insecurity that would result in keeping musicians completely dependent on the state and thus politically marginalized. Indeed, this was not very different from the way in which the regime wielded power over the people in the realm of national politics. Faced with these professional limitations and caught up in an increasingly fierce competition for fans, musicians tried to secure their professional futures by making certain formal and structural changes to the music. These changes manifested themselves most notably in the face-to-face interactions of live performance.

Most of this chapter is devoted to describing what happens in a typical concert setting—what musicians usually refer to as *ndule*. To recreate the live feeling of concert performance in Kinshasa, I will use a slightly modified version of the ethnographic present in certain sections of this chapter.[1] The description begins before the actual concert and concerns itself as much with the ritualism leading up to the performance as with the performance itself (see Fabian 1990). The term *ndule* (slang for "concert" or "live music," but also synonymous with "party" or a "good time") is commonly used in discussions among musicians about their work onstage, but it also refers to the excitement that results from interactions with a live audience. Thus *ndule* is an activity but also a space, and those who create this space (musicians) are known as *ndulistes*. Different forms of performer-audience interaction (dancing, shouting, taking pictures, and spraying money) break down the barriers between musicians and audiences, and the performative mood of the concert setting—characterized by lavish displays of wealth, incessant flattery, and a hedonistic impulse—is linked, both socially and symbolically, to the political culture of the late Mobutu regime.

In her recent book on *jaliya* culture in the Gambia, Paulla Ebron (2002) calls attention to the growing interest in performance, performance studies, and performativity.[2] Indeed, Ebron's own book—which treats not only the performance of praise singing but also the performances of development and tourism—contributes to the expansion of this interdisciplinary object of study. As Ebron argues, however, theories of performance must be situated in the history of social theory. Victor Turner's important early work on "social dramas" (1957) shared much with that of Erving Goffman, who in 1959 published his influential *The Presentation of Self in Everyday Life*. Both authors, in attempting to explain social life in terms other than an idiom of social structure, tried to think their way out of the dominant structuralist paradigm of the day. In the 1980s, anthropology's turn toward a performative notion of practice (Certeau 1984; for an overview, see Ortner 1984) presumably came in response to the structuralism of Claude Lévi-Strauss and the structuralism of Marxist-inspired schools of macro-level analysis such as dependency theory and world-systems theory. Ebron shows that in each of these cases "performance has served as a way for scholars to pursue their concerns with agency in social interaction" (2002, 14). For Veit Erlmann (1996), performance represents the possibility of going beyond the opposition of structure and agency.

Within anthropology, the notion of performance has been mobilized for a number of important fields of inquiry. The first, embodied in the pioneering work of Dell Hymes, occurred at the intersection of linguistics, folklore, and sociolinguistics. This research, often referred to as the "ethnography of speaking" literature, was primarily interested in the performative nature of speech acts, but it also resonated with scholars interested in verbal performance and other forms of "artful speaking" (see Bauman and Briggs 1990). One of the important outcomes of this research was the idea that performance is not simply the enactment of a text but a complex mode of cultural production and social interaction. The second approach, following Goffman and Turner, was more invested in the metaphor of drama and the role that performance plays in various types of transformative—and at times agonistic—ritual. From this point of view, performance has the potential not only to transform individuals (Kratz 1994) but also to influence emerging forms of social consciousness (Erlmann 1996).

Since the early 1990s, and especially since anthropology has become more comfortable with the idea of studying popular culture, there has emerged a significant body of ethnographic writing about the performing arts, or what David Coplan (1994) refers to as "performance ethnography." Ethnographies in this vein have analyzed performing arts from a number of different perspectives: as an embodiment of memories about violence (Taylor 1998), as a relational aspect in the social organization of artists (Waterman 1990), as an ongoing attempt to make sense of various forms of poverty and long-distance labor arrangements (Coplan 1994; Erlmann 1996), and as a matter of negotiation between performers and various state-based agents and institutions (Averill 1997; Askew 2002). Johannes Fabian's *Power and Performance* (1990)—an experimental ethnography at times difficult to read—is particularly important to my reading of performance in Kinshasa, not only because it describes popular theater in the same Zaire that I am trying to capture through popular music but also because his analysis shows the extent to which local artists and performers struggle with the imperatives and dangers of a deeply embedded culture of authoritarian rule.

Big Stars *en Concert*

The Big Stars, a relatively successful local group, used to practice three or four times a week, usually Monday through Thursday from 2:00 P.M. to 5:00 P.M. Practices are themselves performances since they are usually open to the general public, and performance is a particularly demanding kind of practice. Musicians often give the same energy during practice that they do during concerts, but singers often reserve special dress and particular dance steps for the concert occasions, which generally occur at night and attract a different audience (usually older and with more expendable income than people that attend practices). Shows are usually scheduled on Fridays, and musicians receive the afternoon off to rest and to find something to wear. Maneko (the band manager) almost never expected to see the musicians on Friday afternoons. "They're getting ready," he would say. "Getting ready" usually meant doing the rounds of friends and neighbors to find a Versace paisley silk shirt, or a Dolce & Gabbana leather beret, or a pair of Girbaud blue jeans, or an American T-shirt with something in loud letters across the chest. What they acquire does not have to match anything else; it does not even have to be a good fit. It only has to be new or look new. One item will do; one item is enough to show that the musician has fans and that his fans have nice clothes. In most cases, musicians borrow items of clothing from friends, but there are also stories of people who buy expensive clothes and rent them out as a source of secondary income (see Gandoulou 1989). Maybe this is the "getting ready" that Maneko refers to, since if a musician wants to rent something he has to get the money together first.

All musicians are expected to report to the practice space by 10:00 P.M. the night of a show. Everyone knows that we probably will not leave before midnight, but most of the musicians manage to arrive by the prearranged time. Then the waiting begins. Some musicians do their waiting in the practice room; the nonguitarists play guitar for fellow band members who dream of becoming a lead singer and who do not care that someone is sleeping in the corner. In the doorway to the practice space someone always stands with a James Dean pose: this is the space reserved for someone who has spent a lot of time "getting ready." The *batêtes* (junior leaders of the band) are almost never visible. They, the last ones to get ready, prepare in their own private area of the practice space, planning to make an entrance before the band leaves for the show. Indeed, they are what everyone is waiting for.

Outside the practice space, even at 10:30 P.M., there is coming and going. This is Kinshasa. Ngiri Ngiri: home of the legendary Zairian singers Sam Mangwana and Kester Emeneya and the famous neighborhood of the popular painter Cheri Samba.[3] The pharmacy is still open. The old woman selling baguettes and peanuts is still there. Children are everywhere, not only the regulars from the immediate surroundings but also those that went out of their way to buy their bread in front of the Big Stars practice space because of the ongoing spectacle. The river of mud caused by poorly maintained run-off ditches is still there, *en permanence*. Permanently, but it is always new, adapting to changes in the environment such as the rain and the tire tracks of fearless taxi drivers. It is clearly part of the spectacle. We watch as people of all types try to find their way across this baby Congo River; *pousse-pousse* (handcart) drivers, mothers with babies, soccer players returning from a match, vendors from the nail market, nighttime girlfriends, unemployed civil servants, an American musician. All of these people, but never General Defao. Defao is the only person in the neighborhood that never has to cross this postcolonial moat. There is a special mudless path from his studio apartment to the practice space, and if ever he wants to go somewhere else, Ebolo the driver will pick him up in the big red van that reads "Big Stars en Concert."

The people most adept at coming away clean from the mud river are the musicians. Not only because we cross this moat several times a day but also because it is important, given how much time we spend getting ready, that we cross it carefully and with some degree of composure. But no one ever complains about the mud river. Maybe they, like me, think it cannot be real and that it will not be there tomorrow. Or maybe it serves as a kind of divider between musicians and the rest of the world. During the long wait in the practice space, on the musician side of the river, the female dancers pull down their tight body dresses, still well above the knees, and begin to put on the flashy costume jewelry that Defao has provided with their matching outfits. The outfits are an important part of Defao's stage show, which is known in part for its dancing. Many groups encourage their *danseuses* to dress alike, but Defao's dancers are fully outfitted: bumble bee body suits in black, with yellow striped sleeves and sports numbers on the chest, black imitation leather hi-top Doc Martens boots, gangster gold chains with customary bobbing pendants, and blood red lipstick for the face. For weddings they wear high heels, red slacks with a wide vinyl belt, elegant longhair wigs, and a loose, brightly colored flower-design blouse. Despite frequent personnel changes, the outfits always seem to fit. Maybe all the outfits are elastic. Or maybe Defao just bought smalls and mediums to provoke his mostly male audience. Or maybe he chose the dancers according to their measurements.

Eleven thirty rolls around. Midnight. 12:19 A.M. It seems as though we will never leave. When I ask Maneko at what time we should be ready, he invariably replies "soon." Information is provided on a need-to-know basis. If the musicians know the exact time of departure, they will wander off in search of matches or to visit someone and most likely be late. In all honesty, we do not need to know. We are worker bees, musician ants on duty, and if Chef Maneko does not inform us of a time and place, it is because we do not need to know. So we continue to wait. The Big Stars van will take us where we need to go and will bring us back. It is so routine that we often do not know the name of the bar or club at which we are scheduled to play. After all, Kinshasa has so many. 12:42. Finally Montana emerges from the darkness, and in very little time the red van is packed sardine tight—the *atalaku* shouts: "Mother of mine! We are packed in like Thompsons!"—and we are off across the mud river to some unknown destination that will probably not look all that different from Ngiri Ngiri.[4]

I am usually offered one of the spaces in the front with Maneko, but sometimes I travel in the very back with Théo, who sits next to me hoping to trick me out of my sweat towel. Once the junior leaders have given the order, it is important for everyone to get into the van. Not nearby or next to the van, but *inside* the van. This enables Maneko to count heads and to make sure everyone is present. If someone is missing, everyone else stays in the van, which at this point (an excruciating eleven minutes later) is already hotter than a steam bath. But we cannot leave the van because otherwise someone else will stray off and make us all wait again. The *zoba* (idiot) that shows up late has some lame excuse about a missing shoe or malaria—never very believable. He gets sufficiently reprimanded by Maneko (and insulted by the rest of the band) so that he will probably not let it happen again, or not soon anyway. We are off, probably still to make a stop or two for gas, or to pick up a stray band member and one of the *batêtes'* new girlfriends. Once we begin moving, the windows are down and the air once again becomes bearable. Morale rises quickly as everyone, even those previously sleeping, seem to catch a long-awaited second wind. One of the *atalaku* in the far back is making people laugh by changing the words to a popular shout: "Eh-uh-eh a simbi movate" (Oh yeah, she uses skin whiteners). We are so tightly packed that we cannot see outside the van, but we know that we are turning heads. Even at 12:45 A.M. We are the Big Stars and we are going *en concert*. The van says so.

We arrive at the concert venue, and one by one we descend from the vehicle, attempting to stretch our cramped leg muscles with some sense of style. A large crowd is milling outside the bar, watching our arrival. Most of these people are not able to get in the bar because of their age or lack of money, but they will surely find some way to see the show, probably from a nearby tree or the roof of the bar. Locally they are known as *ngembo* (bats), a term that many adults use to describe themselves in the years when they first became interested in music.[5] One of the barefoot children that should have been in bed a long time ago reads the writing on the side of the van in a long, exaggerated voice: "Biiiiiiiiiig Staaaaaaars en Coooooonceeeert" and his companions repeat the mystical sounds, each one laughing and trying to sound more French than the one before. A few people in the crowd yell out names as we saunter past: "Defao!" "Montana!" "Atalaku!" We try to pretend we do not hear them. Maneko is standing at the door with the doormen, pushing us through and sometimes calling out our names so the producer's assistant can make sure we are on the list. Once inside, things are very different. There is breathing room. The crowd is well dressed, about twenty to thirty years old, mostly male, and much better at concealing its excitement at our arrival. Depending on the number of warm-up bands scheduled to play before us, we may wait anywhere from thirty minutes to an hour and a half before we actually start playing. We are sitting off or backstage, with the *batêtes* hidden out of sight. It is 1:07 A.M. The waiting continues.

Most of the places we play closely resemble each other. They have different names (Le Destin, Chez Ya Pecos, Bonbon Sucré) and the layout sometimes differs, but otherwise they seem amazingly similar. Usually, there is a poorly painted white facade with a small metal door that always makes the interior seem spectacular for the first few seconds on entering. Most bars are open air, with some part of the bar covered in case of rain. Inside painted larger-than-life beer bottle labels decorate the walls, as do brewery product flags strung up during the last beer promotion and that no longer flap in the wind. The seats are locally produced welded metal chairs, made with quarter-inch metal rods and a square foot of thin sheet metal. No armrest means one size fits all. They are not comfortable, but with the quality of the local music they need not be, since most people will spend a better part of the night on their feet dancing. When there are no more metal chairs, there are always plenty of plastic beer crates, whose slight dip in the middle (from previous sittings) makes them less stately but more comfortable than the chairs. The stage is usually at one end of the bar, slightly elevated, and almost always too small for the fifteen to sixteen musicians who will occupy it that evening.

The teenage boys who rove around the bar are not just cigarette vendors (figure 34). On their heads they carry cardboard display units that overflow with every imaginable type of midnight snack and late-night utility: cigarettes, gum, bubble gum, mints, coffee drops, lollipops, caramel pops, chocolate candy bars, chocolate cookies, fruit candies, fruit-filled candies, hard-boiled eggs, tissues, toothpicks, matches, nail clippers, key rings, scissors, razor blades, and a complete assortment of local natural stimulants (cola nut, *kitamata*, *biolongo*, and *pili pili* among others). More remarkable than the mobility of these roving vendors (*vendeurs ambulants*) is the way they move:

> Between two transactions, the young "sophisticated streetkid," orphan, or more simply the pariah of Kinshasa society, stops for a moment in front of the neighborhood bar that is playing the latest dance step full blast. Just long enough to demonstrate his moves, much in the manner of the frontmen of Zaiko Langa Langa or Empire Bakuba with whom he could easily compete for the title of best dancer of the year. It's a matter of trying out his technique. It is also, in some sense, his contribution — free of charge — to the theatrical nature of the popular neighborhoods. (Tchebwa 1996, 331)

The bands that play before the Big Stars are local groups not yet well known except by friends and people from the immediate neighborhood.[6] Sometimes two local bands will play, the most local (i.e., the least polished) playing first. Opening for the Big Stars is a big chance for groups that have little or no access to professional equipment and producers, but many young musicians take this to mean that they have already attained stardom. By imitating the gestures of fame (delayed entrances onstage, large clothes and sunglasses, the shouting of names into the microphone), warm-up bands

Figure 34. Mobile vendors sell cigarettes, sweets, and stimulants. PHOTO: SERGE MAKOBO.

seem to lose their sense of time. In theory they are expected to play two or three songs to open the evening as the *lever les rideaux* (curtain risers), but in many cases one of the young singers will plead with Maneko, who, having a very big heart, chooses to ignore the beginning of their next song. It is 1:26 A.M. More waiting. . . .

During all of this waiting, many of the musicians simply find a chair or a crate in a nearby space and curl up to sleep. Before becoming a part of the band, I found this habit surprising. It seemed to me that sleeping on the site of the performance (albeit in a discreetly chosen spot) made the band look tired and overworked. But as I became more involved in the band's regular work schedule, sleeping on-site made more sense. From my notes:

Getting ready for a concert is weird. It takes a lot of mental preparation. You have to have your mind clear. You're going up to perform for four to five hours straight; you've got to be in shape, and there's so much waiting, so you sleep. It's difficult to deal with the schedule. You know you'll be getting home with the sunrise, that your sleep clock will be off until Thursday of the next week, at which time you start to get ready to do it again. So you sleep. It's 1:30 A.M., you only slept for three hours the night before, so you sleep.

The bandleaders never seem to comment on this practice. In fact, they sometimes sleep themselves. To a large extent the need for sleep results from the demanding schedule of full-time practice and performance. Hours of missed sleep accumulate, and during the most ecstatic moments of the night (from 11 P.M.–2 A.M.), accompanied by the pulsating, saturated sound of an endless distorted rumba, the human body falls into a deep and satisfying state of abandon. When I first experience this deep sleep myself, I wake up to the most wonderful second wind I have ever experienced. It is, in fact, the silence that wakes me. The second warm-up band has had the plug pulled, and it is time for the main attraction. It is 1:48 in the morning. It is showtime [video].

We start much more quickly than the warm-up bands. It is a combination of the long wait and the fact that we have done this so many times before. The guitarists know the knobs with their eyes closed and are able to tune discreetly without the audience noticing. They begin with an instrumental piece (*musique de variétés*), often the same piece at the beginning of every show. It has several tempos and complex transitions that show off the skills of the instrumentalists and also help wake up the last few sleepers backstage. It is short, two to three minutes long, and as soon as it is finished, Montana (the president of the band and Defao's number 2) saunters onstage and signals the start of the first song. He is decked out in a large three-piece suit and thick black sunglasses that cover his temples as well as his eyes. Two other singers follow close behind. They pull up their pants around their waist as they prepare to take the mike. Everyone is very stiff and serious; the crowd is murmuring. There are three singers and four microphones, hinting at the imminent arrival of the star and leader of the band.

Defao will not actually arrive onstage until the second or third song. This is standard practice with most bands. The lead singer is the reason that everyone came, and he must be sparing with his presence; he must be *rare*. For similar reasons, he will also be the first one to leave, usually a full thirty to forty-five minutes before the rest of the band. It is 2:08 A.M. and the music for his entry song, "Famille Kikuta"–the closest thing the Big Stars have to a hit this year—is well underway before he arrives onstage. It has a cyclical introduction that can go on until all of his buttons are buttoned and his bleached white hair is matted in place. Then, with all eyes front and center, he floats up to the microphone and removes it from the stand, pushing the cord aside gracefully just in time for the beginning of the next cycle. This exciting moment of arrival gives me goose bumps every time. A strange, inexplicable pride swells in my throat, and just like the barefoot kid outside of the bar I feel the need to say his name out loud: "Deeeeeeefaaaaaaao!" He stands out onstage like a three-dimensional character against a two-dimensional background. "Fondé" has finally arrived (figure 35).[7]

As he begins to sing, the audience is completely transfixed until the first fan approaches with money in his hands, and places it purposefully in each of Defao's front pockets. Defao continues singing completely unfazed. The next fan approaches with one big bill and slips it into Defao's hand as he yells something in Defao's ear. He probably told Defao his name, hoping Defao would sing his praises that night, or told Defao how great he thinks he is ("Def, to sepeli na yo trop!" [Defao, you're the best!]). The next fan follows closely behind and from a wad of bills begins to shell out money on the floor at Defao's feet. He finishes the wad, gives Defao a ritualized civil servant greeting on the side of his head, and struts back to his place in the crowd.[8] By this time a constant flow of people ascends the stage to lay hands and money on Defao's person. Sometimes ignoring their attention, sometimes smiling and showing gratitude, he continues his song despite the people floating around him, putting things in his pockets, speaking in his ear, and striking poses with him. When the transition to the dance part comes he has a few seconds of freedom, as they can see him repositioning himself onstage. But after Defao's famous "wall of dance" is up and running, the crowd is once again all over him, usually two at a time, seemingly oblivious to his music or words.

The Anatomy of a Live Performance

For the most part, song order in concert is improvised. After finishing a song, the bandleader (or the president in his absence) will think briefly and call the next song to be played.[9] In most cases he announces his decision to the guitarists, one of whom relays the information to the other musi-

Figure 35. The bandleader arrives onstage; it is 2:08 A.M. PHOTO: JOHN GRINLING.

cians (drummer, singers, and keyboard player). The only other interaction between the bandleader and the rest of the band comes in the form of the elaborate dance sequences in the final part of each song. Songs usually last twenty to thirty minutes in concert. The two- and sometimes three-part song structure (see chapter 2) that lasts five to eight minutes on prerecorded material is lengthened primarily in the final part of the song, the *seben*, or fast-paced dance part. Audiences depend on hearing the words and melodies of the artist they have paid to see, but a large part of the live concert experience rests on the unpredictable, extended dance sequences that can last as long as forty-five minutes per song. The long repetitive nature of songs makes for an important part of the live aesthetic, which seeks to produce a musical atmosphere conducive to the emotional state making concertgoers want to return again and again. Repetition may be monotonous, but it is not without meaning. The long dance sequences in live performance must be seen as a means of improvisational experimentation that provide the musicians with enough time to match up the right rhythm with the right moves, sounds, and shouts. This constitutes a perfect example of the elusive groove that Charles Keil and Steven Feld (1994) have written about, and a significant number of variables—some of them completely out of the musicians' control—are required to achieve such an emotionally heightened state.

Most songs start with a slow, lyrical introduction, followed by a series of verses (so-called couplets) in which vocals predominate. Percussionists (conga player, *atalaku*, drummer) punctuate with relatively simple rhythmic patterns so as not to detract from the singer or the lead guitarist, who trade the melodic phrases back and forth throughout the verse. During this part of the song the dancers remain offstage, while the cosingers are off-mike but still onstage, each moving within his own space.[10] Each singer dances in a way that suggests he is conscious of the fact that he is onstage, but completely unaware of the people around him. He sways back and forth easily and punctuates his private dance with a series of personalized gestures: spin, dip, hand clap, push up the sunglasses, pull up the pants, tuck in the shirt. His movements are individual moments of expression, narcissistic and consciously uncoordinated with the rest of the front line. Then, when the vocals require three- and four-part harmony, he moves up to the microphone, letting go of his individual identity to once again become part of the powerful front line (*attaque-chant*). Here the singers' movements appear more coordinated. Constrained not only by complex harmonies but also by long, lyric-filled melodies, cosingers bob up and down in time with the beat, their bodies becoming human metronomes. Their hands alternate, first upturned and outstretched, shaking loosely, and then brought in to cross the chest, in a gesture that has come to signify the passion of the popular singer. Except for the percussionists, whose instruments require some upper body movement, the instrumentalists stand still as they play.[11] Whether the stoicism of the instrumentalists is a question of temperament or simply a result of the concentration required to play this style of music, their relative motionlessness stands in stark contrast to the singers and to the usually very excited crowd in front of them.

During the slow part of most songs, people dance together as couples (figure 36). A particularly slow or romantic song will lead most couples to dance *collés-serrés* (lit. "stuck together tight"), with her hands around his neck and his hands around her waist, attached at the hips: "Actually, people dance together or no one dances at all. People consider it embarrassing to be the only couple on the dance floor . . . truly ridiculous, almost humiliating. Everyone looks at you and this is not very stimulating. Here [in Zaire] people prefer to dance in a large group, close together" (John Grinling qtd. in Tchebwa 1996, 339).

Figure 36. Couples dancing during the slow, lyrical section at the beginning of a song. PHOTO: SERGE MAKOBO.

If the song is more upbeat, or as the verse moves into a more upbeat chorus, less intense couples will separate, either liberating their upper bodies, or separating their bodies altogether but keeping their arms in place. It is usually during the chorus that tension builds, leading up to the transition to the *seben*, where couples almost without exception separate completely and begin their personal variations on the most well-known dance steps of the day (figure 37).

> And what is dancing? Simply exuberance? Not at all. The man displays composure and self-control. Even when he excels it is with some reserve, his expression very serious, that he appears on the dance floor. . . . The woman sways, swinging her pelvis, while the man leads her in a nonchalant way. Then, at a more or less precise moment, sometimes within a beat, the couples separate. It is the *seben*. Women take this chance to retighten their wraparound with a large gesture that attracts attention . . . but they also want to keep their clothes from coming undone. (Grinling qtd. in Tchebwa 1996, 339–40)

As the end of the chorus draws near, the dancers and the *atalaku* come closer to the stage and the instrumentalists back up to make space for the

Figure 37. Couples separate and dance individually during the *seben*, the fast-paced dance sequence. PHOTO: SERGE MAKOBO.

seben. Every stage has a number of concentric layers. The backstage is usually made up of a ring of observers, cousins, friends, and sound engineers. The "defense," which basically corresponds to what we call the rhythm section (percussionist, drummer, keyboard player, and guitarists), forms a kind of human backdrop for the movements of the dancers and singers. Defense musicians have limited movement not only because of the restrictive space of rented or improvised podiums but also because of the ever-encroaching backstage entourage. Singers perform in two layers, the first of which is the domain of the cosingers. They are always a little bit off the microphone, even when their responses form a counterpoint to the lead singer's displays of vocal virtuosity. During many songs the lead singer and his cosingers occupy the front line together. In other songs, the lead singer takes up the entire front line himself, and the cosingers do not approach the microphone until the chorus or until after the transition into the dance segment. In front of the front line is a kind of *avant-scène*, almost exclusively used by dancers, who occasionally move there from tightened positions in the front line to perform with greater ease, sometimes as soloists. The *atalaku*, the most flexible of the musicians in terms of the use of space, darts back and forth between

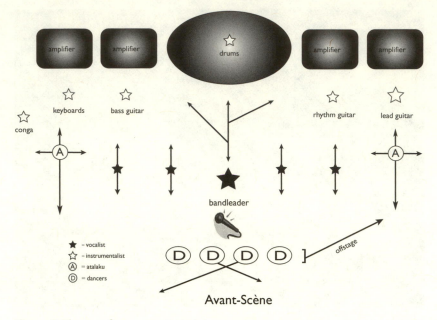

Figure 38. The use of space on a typical stage. ILLUSTRATION: BOB W. WHITE.

all of these layers, spending most of his time between the defense and the front line, but also making strategic advances into the *avant-scène*, especially to interact with the *danseuses* during the *seben* (figure 38).

The magic of the *seben* is due in part to the fact that it tends to sneak up on the audience. Musicians, intimately familiar with the structure of each song and with the cues in the chorus (both vocal and instrumental) that lead them into the *seben*, are comfortable enough with the transition to ably mask its arrival. But from the perspective of the audience, the chorus spills into the *seben* almost unintentionally, and the accompanying increase in intensity often leads to excited crowd reactions. At this point, if any space is left on the dance floor, it will soon be filled. For the musician, the transition, although not unexpected, is just as exciting. After the singers have finished the last lines of the chorus, the lead singer steps away from the microphone and raises his arm, sometimes looking around to make sure all the musicians are prepared for the change. The lead guitarist then kicks off the *seben* with a slightly accelerated guitar riff, and the drummer's snare, the *atalaku*'s maracas (now played like a rattle), and the on-mike scream of one of the singers or the second *atalaku* soon join him. Within this space of roughly thirty seconds the song changes from words to motion, with the guitarists playing fast paced and nonstop and the singers falling into a formation of choreographed release through dance. This is what I came to call, much to the pleasure of the other musicians, "thirty seconds of joy."

Dancing and Shouting

The *seben*'s mood of controlled frenzy is maintained in large part by the *atalaku*, whose job, having taken the microphone from one of the singers, is to arouse and encourage people to dance through a careful combination of shouts, sung shouts, and the vocal gymnastics that make up his bag of tricks. An intimate relationship exists between shouts and dances, and at the center of this dynamic stands the *atalaku*. As in the previous parts of each song, the crowd-pleasing *atalaku* has a great deal of flexibility during the *seben*. He is an instrumentalist, playing the maracas as an important complement to the driving rhythm of the snare drum. He is a vocalist, using the microphone both to sing and to shout. And he is a dancer, sometimes leaving aside the microphone and the maracas to join the front dance line, and sometimes dancing solo or alongside the *danseuses* in the *avant-scène*. Thus the need for two and sometimes more *atalaku*: while one is shouting, the other can continue playing the maracas. Occasional call-and-response shouts require that both *atalaku* shout at the same time. To do all this, and to maintain the energy of an extended *seben*, the *atalaku* must have incredible stamina. After the instrumentalists, the *atalaku* is the first musician onstage as he accompanies the band with high-energy shouts, dance moves, and maracas during the instrumental *variétés* music at the beginning of the show. He is on the microphone for at least two to three times as long as the singers, and during technical problems (such as instrument failure or blackouts), he will sometimes continue shouting even if his microphone stops working. It is he who "chants the hysterical shouts that are supposed to punctuate the music and direct the dance steps and physical contortions" of live performance (Tchebwa 1996, 206).

Although people commonly believe that the *atalaku* is responsible for calling dances and shouts, this is rarely the case. The succession of dance steps is determined by a number of actors and factors in the musical environment of any given performance. First, it is important to remember that dances are almost always accompanied by shouts. The motion of the dance does not always correspond directly with the content of the shout, but in most cases the two have an automatic association. There are examples of shouts that have become more well known than the dances they accompany (e.g., Super Choc's *mandundu*, Edi Gar's *makiese*, and *bizelele* sung by Nono of Zaiko Langa Langa). When shouts of this type are performed by other groups, dances from the group's own repertoire are substituted. Each song has a series of predetermined shouts (usually three or four) that come directly from the album on which the song was released. After the predetermined shouts and dances have been exhausted, anywhere from three to ten additional shouts will be added to complete the song in concert. The exact number of shouts will depend on those that are chosen (since some last longer than others) and on the point at which they are chosen, since some *seben* are shortened if the groove does not feel right.

In most bands, the most senior singer takes on the role of the dance-line leader. In this capacity he decides who calls the next dance step, which in turn signals the next shout. But his decision is constrained by a number of factors, most important of which is the structure of the song. Partitions within the *seben* correspond to motifs from the lead guitar and thus partition length and transitions between partitions are usually determined by the lead guitarist. Most dance-line leaders will call a change in step on hearing a change in partition or when seeing the lead guitarist's signal to the instrumentalists to prepare for such a change. Apart from this technical/structural constraint, the dance-line leader also pays attention to audiences' preferences for particular dances. His job is to manage dance sequences so that they will not only entertain but also appear familiar, since many members of the audience dance what the band is dancing. Certain key dances of the moment must be used sparingly so as not to wear out their popularity, and they must be well timed to maintain a certain level of excitement throughout the performance (figure 39).

The dance-line leader also holds responsibility for organizing the *danseuses*. Female singer-dancers, present in the music since the days of the vaudeville-style variety shows of the 1940s (see Fabian 1990), were first used in a systematic fashion by Tabu Ley Rochereau, who along with his Rocherettes conquered the Olympia theater in Paris in 1970. Since then, female singer-dancers have become mainly dancers, and their now ubiquitous presence (both in videos and in concert) plays on female eroticism and male desire (Biaya 1994; Chiwengo 1997). *Danseuses* are almost never onstage during the

Figure 39. The Big Stars' front line during a concert at sob's in New York.
PHOTO: SETH CASHMAN.

first parts of songs.[12] Invariably they wait backstage, preparing themselves to appear during the transition to the *seben* or during the *seben* itself. Their placement and movement onstage is directed by the leader of the dance line (either the lead singer or the most senior singer onstage at that time), but in the case of an extended dance sequence (usually in the *avant-scène*), the head *danseuse* may choose particular dance steps and positions.

Danseuses are not present for every song. When they do appear, it is usually in groups of two or more, preferably dressed in similar or complementary outfits and dancing in unison (figure 40). Compared to male dancers (most often singer-dancers), who joke with each other and exaggerate dance steps to please the audience (*mettre l'ambiance*), *danseuses* are generally more subdued in expression. They are admired for having a full figure ("tala santé oyo!": "look at how healthy she is!") and for their ability to isolate and control the movement of particular body parts, especially the hips and buttocks. *Danseuses* who smile or maintain eye contact as they dance are appreciated for their charm ("aza na charme": "she is charming"), but most dancers prefer to charm with their hips, maintaining a concentrated, indifferent expression during performance. After their arrival onstage, individual *danseuses* can

Figure 40. The Big Stars' *danseuses*: Jeancy, Monique, Mami. PHOTO: BOB W. WHITE.

break away from the small group for dance solos, often to wander into the audience to provoke men and solicit money (figure 41). Some groups will have troupes of *danseuses* (anywhere from eight to ten) and designate a special place in their show to introduce them to the audience one by one.

The dance solo gives each *danseuse* an opportunity to be noticed for her individual skills as a dancer, but it also offers a chance to make extra money. During solos the *atalaku* spurs the *danseuses* along by improvising shouts that correspond roughly to their performances. The *atalaku* pays close attention to the dancer's moves, since she often uses a step of her own or something completely improvised. He fills in the gaps by improvising shouts spiced with her name: "Mami! Would you check out Mami!" or "Jeancy! She's dancing! She's dangerous! She's dancing!" Like some singer-dancers, the dancer often uses predetermined cues that tell the drummer to accent certain gestures. One dancer shakes her hands above her head to signal a full-arm downward motion that will end in the slapping of her rear; the drummer gives her two hits on the snare drum. Another dancer gets cymbals for her footwork and the bass drum for her hips. These highly personalized solos, however, are usually no more than a prelude. Dancers know that their best chance of making extra money comes from attracting attention (not only male) on the dance floor, and the best way to do this is with suggestive gesturing.

CHAPTER FOUR

Figure 41. The Big Stars' *danseuses* venture out into the audience. PHOTO: BOB W. WHITE.

Monique, nicknamed B-52, is the tallest of the dancers, and her slow, graceful movements match what appears as demure demeanor. Her solos, however, are far from demure. After a rushed series of standard steps and breaks, she cuts the beat and walks calmly to the center microphone stand. She places the microphone on the ground and calmly carries the stand out to the middle of the *avant-scène*. Still holding on with one hand, she circles the stand until her back is facing the audience. With very little ceremony she slides both hands up and down the length of the microphone stand and starts to wind her rear in slow, exaggerated figure eights that seem to dictate the rhythm of the music. All except the distinguished guests in the single ring of front-row seats are now standing on their toes, anxious to see her next move. With skillful and suggestive gestures, the microphone stand goes from being a horse to a scratching post to a fire hydrant. The audience is delirious and has already begun to spray her with money.

She leaves the microphone stand and begins to focus on a live subject, having already spotted a wealthy-looking older man who up until now has shown no signs of being impressed. Only a few feet from his face, she turns her back to him, doubles over, grabs her ankles and begins to move her rear at almost exactly eye level. The man in the audience can remain straight-faced no longer and finally cracks a smile. His friends on either side are howling with glee and wildly encourage him to pay something for his not-so-private dancer. But before he can reach for his wallet, she has already changed positions. She hovers above his lap, facing the band and forcing him to acknowledge her presence. After she senses the bill placed nervously between her skin and her elastic body suit, she jumps up, claps her hands, and turns again to face him. Now she rejoins the rhythm already in progress and performs a dance of joy swinging her hands behind her head. She does not look at him directly, but her continued close attention acknowledges his importance relative to the rest of the audience. He is obliged to shell out more money before she agrees to move on.

Not all dancers will venture so boldly into the audience, but those who do will often perform similar acts of solicitation.[13] Mami, a short stout dancer with a fake Madonna beauty mark and overpainted feline eyes, is known for a step called "Cupid." As she steps through the *seben*, she pantomimes pulling a love arrow from her quiver, draws it in her imaginary bow, and roams around the dance floor in search of a target. Once the target is chosen, she sends him the arrow and carefully works her way to where he is sitting, zigzagging a slow, deliberate path across the *avant-scène*. Mami's finale usually has her standing on the armrests of a distinguished man's chair, slightly bent at the knees, with her pelvis dancing circles around his field of vision. The acrobatics of the Cupid dance made Mami extremely popular with the audience, but her "Coca-Cola" was also a crowd-pleaser. After having placed an empty Coke bottle in the middle of the dance floor and circling it several times with a suggestive, low shuffle, Mami places the bottle in between her legs and starts to work the crowd. With one hand behind her head and the other holding the bottle in a loose, bobbing motion, she shuffles slowly toward the audience members who are the best dressed and/or have the largest number of beer bottles on their table. Sometimes before she arrives they are already lining up in front of her. They want a chance to dance this moment of humor, and in addition to some money, they each bring their own bottle.

Danseuse solos are ecstatic high points of concert performance, but they are relatively short compared to the total time devoted to dance in a concert; some concerts do not even feature these extended solos. A variation on the *danseuse* solo is the group dance solo in which individual band members (sometimes the entire band) are pushed by fellow band members into the *avant-scène* to display their dancing skills. Male dancers usually display agility, athleticism, and humor, while *danseuses* combine technique with playful eroticism. This variation is relatively common (occurring in one of every five Big Stars' concerts), but by far the most common dance formation is the loosely choreographed line of dance performed by the front line of singers. Their movement, coordinated by cues from the dance-line leader, is tightly synchronized, but individual dancers vary motions or add accents to highlight individual style. This dance line can also include the participation of the *danseuses* (either in between or in front of the singers), and in full force can involve as many as sixteen people: eight *danseuses*, five singer-dancers, and three *atalaku*. This is known as Defao's "wall of dance."[14]

Defao has always been known for his skills as a dancer, in fact in the early years of his career he was better known as a dancer than as a singer. As the leader of the Big Stars, he managed to continue this tradition through the wall of dance, which fills the stage during the majority of his performances. In the back line, the defense moves gently, slightly changing the backdrop behind the *attaque-chant*, which is five to seven people wide and moves like a Chinese dragon: together, individually. In front of the singers are two lines of four *danseuses*, loosely synchronized but dancing a step completely different from that of the male dancers behind them. In this complex formation, the lead *danseuse* turns her head back periodically to see what the singer-dancers are doing and from time to time calls the same step for her team. When the dozen or so dancers finally sync up, it is music for the eyes. Time seems to stop and the stage floats under the weightlessness of the band. From center stage shouts of joy soar that match the volume of the *atalaku*, who by now has worked up a full sweat from his singing and dancing. The layered effect of this wall means that the spectator always has something new to watch, and on many occasions it is not clear who will tire first, the dancers or the audience.

During this dance spectacle movement also occurs in the audience. Almost all of the dance steps performed by the front line are recognized and followed by most members of the audience. Even if some people are too far back to see the exact dances, they hear the corresponding shouts over the PA system and can follow the people in front of them, all dancing in a similar fashion. Many audience members also sing along with the shouts. Of course people participate to varying degrees. Some people position themselves in front of the singers and try to impress the musicians by following the dance sequences and shouts very closely. Others know the dances and the repertoire so well they need not even look around before changing steps. This category of fan (more often female than male) will sometimes join the front line onstage, either dancing directly with the lead singer or together with the lead singer and the *danseuses* in the middle of a song. Some people dance the easiest or most obvious dances and do freestyle for the rest of the *seben*; others simply stand up with an oversized beer bottle in hand, unable to control the urge, and dance in place in front of their chairs.

Due to the frenetic pace of musical creation in Kinshasa, the most popular dances change constantly. Only a small number of dance steps earn the distinction of staying on the market for more than a year (Djuna Mumbafu's *moto* and the suggestive *mayeno* offer two good examples) and even fewer are considered good enough to be picked up and used by musicians other than those who created them (e.g., Rajakula's *kitisela*, Nouvelle Image's *kibinda nkoy*, and the 1997 rage *ndombolo*, author unknown). Relatively well-known dance steps that do not attain this level of mass popularity may last for three to six months (about the same time as the album or music videos) and are automatically associated with their creators; other musicians do not pick them up for use (e.g., Djuna Mumbafu's *bidenda*, Defao's *simbaka motema*). Thus no more than about one dozen recognizable dance steps with shouts circulate around Kinshasa at any given time. Almost all bands draw from this common pool of dances and shouts to complement their own repertoire. As a general rule, however, the number of borrowed dances should not surpass those created by members of a given band, and borrowed dances are usually adapted to bear the band's own signature.[15] Many musicians feel pressure to include at least some of these popular dances and shouts to maintain the support of Kinshasa's fickle audiences.

The majority of new dances come from unknown musicians. Most famous bands borrow from up-and-coming groups that have their pulse on youth tastes and fashions but do not yet have the legitimacy of the larger, better established bands. The band Nouvelle Image may serve as a case in point. This group of musicians took Kinshasa by storm in 1995, only partly because of their unique mixture of modern and folklore styles, and was one of the most borrowed-from groups in Kinshasa in the 1990s. Almost no professional group in Kinshasa was able to resist their trademark dance/shout *kibinda nkoy*, which when performed was usually clustered with several other nuggets from the young group's repertoire (such as *zekete* or *zitutala* and the hugely successful *ndombolo*). Examining how steps spread proves helpful for understanding how dance styles change so rapidly. Music videos have a prominent place in television programming, and dancing constitutes the key element of most videos. But before dances make it onto the television screen, they have already circulated throughout the city in bars and live concerts. Some dances are created by spectators and picked up by musicians for performance, while others make for a kind of creative borrowing between musicians (White 1999). Occasionally musicians will arrive to band practice with a new step they want to try out. The step will be shown to a fellow musician or stage companion, and if enough musicians from the dance line express interest, the step may be incorporated into the group's regular repertoire of dances.

But new ideas can also be tested during live performance in a concert setting. This was the case with a dance emerging in May of 1996 that was introduced to the Big Stars by Bleu, one of the band's lead singers. During one of the band's first shows on tour in Bas-Zaire, Bleu stepped back from the microphone, standing still, and looked around the stage. Taking advantage of a temporary calm in the dance line, he lunged forward with his arms tight to his side and took three giant steps, each with a rhythm of their own, independent of the pounding backbeat. All eyes were on him as he started to shuffle backwards with his shoulders shrugged and a huge smile on his face. His hands were spread out, with his wrists on his hips and his fingers stretched out like feelers. No one in the band was quite sure what was happening, but everyone seemed to like it. A few minutes later he lunged forward again, and the musicians egged him on as they began to realize that this was not a freak occurrence, but a new dance step. The *atalaku* identified the step as a variation of a new dance for which he knew the shout (*mobondo sabina*), and he began to shout accordingly. After Bleu had performed a few cycles of the step, various members of the band joined him in the *avant-scène* to try it out, each with his or her own version. The novelty of the step, together with the catchy shout, made it a great source of interest for the band. From my notes on May 6, 1996:

> This dance, this Bleu dance with the Monty Python silly walk, this dance is taking over our shows . . . we did what seemed like at least a forty-five-minute *seben* just to elaborate the new step. The best is Bleu, with his

Bleuettes. Théo dances it pretty well, even Mami and Jeancy have their own little version! [The musicians say] it's a dance "qui a fait plaisir"; nice to watch, very cyclical. *Kitisela*, our most popular dance, is dead; dead and buried.

The dance usually begins as a root idea or motif and then is elaborated by various members of the band, each adding his or her personal variation to the theme; a dance's longevity is directly proportional to its ability to support versions. The particular dance and shout combination here was borrowed from another band, but it was adapted and elaborated in concert and would later become an integral part of the Big Stars show. Soon the dance completely overran the previous most popular dance (*kitisela*) in terms of the performance time it occupied.

Stylistic innovation in Congolese music occurs mostly in dances and shouts. Song structure, although changing gradually over the past thirty years, has shown relatively little variation within the past decade. Lyrics also have remained very formulaic. Musicians express the fear of losing an already precious local audience base as a reason for not straying too far from standard themes about love and male-female relations (chapter 6). Thus dances and shouts are the most effective way for local musicians to express their creative impulse and distinguish themselves in a highly competitive milieu. Dances and shouts are inexpensive to create, and they require no props or costumes. They are highly mobile, easy to remember, and impossible to copyright, all factors which make them central to the dynamic of music production and consumption.

It is generally believed that well-known musicians, tired and lacking inspiration, actively seek out fresh ideas from younger and less experienced music groups or musicians. Stories abound about how well-known musicians exploit young lyricists (*paroliers*) to beef up their material and add to their repertoire.[16] But there are also many examples of less well-known musicians, even nonmusicians, offering ideas to the stars. The Big Stars repertoire of shouts and dances, totaling about thirty during the time of my fieldwork, was composed in the following way: ten of the current band's creation, eight from up-and-coming groups (Nouvelle Image, Super Choc, and Rajakula), seven from Defao's previous band (Choc Stars), and four from various unknown neighborhood groups. Part of the reason behind "borrowing" is that lesser-known and unknown groups have no recourse when profit is made from their creative energies. Established musicians enjoy performing the shouts and dances they borrow from younger groups, but they also see borrowed material as a strategy to please young audiences, and as proof of their willingness to listen to new trends and tastes.

"We Go to Be a Part of the Show"

Music, shouts, dances, and the visual overload of live music performance penetrate the personal universe of the people who make up the audience. The physical and sensual experience of loud music, alcohol, and large numbers of dancing bodies enables individuals to take part in the strange and wonderful space that musicians occupy. But people in the audience also penetrate the space of the musicians. As a local music promoter once explained to me: "In Europe you all go out and watch a show, but here we go to be a part of the show. I went to see Wemba last night and didn't even notice what color he was wearing" (personal communication, Gaby Shabani, May 8, 1996).

Various kinds of identification strategies (singing along with shouts, taking pictures with the artists during performance, placing money on the artists in various ways, etc.) enable the nonmusician to participate in the performance and at some level to identify with the musician's personal power and gestures of individual distinction. The symbolic space that separates the two, often no more than a slightly elevated stage and a set of four microphone stands, is porous, and the ease with which some members of the audience arrive onstage blurs the distinction between the stars and their fans.

Interaction among musicians and fans can be completely spontaneous, but more predictable forms of interaction also occur in concert. While waiting for musicians to change places or tune their instruments, Defao will often take the microphone and appease the audience by talking about how late he intends to stay: "OK, the music is gonna keep coming. We're going to play until . . . 6:00 in the morning." Short pause. He looks back to see if the musicians are ready. Seeing them still fumbling with their guitars, he continues to stall for time on the microphone: "We're here until 7:00 in the morning, and we're going to play all your favorite songs . . . [someone whispers something in his ear]. OK, no problem whatsoever, we're going to keep going until 9:00 this morning . . . [he turns again]. . . . You guys are a great audience, the music is gonna keep coming." On some occasions he takes requests from the audience. The requested songs do not vary much from a set of three or four Defao hits, but this strategy gives the impression of great generosity and creates an atmosphere of audience participation that heightens spectators' involvement in the performance. It sometimes happens that audience members are invited to sing the words to one of Defao's well-known songs or to play along with the band as guest musicians.

Near the end of one of our shows all of the equipment and lights in the area in which we were playing went dead due to a power outage. Suddenly we felt the darkness around us, and the full pounding sound of our fifteen-piece electric band was reduced to its naked humanness, the drummer and the *atalaku*, the only two musicians who do not need electricity to play a *seben*. Despite this temporary technical difficulty, they continued to play. The *atalaku* was unsure at first, but when he saw that the drummer had no intention of stopping, he put his microphone back in the stand and continued shouting without it. He approached the edge of the stage to get closer to the audience and started to lead them in a Big Stars shout they seemed to know: "Otoki te! Okozuwa mosolo te! Otoki te! Okozuwa mosolo te!" (If you don't sweat, you don't get paid). The crowd answered back for each response section, and then he gave them a chance to do it on their own, "Otoki te! Okozuwa mosolo te!" They were yelling at the top of their lungs, almost drowning out the drummer who was experiencing the closest he will ever come to a drum solo. Such unexpected occurrences are part of the reason that African audiences feel so attached to live performance. From my notes:

> Everybody was happy. Despite the rain, which was relatively heavy, we continued playing. At first I didn't think we would last, but then all of the sudden I said: I'm with a Zairian band playing rumba in the rain, and the show was as hot as any I had seen. What a great moment. Kabosé came over and prodded me into dancing. Chef Man just sat there playing his solo, stoic like the night. Ladi smiled, always with a slight delay (you can't smile in the middle of a Zairian chord change). Defao turned to look at me with a glimmer in his eye. I felt very happy and very lucky. (April 11, 1996)

The rain that began to fall was a moment of intimacy shared between musicians and fans, and neither it nor the blackout was able to stop the show. As the show finally ended at around 5:00 A.M., the musicians hustled into the minivan waiting nearby, and the last few musicians to leave the stage were accosted by fans who had been trying since midnight to get a picture with someone from the band: "Massa, carte moko, pardon!" (Hey, can we get a picture? Please?).

For fans at this particular concert picture taking was rendered very difficult by the elevated podium commonly used in larger, outdoor concert settings. Concerts are more commonly held in small, open-air bars with stages set back from the dance floor with little or no elevation. In this setting the atmosphere is much more intimate: the crowd is smaller, the audience is physically closer to the band, and fewer obstacles obstruct the way for audience members who want to go onstage. Thus, when pictures are taken, they are not taken *of* musicians, but *with* musicians. In most concert settings, fans simply walk onstage, stand next to the star or musician of their choice, and have their picture taken together with him or her in the middle of a song or dance number.

As soon as the lead singer arrives onstage, he is usually bombarded with members from the audience who want a picture with their favorite star. The flow of audience members is not continuous, but at particular moments (immediately after the star arrives onstage and at the beginning of subsequent songs) the stream of people wanting to pose with the star is unbroken and can easily last the entire length of a song (up to thirty minutes). People approach the stage on an as-ready basis and tend to stagger themselves, waiting at the edge of the stage until the previous fan has finished. Women seek pictures as well as men; the rich do as well as the poor. It does seem that women tend to take pictures in groups of two or three, while men usually take pictures alone. It is also more common to see younger than older people, but this might result from the makeup of the concert-going public, already relatively young. In some concert situations, picture taking can become very unruly and security guards either stop pictures all together or insist that people form a single-file line on either side of the dance floor. When the *avant-scène* becomes too crowded, some security guards will position themselves near the musicians in front of the microphone stands and act as a turnstile for one or two people to come onstage at a time.

No matter how many people want pictures, the process itself is clumsy and cumbersome (figure 42). The fan arrives onstage, usually with a very self-conscious strut, places him- or herself immediately next to the star

Figure 42. A fan of Werra Son appears onstage to have a picture taken with his favorite artist. PHOTO: SERGE MAKOBO.

he or she wishes to pose with, and proceeds to try to look natural. Young men will often put on sunglasses or adjust their clothes before the picture is snapped. Older more distinguished types will place an arm around the star's shoulder or freeze a handshake in the style of heads of state during photo opportunities. Women will stand close to the star, usually one on either side, with the star's arms wrapped around their waists or shoulders. Pictures are taken by independent photographers who move from concert to concert in search of people who want photo souvenirs of their evening: a kind of visual autograph. For about US$1.00, the photographer will take a snapshot of you with the star, take down your name and address, collect a partial payment for his services, and deliver the picture to your home in person, at which time you can pay the difference.[17] Despite the fact that most concerts have two or three different freelance photographers working simultaneously, picture taking makes for a complicated process. Photographers rarely have equipment reliable enough to take pictures in rapid succession (flashes recharge slowly, winders get stuck, etc.). Since they have very few repeat customers, there is always some discussion once the customer is onstage about who has been commissioned to take the picture.

Musicians, especially the lead singer who most often finds himself at the center of this commotion, are amazingly tolerant. Sometimes they stop what they are doing (singing or dancing), and sometimes they continue, completely oblivious to the people around them. Singers are more likely to stop midaction during the dance section of the song, since the other singers present can continue to dance while the picture is taken. Fans, however, usually prefer to arrive onstage during the first part of the song. At this point, there are usually fewer people onstage, and the fan has a better chance of getting a good picture (i.e., with the singer singing or a private shot of just the fan and the singer). This part of the song is also easier for photographers since the dance floor is not yet full. When asked how they feel about this practice, many musicians admit that they find it a great nuisance and that it tends to upset their concentration, but they also insist that it is important to the fans and thus should not be discouraged. In touring situations, where fans rarely have the chance to interact with their favorite stars from the capital, musicians appear particularly patient. Perhaps they see photographs as an important part of their ongoing efforts to maintain popularity and a positive public image, or perhaps they view it as a manifestation of their personal power and legacy as artists. A free flow of people onstage and unlimited, free photo opportunities may also create an atmosphere that encourages members of the audience to place money on or around the artist (spraying). Although fans wanting pictures and people offering money are generally not the same, there is some overlap between the two, especially given that spraying and picture-taking activities occupy roughly the same time and space in most concert performances.

The practice of spraying is always most intense immediately after the star finally arrives on stage. Spraying, as well as picture taking, occurs with varying levels of intensity throughout the show, but it becomes less common as the evening progresses.[18] Given difficult economic times, money offered to the musicians onstage is often a symbolic gesture of appreciation. Larger single bills are preferred since they lend greater prestige, but it can also prove effective to shower the musician with a large number of smaller bills, since most will fall to the ground before people in the audience can identify the denomination. Most fans give somewhere between the equivalent of seventy-five cents and a dollar, about the price of a bottle of beer. Amounts can be larger, but more significant sums of money are usually given to the musician in private, either before the show or at the musician's home, as part of an ongoing patron-client relationship (see chapter 6). Amounts can be kept discreet by simply placing the money in the musician's pocket, or directly in one of his hands. More conspicuous displays of wealth (especially those done in foreign currency such as U.S. dollars) are spread or slapped on the musician's sweating forehead. Musicians that get sprayed by many people at one time often let their entire earnings drop to the floor and pick them up at the end of the song.

During one performance a young man wearing flashy sunglasses and an oversized American T-shirt began to make repeated trips to the microphone to lay money on Defao. Each time he sprayed Defao with 5,000 NZ (the equivalent at that time of about fifty cents US), which seemed generous considering that this was only a practice session and that he returned to give money several times. After his 5,000 NZ notes ran out, he began giving 1,000 NZ notes, at which point Defao approached the microphone and started to tease, speaking to no one in particular:

"Okay, thank you, thank you. Thank you for your support. Please keep the money coming, especially the red ones [5,000 NZ notes are red, 1,000 NZ notes green], the green ones are OK, but we really prefer the red ones." The young man immediately stands up in protest:

"But I gave 12,500! The green ones added up to 12,500!" Defao backs off a bit from what he intended as a harmless joke:

"Okay, thank you, thanks friend." When the young man returns to give money again, Defao stops the music and has him come and introduce himself at the microphone. He says his name in a deep voice, kind of bending over and bobbing as he repeats it. People start to laugh and when he returns a fourth and a fifth time, they laugh even harder. It is not clear if they know him and are laughing because they see him interacting with Defao, or if (like me) they find something very exaggerated and narcissistic in the way he carries himself every time he repeats the action of laying money on Defao.

"Général! 'Hitachi'! C'mon Général, 'Hitachi'!" he yells out the name of his favorite Defao song from his seat at the front of the crowd. Defao consults his lead guitarist, flashes one of his charming underbite smiles in the direction of the young man and says: "Next song, OK?"

Spraying comes in many forms. Women will spray money on the forehead or chest of their favorite singer in the band. The *danseuses* sometimes spray their favorite singers or the junior bandleaders, but it is rare to see male members of the band spray each other. Sometimes close friends or regular fans of the band with sufficient means will spray sections of the band (for example, the singers, the guitarists, the two *atalakus*, etc.), or on special occasions the entire band. Singers are without a doubt the most heavily sprayed among all the musicians.[19] Much to the pleasure of the nonsingers in the band, I used to joke that the problem with singers is that they stand between the rest of the band and the audience. Musicians tell stories about singers, especially lead singers, capable of making as much as US$100 per night just from spraying, some from a single fan. In addition to singers, the lead guitarist, solo dancers (both male and female), and the *atalaku* are also regular recipients of sprayed money. The practice of spraying is always a high point during live performance, confirming not only that the music is good (*kitoko*), but that the musician is worthy of praise. Fans in this context are spraying more than money; they are spraying love, adoration, and their desire to be a part of the show.

5
MUSICIANS AND MOBILITY

ANY ATTEMPT TO TALK ABOUT THE ROLE OF MUSI-
cians in African society must address not only the social
position of musicians but also their mobility relative to
other social-occupational categories. In this chapter I
present a number of different types of musical and social
mobility. Some musicians have early fame in their career
and end up poor. Others have little fame until their careers
are further along. Others struggle for years and never
break through in spite of their efforts. A limited number
of musicians have boasted significant late career come-
backs, as in the case of Wendo Kolosoy (figure 43). By
focusing primarily on my own activities in Kinshasa, this
chapter attempts to shed light on certain aspects of life
as a musician in Mobutu's Zaire. Of course my personal
experience can hardly be seen as representative; indeed
the story of my involvement in a relatively successful local
dance band says as much about the privilege of white foreigners as it does about life as a Congolese musician. The
access I obtained as an outside observer and the ease with
which I was able to move between musicians and between
bands provided me with a wealth of information about
musicians' conditions and aspirations. In this sense, my

Figure 43. Wendo Kolosoy with Order of the Leopard medal.
PHOTO: BOB W. WHITE.

presence as an ethnographer functioned not so much as a filter or mirror but rather as an instrument of knowledge (Powdermaker 1966). Before explaining what I mean by this, I would first like to discuss some of the possible trajectories followed by Congolese who are trying to make a name for themselves in the world of music.

Trajectories of Fame

As some musicians are rising up or riding a wave of popularity, others are on the way out or completely forgotten.[1] Such was the case with Charles Mwamba Dechaud, the once famous guitarist and composer of Grand Kallé's African Jazz and the elder brother of the legendary Dr. Nico. When I met Dechaud he was living in the house that Nico built. Actually, he was living out back in what looked like the servants' quarters. When I arrived at the family compound, Nico's son told me to go out the same way I came in and knock on the next door over. The uncut tall grasses and manioc brush reminded me of summers spent in Mississippi as a child. I knocked lightly on the slightly opened door and after a pause a voice answered faintly from inside. I knocked again, this time on the frame of the door, and Dechaud emerged from the back room, gaunt, severe, emaciated. "Oui?" he said. "Um . . ." I was nervous. "My name is Bob White. I'm doing research on Zairian music. I was told that I should see you." He gave me a long blank stare as I proceeded to unfold my letters of presentation. I kept going even though he did not seem the least bit interested in my credentials and sat down on the tired cushion chair facing the door. He saw me looking at the 8 x 10 picture tacked to the otherwise bare walls. "You see that picture?" he asked. "That's me with the American ambassador. He gave me that guitar, the same one in the chair." The guitar was sitting in the chair upright, a tired but faithful companion, covered with a fine layer of dust. Dechaud said he was sick and that he had asked someone for money to buy medicine, but that they never gave it to him, so I instinctively pulled some money from pocket and handed it to him. He thanked me, stood up, and told me to come back whenever I felt like it. "We'll do something good," he said, visibly energized by my gesture, which in real terms was little more than symbolic. As I was leaving, I felt as though I had seen a ghost. Nico and Dechaud were two of the original members of African Jazz. It was hard not to be struck by the difference: one had built an expensive house in a well-to-do neighborhood, while the other one lived in it, hidden in the back, completely forgotten.

At about the same time that day, Lofombo, one of Kinshasa's brightest rising stars, the bass player and musical arranger for Pépé Kallé's Empire Bakuba, was putting the finishing touches on his newly rented apartment in Bandal. Up until now he had been staying at his mother's house with his seven-odd brothers and sisters, one of whom used the house as the home base for his own band. Lofombo was starting to feel the pressure to move out, not only because of his age or the fact that his wife was expecting their first child but also because the number of people who solicited his advice and services was steadily increasing, and he felt the need to live in a neighborhood with easier access and more prestige than Bumbu, a heavily populated and somewhat remote neighborhood. More and more people had begun to recognize him on the street, partly because of the fashionable intellectual look he cultivated (oversized corduroy button down shirts, baggy pants, and small round eyeglasses over a partial goatee), but also because he had appeared in several high-profile music projects and was starting to make a name for himself as a studio programmer and engineer.

Moving into a new apartment and planning the wedding with his high school sweetheart required considerable amounts of money, but these were moves he was expected to make given his relative renown as a professional musician. Lofombo was careful to invest his money in ways that would help his career as well as his image: he had two VCRs (which he used to copy videocassettes), a large-screen TV, three guitars, two guitar effects boxes, two microphones, a double audiocassette deck, and two Roland R-8 programmable rhythm machines. Unlike most musicians, he was saving the car for last. As a first-string musician in one of the capital's top dance bands, Lofombo was able to take advantage of a busy touring schedule, regular paid projects on the side, and the adoration of wealthy fans who sprayed him with money for his ability to make them dance. When his first son was born in the fall of 1996, Lofombo was well on his way to becoming a star.

For every successful popular musician in Kinshasa, there are hundreds—if not thousands—that did not make it. Young aspiring singers bob up and down as they sing, precociously imitating their musical idols, perhaps hoping that one day they, too, will be a source of adulation, inspiration, and envy. This motion, repeated hundreds of times every weekend by countless singers, is intended as a sign that the singer has star potential and that the music is *kitoko* (good or pretty; see Pwono 1992). The motion may be related to the need for the singer, faced with complex harmonic and rhythmic combinations in vocal lines, to become a sort of human metronome. Or maybe it is an ecstatic response: the hands also bob up and down—palms open—with their own rhythm, and together with a slight tilt of the head, they recall the gestures of receiving that are common in charismatic Christian churches. It is a motion that has become a necessary part of most artists' stage presence and (ironically enough) an important expression of individual style [video]. Other accompanying gestures also punctuate the performance: the way that singers look to the side or behind them during other vocalists' solos, the raised eyebrow and arm to signal the transition to the *seben*, the handkerchief delicately dabbing a sweating chest or forehead, the distinctive bad-boy walk (exaggerated steps, head tucked in the neck, arms dangling at the side), and the almost compulsive habit of twisting pant waists and pulling them above

Figure 44. "I love music, that's why . . . I want to be a real singer!" SOURCE: BARLY BARUTI, *PAPA WEMBA: LA VIE EST BELLE* (KINSHASA: AFRIQUE ÉDITIONS, 1987).

the hips. All of these gestures intend to give off an aura of celebrity, as if to say: "Do you see this? I'm a star up here!"

Not surprisingly, the historical register on popular music is filled with writing about those who succeeded against the odds. This story, told count-less times for every generation of aspiring Congolese musicians, is immor-talized in Mwenze Ngangura and Benoit Lamy's 1987 film *La vie est belle* star-ring a young Papa Wemba who can think of nothing but song lyrics and records (figures 44). While these success stories are to be understood as the exceptions to the rule, certain patterns do emerge when one listens to people tell these stories. Everyone knows, for example, that Wendo used to be an en-gine greaser on the state-run riverboat transport system. Or that Franco used to sit on his mother's lap while she sold donuts in the nail market. Or that Koffi got his start writing song lyrics in secret for Papa Wemba. Stories and their details vary considerably, but those that emerge from popular versions of musicians' trajectories often correspond very closely with the stories that musicians tell themselves, suggesting that these narratives have most likely resulted from a co-construction among musicians, journalists, and fans.

In Kinshasa people constantly reminded me that musicians are considered roguish, uneducated, and hedonistic. Arguably musicians' position in Zairian society has improved somewhat as the industry has become increasingly professionalized and as certain stars have become independently wealthy through their work. But to this day musicians project an image that often casts them as *voyous* (hoodlums), *bon viveurs* (pleasure seekers), or as morally suspect. Most people do not expect musicians to read, write, or express themselves in French. They are thought to be impulsive, frivolous, and are expected to spend their final years in a state of abject poverty. Stories abound about how parents attempt to keep their sons away from music and their daughters away from musicians, the implication being that wealth or social status not earned through more noble means is unsustainable and most likely tainted by the ills of illegality or, worse, of witchcraft.

Despite the threat that musicians supposedly pose to public morality, their outrageous self-presentation and attitude make for interesting conversation and for many people constitute a regular source of entertainment (White 2004). Some people take issue with the musician's lifestyle (working at night, multiple sexual partners, drugs and alcohol, etc.) yet they are also eager to explain that the musician serves an important role as a social commentator or moralist. The late Franco, cofounder and leader of O.K. Jazz, is often given as an example. People speak of the forceful social commentary in his music as somehow related to his marginal position in society. Popular accounts of Franco's story usually focus on the importance of his message and how his ability to convey it was related to his humble beginnings. The following are common statements about the musician: "Franco was poor, so he told it like it is." "He came from a poor family; he used to sit with his mother as she sold donuts in the Bayaka market. In his songs he used to criticize everyone and everything, to such a point that he was everybody's friend." "Franco gave us music with advice that we could learn from, and that's what matters most about music."

Professional musicians in Kinshasa are sensitive to the fact that becoming a star does not come easily. In fact, they tend to see this process as just that, a process, one that evolves over time and that requires not only talent but also determination and strategy. Musicians groom their star status in much the same way they groom their hair, carefully constructing an effect or an image that will increase their chances of being noticed. As people in any career, musicians are concerned with making the right moves at the right time to ensure their continuous path to stardom, or what they refer to as *védettariat* (from the French word *védette*, meaning "star"). One musician friend of mine asked if I would consider appearing with him on a local music television program. It was his first time on television, and he felt that my presence would help his image in this important debut appearance. He already had a small fan club that had formed around him, and he was beginning to compose songs and sing extended solos, all important aspects of any professional singing career. Musicians listen very closely to what is said about themselves and other artists in bars, taxis, and on television, and they often scan the local press for references to themselves or their bands (figure 45). Many musicians judge their success at any given moment simply by the amount of money they receive during performances or by the number of gifts fans give them.

Most lead singers and even some second- or third-string singers in Kinshasa's biggest bands have fan clubs. In most cases these are people who are already fans of the group but have decided to organize around their special interest in a particular member of the band. Musicians benefit from saying that they are enough of a star to merit their own fan club, and fan club members generally expect some kind of preferential treatment, especially with regard to attending certain shows and private engagements. Several singers explained to me that the fan club's main responsibility is to manifest its admiration for the star, but in some cases the fan club members can even help the star further develop his *védettariat*, joining together to collect money or clothes to be given or lent to the star. This activity takes on a very public quality, with members of the fan club hanging banners and conducting caravans (*carnaval* or *cortège*) in the star's honor and appearing on local television programs to speak publicly about their commitment to the artist. Fan club members are among the most active audience members in terms of spraying money. On some occasions, artists will "plant" money with key members of the fan club organization, hoping that if others see a musician getting sprayed, they, too, will be moved to give. Most young artists will approach close friends or acquaintances to form the core of their fan club, but some fan clubs (especially for musicians already well known) come into existence without the musician's involvement.

One afternoon I found myself seated with Shora Mbemba (the leader and

Figure 45. Front page of a fanzine with General Defao in the center (*TRIBUNE DES STARS*, NOVEMBER 1999).

founder of the group Super Choc) at an open-air bar in the neighborhood in which he lives, and I was soon taken by the way that sound and people quickly filled in the empty space around us. Before we arrived, the bar had been almost completely empty. It was 7:00 P.M. and the music was playing, although not very loudly. There was plenty of movement in the street, but no one had as yet sat down to have a beer. As soon as we arrived, the bartender came out, wiped down the table with a rag and a bottle-opener keychain in one hand and with his other hand placed several glasses on the table in front of us. He greeted Shora discreetly and took a few steps back, politely waiting beside the table until we were ready to order. After he returned inside, the music changed to Super Choc's latest album, and the volume was pumped up to its normal saturated maximum. Shora did not react except to say, almost under his breath, "that's our album."

After the beer was served the flashing lights and sirens attached to the inside of the patio roof began to go off, but this was not what attracted so many young children to where we were sitting. They had started coming close almost as soon as we arrived. They tried to sneak up behind the wall surrounding the elevated *terrasse* overlooking the street nearby. They listened to our conversation and tried to imitate some of our sentences, giggling in between. The bartender would shoo them away from time to time with a feigned expression of anger: "Go on! Get out of here! Little brats!" Those too afraid to get close had formed a two-tiered wall of dance in the distance and were practicing the dance steps that corresponded with the shouts blaring from the loudspeakers. Shora called my attention to the children: "You see the kids? They know all the dance steps." And they did. They could have been his front line. When they saw him pointing in their direction, and both of us turning to watch, they picked up the pace, exaggerated their movements, and smiled vigorously.

Most fans were not nearly so timid in approaching their favorite stars. I remember a taxi ride with Lofombo in which the taxi driver immediately recognized the rising star in his rearview mirror and, after agreeing to drop us off on the other side of town, proceeded to lecture Lofombo on how, as an up-and-coming public figure, he should behave with restraint:

"Lofombo, you're very good. Everybody says that you're good. You take your work seriously, you know the latest technology, and you can really make people dance with that bass of yours. But I have something to tell you. You have to be careful about how you carry yourself. It's important to stay humble, listen to your fans, and most of all don't let it go to your head. Do you hear what I'm saying?" Lofombo smiles and nods in a gesture of acquiescence. "You have a long career ahead of you. It's important not to let it go to your head. Do you hear me, little brother?" He answers without hesitating: "Yes, big brother." (Field notes, April 30, 1996)

But musicians in Kinshasa are not known for their humility. In many cases, popular musicians' popularity goes straight to their heads, altering their ability to see themselves or their actions in an objective manner, and this is when people start to say that musicians *friment* or *basalaka fière*, meaning they show off. *La frime* can take many forms, some more conscious than others, some taking on the status of a strategy. The bandleader, for example, must not arrive on stage at the same time as his musicians. In most bands, different levels of musicians arrive on stage in roughly the same order that they appear in the band hierarchy: rhythm section (sometimes with the dancers and the *atalaku*), second-string singers, first-string singers, and finally the lead singer and/or star of the band. Similarly, the stars of the band should be the first to leave the concert. Private transportation to and from the concert is standard, tinted windows and Mercedes are preferred, but any car is better than none. Bandleaders often instruct musicians to arrive as a group at the concert venue well before the beginning of the concert. This ensures that the group does not lose spectators skeptical about the band's arrival, but it also makes the bandleader's arrival more grandiose. At the end of the concert, the departure occurs in the reverse order of the arrival: first the bandleader, then the junior leaders, then the rest of the band.

During one of the few weeks I had a vehicle at my disposal, I was often solicited for help with transportation. A musician friend of mine asked if we could spend the morning together so that he could drive around the city. "I have some important business," he said. At first I refused, saying that I would be responsible if anything happened. But, as usual, the hot weather and the musician's insistence wore away at my resolve. As we drove around Kinshasa, I began to think that the singer did not really care where we went: "I just like to drive," he said. Judging from the type of errands we were doing (mostly dropping in on his girlfriends), it became obvious that he also liked to be seen. As we returned to the car each time, he would carefully place his wide-rimmed dark sunglasses, look at himself in the mirror, roll down the windows, and turn up the music. He drove around at a slow cruising speed, his left arm hanging over the driver's door, slapping hands with adoring friends and fans and stopping to joke with traffic police. "Everybody knows me," he said as a matter of fact. "That's the way it is in Kinshasa." Musicians know that as soon as they venture into public, and for a better part of the day, they will be the object of attention and scrutiny. Some people will call to them, some will ask for money, some will cheer and send the thumbs up. Others will simply stop what they are doing and stare.

The way that most popular musicians carry themselves in public and the attitude they exude express their personal style. All of the visible signs of musicians' *védettariat*—their means of transport, their way of walking, the clothes they wear, the way they wear them, the company they keep, and so on—are tied to an internal power that despite its sometimes outrageous external appearance is supposed to be topped off with a thick layer of *maîtrise* (mastery) (Friedman 1990). A considerable amount of research has been conducted on the Pool region's youth fashion phenomenon known as *la sape*. The term itself comes from the acronym of Brazzaville's Société d'Ambianceurs et Personnes Elégantes (Society of People Who Like to Have a Good Time and Who Are Elegant). Members of this movement, or *sapeurs*, hold periodic competitions in the form of fashion shows, but instead of highlighting designers, they highlight themselves, or rather their ability to mix and match the brand names of high fashion that make up their performative repertoire. I will only devote limited attention to the *sape* phenomenon, because *la sape* is less institutionalized in Kinshasa than it is in Brazzaville, making it more of an idiosyncratic personal expression than a coherent form of social organization.[2] In Kinshasa, participation in formalized *sape* organizations or competitions does not exist in the way that Justin Daniel Gandoulou has discussed for Congo-Brazzaville (1989). However, musicians in Kinshasa are on the whole very conscious of what they wear and clearly compete with each other when it comes to their clothes and their look. The naming and showing of labels (*griffes*) during live performances is one of the ways in which *la sape* manifests itself in the Kinshasa music scene. This practice, though sometimes done with an ironic tone, may be seen as a means by which musicians symbolically insert themselves into the prestigious lineages of international high fashion. Although very few musicians in Kinshasa refer to themselves as *sapeurs*, they nonetheless cultivate the outward signs and gestures often associated with the movement. A heightened sense of awareness with regard to clothes and clothing labels makes clothing a common topic of conversation among musicians, and much of the language of the *sapeurs* from Brazzaville has been registered among musicians and their fans in Kinshasa (Tchebwa 1996).

Getting in the Band

When I first met the singer General Defao, he was at the peak of his musical career. Earlier that day I had been having a beer with my friend John, the founder of a local NGO for children who had lost their parents to HIV-AIDS, and also a keen observer of Congolese popular dance music. I announced my decision to approach Defao to see if I could play with his band. John already knew Defao, so he said simply,

"Great. Shall we go see him then?"

"Now?" I asked, caught off guard.

"Sure, why not?" He finished his beer and began to get up from his chair.

"But I'm not ready . . . I . . ."

"Of course you are. . . ." I recognized his mischievous grin, and decided to accept his challenge.

Defao's group had a reputation for discipline, and I thought this would facilitate my research. His Big Stars worked on a regular basis (four practices and two to four concerts per week), and they were known for playing very often in les quartiers populaires (lower-income neighborhoods), a practice I expected would expose me to the way the majority of people in Kinshasa lived. The band, which began in the early 1990s, was already well known in Kinshasa, but was only starting to make its name in other parts of the world. When I arrived in Kinshasa, the Big Stars had just finished their first European tour, and they were starting to attract more contracts in other parts of Africa, especially in Zambia. The band had never managed a truly big hit song (un tube), but when I arrived, it had already produced six full-length albums. Despite the fact that Defao's operation faced financial struggles, his careful management of band resources meant that the Big Stars was one of the few bands to have its own equipment and practice space (occasionally rented to other bands), and the only band at that time to have its own transportation. Thus I saw the Big Stars as a group clearly on an upward swing, and I thought this mobility would give me valuable insight into the cultural and social aspects of being a popular musician in Kinshasa.

On our arrival, John and I had to make our way through five gatekeepers, people supposed to keep a distance between Defao and the general public. Finally, after gatekeeper number four, we arrived at what seemed to be Defao's front door. "Is Defao here?" John asks. Gatekeeper five: "Who is it?" Without hesitating, he replies: "Monsieur John." "One moment, please." He went in quietly, came out again a few moments later, closed the door behind him, and said, "You can go in now."

And there we were, face to face with General Defao, in what seemed to be a living room, although it was hard to be sure since the furniture was covered with piles of clothes, all of them new, some still in their packages. There was barely a place to sit down, so we stayed standing. Defao was not tall, but he was big. He had an underbite smile and a pleasant demeanor. He was wearing black and a Chicago White Sox baseball cap, just like in the video I had seen in Montreal. He said he had just returned from a year in Paris where he had gathered enough material for three albums and produced two. He had also returned with some clothes. In between our awkward, broken bits of conversation, he was talking to the other two men in the room about what items they would take, though I am not sure if they were buying items or choosing their gifts. It was very strange, the three of us standing there: Defao with a big smile on his face, not sure why we were there. John was a bit nervous. He had introduced me as his friend: "This is Bob; he's a musician." Defao started talking about their practice time, and I asked if I could sit in on one of their practices. "Pas de problème" Defao said, smiling and looking at the clothes on the floor, nodding his head. "No problem."

The next day I showed up promptly as agreed. "Come and sit down, Monsieur Bob." I walked behind the person who was leading me by the hand, a little embarrassed at being pulled through the very tight crowd to the front-row place d'honneur. I expected that people would gawk at me, commenting on the fact that there was a mundele (white/foreigner) in a local band practice in Ngiri Ngiri, a relatively poor neighborhood near Bandal where I was living. For once, to my surprise, nobody seemed to notice me at all; everyone in this room was watching the Big Stars. The practice room, already half filled by members and friends of the band, was about the size of a large living and dining room area combined. The performance space itself (including several rows of dancers) took up almost half of the room. A row of seats was placed in a U-shaped formation, some against the walls near the front, some facing the band. The space behind the seats was used for standing room. When I scanned the audience, its members continued looking at the band. My seat was the corner section of a locally fabricated living room set that some years ago must have been someone's status symbol. It was pushed against the wall of the practice hall, stage left, just in the perfect place to let me see both the band and the audience.

At first I expected "practice" to be the somewhat intimate, exclusive activity common to my own musical culture. Most American musicians only practice with close friends or other musicians present. Practice is not a place for onlookers, but a session for work—a place in which mistakes are acceptable and problems are ironed out. The Big Stars' practice, however, was filled with people who had come to see a show. In fact, the band even charged admission at the door. Many full-time professional bandleaders have taken up this activity to subsidize the cost of maintaining large bands, which often have upward of twenty-five members. In the words of the band manager, Maneko: "Practice is difficult because people are there [watching the practice], so I can't really stop the show; they pay their entrance of 5,000 NZ [US$0.50]. We started at 2,500 NZ, but there were just too many people, so we put it up to 5,000. Soon we'll have to go 10 or 15; it's a way for us to make a bit of money to get by." Money from "the door" would sometimes be distributed to musicians to help pay for food and transportation. This practice makes it possible for the group's leader to use admission money from concerts for other (often personal) purposes, and also serves to reinforce his image as a good boss (see chapter 7).

After I sat down, I gestured hello to Montana (Defao's most high-ranking band member), but he was nestled in the opposite corner of the room, sitting behind the mixing board and speakers, remaining somewhat aloof from the spectacle going on in front of us. He was dressed in all white except for the thick black sunglasses that only further accentuated his white hair. White hair was becoming a bit of a fad with the Big Stars. Defao had been the first to completely bleach his hair, and Montana followed suit not long after. Later, other band members would do the same, although they usually only had enough money to bleach one part of their hair or to partially bleach all of their hair, leaving reddish stripes and patches. Besides making a fashion statement, the members of the group, it occurred to me, must have performed this bleaching ritual to express their loyalty to Defao, whose short-cropped cotton top had become one of his trademarks. I motioned to Montana again, and he gestured that he would come to see me in a minute, though he never came. At that point in his career he was a young leader in the group, and was gradually becoming a star in his own right; I think it was understood that I was supposed to come to him. After the first song, I started feeling the music take me over as it usually does, but having been in the region for several months, I was beginning to make considerable progress with my self-control. In this setting it is not very common for adult men to show physical signs of enjoying the music (foot tapping, head bobbing, finger snapping, etc.) on the dance floor or onstage. So I sat. It was difficult because the atmosphere was very intense. The crowd of mostly young men, but also some young children (five to ten years old, both male and female), was in a kind of frenzy, each one alternating between dancing in place and watching the antics of the very spontaneous choreography of the front line. The crowd was advancing slowly, spilling into the singers' performance space, and this led Montana to stop the music.

"Okay," he yelled, "woah, woah, everybody just relax. You guys have to take it easy, this is not our space. You people that come over from Bandal, this is not Bandal. This is Ngiri Ngiri. Just relax, okay?" Holding onto the microphone, he turned his head back to double-check that all the musicians were still in place, then took the microphone again: "The dancers, where are the dancers? Are they ready?" There was a commotion in the crowd, as the people in the audience tried to locate the person who wanted to try out for the band. A young woman, very modestly dressed, stood up, grabbed her handbag, and pushed her way through the crowd outside of the building. There was more talk inside the steaming room until a few moments later she returned garbed in a garish turquoise and violet bodysuit, a somewhat ordinary costume for female dancers in Kinshasa. Montana brings her to the microphone:

"What's your name?" he asks, pointing the microphone at her.
"Olga."
"Married yet?"
"No."
"Where you from?"
"Ngiri Ngiri." Montana motions the audience to give her a round of applause. She is not being judged on her oratory skills.
"Okay, okay. Let's go. *Seben!*" He turns to signal the start of the music.

She started dancing almost immediately. She probably understood that chances like this do not present themselves often and that if she wanted to be selected she would have to act fast. She stretched out her arms, put her hands together in front of her, tilted her head back and started to shuffle toward the crowd. It was the dance of the day, *kibinda nkoy*. She turned and floated one half of her behind on the fourth beat of every measure. Her hips jerked with a pattern difficult to discern, her eyes looked to the sky, her nostrils flared. Before very long the crowd started to react. She dropped to the ground face first with her arms in front of her and began a grinding motion between her pelvis and the cement floor, sending a wave of cheers through the audience. She and her crowd were playing off of each other; even Montana was laughing. Already a half a dozen teenagers had come to place money on different parts of her body; some went in her nylon body-suit, some stuck to her skin where she was sweating, the rest made contact on her forehead and then fluttered lazily to the ground in a pile around her. The people in the audience were on their feet. There was a constant flow of people walking up to lay money on her.

To all of this she remained indifferent, so concentrated on her movements that she seemed almost unaware of the frenzy she had provoked in the audience. Montana rarely looked at her; he was more interested in seeing the audience's reaction. He approached the microphone and signaled for the music to stop as she got up from the floor and brushed off the dirt on the back of her tights, not noticing that it was mostly the front that needed whisking. Montana then took the microphone: "So what do you think? She's good, huh?" The crowd roared and whistled. "Can she dance or what? Do we take her? What do you think?" The volume was rising. "Do we take her?" Everyone, especially the teenage boys, were yelling in unison, "Oui!" "Do we take her?" "OUI!" "OK, we'll take her." The crowd roared again, and the dancer clasped her hands together over her head in a victory sign. She made the audition. Montana gave her the same interview as in the beginning, but this time she was smiling. She went over to the other dancers who congratulate her with artificially friendly pecks on the cheek. They all had the same look on their face, something similar to the expression of young women competing in a beauty pageant. With that the practice-performance ended, and for whatever reason Olga was never heard from again.

That week I attended several practices, and before the week was up I received a special invitation from the administrator and lead guitarist of the band, Maneko, who was interested to know what had brought me to Zaire. I told him I was a musician:

> "Really? What instrument do you play?" he asked.
> "Guitar," I said.
> "Ah, *bon?*" His face lit up.
> "Do you play?" I asked, since I did not see him onstage that day.
> "Yes, well, I'm the lead guitarist." Changing the subject: "Hey, do you know any blues?"

"Sure, blues, rock, you know, the basic American stuff." He had a distracted look on his face; he saw Montana leaving and grabbed him to introduce us.

"Président, this is Monsieur Bob, he's a guitarist."

"Alright, well this is our *chef*, the lead guitarist, you can practice a few songs with him and then come play with us." I tried to keep my cool, but I was excited inside.

"Hey, that would be great," I said. And I didn't even have to audition, I thought to myself. This was the color of privilege.

In my first meeting with Maneko, I explained my research and expressed interest in joining the band, and almost immediately he began talking about setting up a regular training schedule. The fact that I did not have to audition to play with the band said much more about the role of white foreigners in Zairian history than it did about my credentials: I had no formal musical training to speak of, and based on our conversation neither Maneko or Montana knew anything about my musical talent.

Mundele ya Biso ("Our White Person")

Foreign (i.e., white) musicians have a long history in Zairian music (Tchebwa 1996). The first whites were influential in early studio recordings, especially with wind and brass instruments (Fud Candrix on saxophone and clarinet; Gilbert Warmant on solovox), guitar (Bill Alexandre), organ and piano (René Pilaeis, John Werk), and especially as sound engineers and protocol managers (Charlie Hénault, who also played the drums with African Jazz). In the years leading up to independence, and especially after independence, white musicians became less common in Congolese ensembles, although there are some examples from the 1980s (there have been several European and Asian instrumentalists in Papa Wemba's European formation of Viva La Musica and Boketchu Premier's Swede Swede used a white dancer in the lineup for a certain period of time).[3] Apart from those who participate as dancers, most white artists have played imported instruments or instruments thought to be more technical or at least more technological, especially keyboards and guitars. This phenomenon, I suspect, results not only from the shortage of local expertise on particular instruments but also from the local perception that particular instruments require formal musical training and greater familiarity with recent technology. Given that I had played the guitar since the age of thirteen, and with the prominent role of the electric guitar in Congolese popular music, I assumed that if I played with a local band, I should play the guitar.

Chef Maneko felt very strongly that I should start by learning the rhythm guitar, "because that's the base of the music," he used to say. "There are too many people who think it's really cool to play lead guitar so they go straight to lead, but they never learn the really important stuff like the names of chords or the structure of a song." At my first training session, Maneko sat me down under a little thatched-roof structure next to his house that served as a kitchen and a hair salon in addition to being a practice space. The first song we started working on was not difficult per se, but I quickly became frustrated due to a small group of onlookers forming around us and not being accustomed to an audience practice, especially in the early phases. I imagine that they were not accustomed to seeing their friend Maneko giving lessons to foreigners, and so they stayed. It was disconcerting, but I decided that in this case I had to adapt. When I finally got past the initial discomfort of being watched doing something very poorly, I was able to assimilate a few phrases and to begin learning the structure of the song. But my concentration was broken again by interventions from the small crowd, with individual members trying to sing the notes I was attempting to locate on the guitar.

Even before the end of this first practice session I understood that this style of guitar playing differed substantially from anything I had ever before encountered. On the surface Congolese guitar playing appears relatively simple because the number of chord changes within any given song remains somewhat limited (song patterns such as I–IV–V intervals or I–IV–I–V intervals are the most common). But the elaborate ways in which these chords are exploited (arpeggios, variations, and polyrhythmic accents) make playing rhythm guitar in the Congo extremely difficult. In a typical popular song, there may be no more than three or four basic chords throughout the entire piece, but the number of chord variations (the same chord in a different position or on a different part of the neck) can be anywhere from three to five times that number. In addition, each variation has its own particular set of rhythmic accents, which often runs counter or is complementary to the melody and the parts being played by the other guitars. I was faced with the mystical, almost mythical African polyrhythmic that I had read so much about (see, e.g., Chernoff 1979) and that I had hoped to escape by playing the guitar instead of the drums. My lack of formal musical training, something that came as a great surprise to my fellow musicians, seemed to have finally caught up with me.

Polyrhythmic elements, to me the most difficult obstacle to overcome, were generally taken for granted in this setting. My various teachers' explanations of what I was doing wrong often overlooked the complex sets of rhythmic guitar strokes I was trying to perform. Instead, their comments usually had something to do with the speed at which I played, the hand position, or inevitable "missed notes." When it became obvious that I was being held up by the *battement* (the rhythm) and not by the notes themselves, the person working with me would almost invariably take the guitar and try to show me by example (as opposed to trying to correct what I was doing through verbal explanation). This rarely worked, however, since the basic problem was one of comprehension: I simply could not hear the rhythmic pattern being played for me, and thus remained unable to reproduce it.

Trying to learn the guitar for the Big Stars proved difficult, for social as well as technical reasons. I had hoped to work closely with one of the band's six guitarists, but every time I arrived to practice, the guitarist had either "stepped out for a few minutes" or was sleeping. It was not until later that I realized, pained with embarrassment, that it probably was so hard to learn the guitar with them because I did not pay them. Most of the musicians were working for a monthly salary that amounted to little more than a symbolic pittance — certainly not enough to pay their living expenses — but they were afraid to leave the band. So what did they do? They slept. Why should they provide extracurricular training for someone imposed on them from above when they barely even received pay for their work as performers? If I had understood this from the beginning it would certainly have changed the nature of our working relationship.

Maneko put no pressure on me to learn quickly. In fact, he seemed more concerned that I follow a certain progression of steps and take the time to get each one right. In my case, pressure was usually self-imposed; the end of my fieldwork was almost always on my mind. One day Maneko heard me in the practice room working on a solo part I had taught myself the night before. He came in later, sat down next to me, and said, "Monsieur Bob, you're a guitarist with the Big Stars, and as a guitarist I have to say that I think you should take things one step at a time," suggesting that by working on lead parts I was not following the proper order of learning. The famous guitarist Lokassa ya Mbongo tells a similar story of when, during his training under the African jazz guitarist Mwamba Dechaud, he inadvertently stumbled on a minor chord and attempted to integrate it into his composition. "One day I touched an A minor by accident. He looked at me and said, 'Who told you to touch an A minor? Who said you had the right to touch that chord?" From then on I only played minor chords when I was alone" (interview, June 30, 1997).

My forays into this forbidden territory partly derived from the frustration I was feeling with my slow progress on the rhythm guitar. There was very rarely someone with whom I could practice, and it was especially rare to be able to practice with a singer. Furthermore, it took me almost a week to learn my first song, an inordinate amount of time when compared to the one to two hours it usually takes me to master a song in my own musical culture. Learning this way of playing the guitar almost proved a full-time job. I used to watch Vieux Ladi and Maneko in practice and onstage, overwhelmed by the seemingly endless number of fingerings and positions they mastered, thinking to myself: "No wonder Maneko barely moves onstage. No wonder you rarely see a guitarist who is also a singer. No wonder guitarists don't dance; this guitar requires total concentration." The first time I performed in public was during one of our weekly open rehearsals. I was disappointed with my performance and decided that I would have to do better next time. Next time did not come for a while (almost three weeks), but when it finally did, I was much more prepared and somewhat more confident than the first time. This time it was a real concert setting, and I played for the entire length of a twenty- to twenty-five–minute song. There was something reassuring about forming part of the rhythm section, but I also felt removed from the audience and closed in between the amplifier stacks and the singers in the front line. My movement was limited, and I envied the musicians in front of me who could move around freely onstage. Standing only a few feet behind the dance line, I felt weighed down by my guitar.

Prayer, Leopard, Insecticide

About halfway through my research, my fiancée came to visit me in Kin-shasa. Since I knew she would be staying for a full month, I dragged her along during my everyday activities. I am not sure whether it was the heat that day or the fact that she was present, but I was having a particularly hard time with one of the partitions that my guitar teacher Ladi was trying to show me. I had been practicing at home and felt extremely frustrated by the fact that I seemed to have learned the partition incorrectly, which meant that the first thirty minutes of our session were devoted to unlearning what I had taught myself over the previous week. We repeated the partition dozens of times: first Ladi playing, then me trying to imitate, then Ladi playing again, then me trying to imitate, then Ladi singing the partition, then me trying to imitate. But no matter how hard either of us tried, I could not make my fingers do what this song required of them. I was sweating and frustrated and could see that my fiancée was getting uncomfortable on my behalf. She suggested that I take a break, but I insisted that I was close to getting it. I was determined to stay in that steaming practice room until I got it right.

In the end I never got it right, and we left that day with a heavy cloud hanging over both of our heads. She knew that in this state of mind I was not receptive, so she waited until later that evening to talk about what had happened:

> "Bob," she said carefully, "is learning the guitar really important for your research?"
>
> "What do you mean?" I was caught off guard by her question. "This is the most important part of the music. The music is nothing without the guitar."
>
> "Yes, but is it the most important part of your research?"
>
> "Of course it is. I'm a guitarist. What else could be more important?"
>
> "I don't know, what else is there?"
>
> Long, pregnant pause . . . then I turn to her and say:
>
> "You think I'm wasting my time. . . ."
>
> "I think you're banging your head against a wall, and I think you have a lot of work to do before you come home."

We continued talking about my frustration with the guitar, and it came out that what interested me most about Congolese popular music, in fact what had drawn me in from the beginning, was the phenomenon of *animation*, the fast-paced dance section of each song driven by the words and movements of the *atalaku*. The *atalaku*'s potential to provide particular ways of understanding popular music in Kinshasa, not only in terms of the third space that music creates between tradition and modernity (White 1999) but also because of the degree to which it is embedded in local ways of doing and thinking about politics. Later that week I decided to sit down with Chef Maneko and tell him that I was giving up the guitar. I was not sure how he would take it, but I knew that if I continued to struggle with the guitar, I would never have enough time to learn what I wanted to about the social and cultural aspects of the music. I needed to play an instrument whose mechanics were simple enough to allow me to focus on the mechanics and meanings of other things, primarily the interaction among musicians and among musicians and the rest of society. The instrument that would allow me to do this was the insecticide spray can maracas (figure 2). When I broke the news to Maneko he seemed genuinely excited. I think that he, too, felt my training as a guitarist was not going as well as we had hoped, and my intention to train as an *atalaku* seemed to strike him with a sense of novelty and relief.

Immediately we started talking about the advantages of being an *atalaku*. Maneko thought that my experience as a guitarist would give me a considerable advantage since, as someone who was already familiar with notes and scales, I would be less likely to sing or shout out of key. He also suggested that my presence as an *atalaku*, a more visible presence than the guitarist, would attract more people to concerts, especially because I would become the first non-Congolese to take on such a role. I countered his points by giving my impression that the *atalaku* did not get the same respect as did singers or guitarists. *Atalaku* rarely figure prominently in music videos and concert footage, and despite the fact that most people are familiar with the products of their labor (shouts), very few are recognized as singers or artists (White 1999). They represent a paradox because their shouts form an integral part of the expansion of commercial dance music in an urban setting yet they are usually associated with traditional musical styles or *folklore*. Because of this association and because they often come from very modest backgrounds, *atalaku* often face stigma in band hierarchies.

"You have to admit they are strange," I said, "and it just doesn't seem like people take them seriously." Maneko nodded his head in agreement. "Yes, yes, but you must know that it's not their fault, they're just taken by the moment." After some more discussion, I told him that I had made plans to meet with a well-known (then unemployed) *atalaku* who lived close to my house and that we had plans to start my training as soon as possible. Maneko seemed very excited about my initiative.

As planned, Bébé and I met at my place on Saturday. He would always arrive when he said he would, and in this land of broken digital watches and transportation tales, his professionalism encouraged me. On our first day he brought his own maracas so that we could start working. Unfortunately, there was no electricity that day, so it meant that we would have to practice without music. He showed me the first rhythm I would have to learn, and I played it on my leg until I had it close enough to try it on the maracas. I remember the strange metallic feeling of the instrument. It resonated so strongly that I was a bit embarrassed to play it loudly. It was made out of an emptied pesticide spray can (Mobil, but Raid and Kilit! are also used) with several lines of perforations that serve as sound holes, and a triangular cut in the bottom of the can for inserting the hardened red seeds from a locally indigenous tree. Bébé had already prepared a can for me, but he did not have any seeds. He explained eagerly: "We have to look for the seeds. The seeds are the most important part. If you don't get the right ones, it won't sound right. But it's OK, I know a few places where we can find them."

The day that we went to collect the seeds, we strolled through Gombe, one of Kinshasa's rich neighborhoods, and Bébé played on his status as Zaiko Langa Langa's first *animateur* to convince the military guards sitting at the bottom of the tree with red seeds that they should let us collect some for my research. We gave them a little tip, and Bébé made them laugh by telling them that I was his student to become an *animateur*. Suddenly, as is often the case in Kinshasa, they acted as if we were all old friends. They even pointed us to a place down the road where a young man was already collecting red seeds, and when we arrived, he already had a pile of shucked red seeds about three feet wide by two feet high. He was so surprised by our excitement that he let us walk away with a milk carton full of red seeds without asking anything in return. We gave him a couple of small bills anyway, took a picture (figure 46) and—very proud of ourselves—started back on our way home. Bébé inspired confidence in me because of his ease in talking with complete strangers and because of the commitment he had not only to his own work but also to mine. The next time we met we would be able to practice with electricity and two fully functional maracas.

Figure 46. Collecting seeds for a maracas with Bébé Atalaku. PHOTO: BOB W. WHITE.

Formal training for the position of *atalaku* was hard to imagine because most people were busy trying to learn the art of singing or guitar playing. Bébé and I would get together three or four times a week, start with loud music and two large, cold beers, and when the mood hit us we would begin. I would put on an old Zaiko cassette and Bébé would stand up and start playing. It was better, I learned, to practice at my place than at the place where the band practiced (as I did when I was trying to learn the guitar). Although we were surrounded by the comings and goings of the other people in the compound, it was invariably less distracting than being caught up in the spectacle of the musicians' practice space. We worked first on the rhythm from the words segment of songs, which was very straightforward and basically the same for most songs. For the *seben* he had me listen to two rhythms, which he referred to simply as "number one" and "number two." Number one was relatively easy, but it was number two that sounded typical of Zairian dance music and proved difficult to master [audio].

Bébé was an excellent teacher. He would let me play more than he did so that I could practice and so that he could monitor my progress. He was very patient, but he let me know when I made mistakes. "Playing this instrument is very difficult, Monsieur Bob. There are very few *animateurs* who are able to play like me. Most of these young guys, they don't know a maracas from a microphone. But what they don't understand is that you can't be a real *animateur* if you haven't mastered this instrument. It's very important" (field notes, February 21, 1996). I would take a break, sitting down in my chair to watch Bébé as he played alone. Sometimes I would try to join in, but remained unable to get the rhythm. He would egg me on, continuing to play, and I would get it back for a matter of thirty to forty-five seconds. It seemed so fleeting; I did not see how I would ever be able to generate this rhythm at will, especially in front of a crowd for an extended period of time. We would stop, and Bébé would have me do some exercises. He tried to get me to play with only one hand. Impossible. He had me play with a Christian prayer maracas (made with straw and filled with bottle caps), and the difference proved amazing. Now this is easy, I thought. Back to the insecticide maracas: easier than before, but still difficult. Try the matchbox. I tried, but nothing resembling rhythm number two would come from the small box of Leopard brand matchsticks. "No way," I said, feeling somewhat silly trying to make this rhythm with a box of matches. Try the insecticide. Try the prayer. Try the Leopard. He was firing the different instruments at me one after another, never giving me enough time to get comfortable with any one. Prayer. Leopard. Insecticide. Prayer. Leopard. Insecticide. Something about completely unsettling my level of comfort and the feel of these objects in my hands made me more sensitive to the motion I was supposed to reproduce. It was not clear to me if Bébé was doing this on purpose, but it seemed to work. The last time I picked up the insecticide maracas I went off into an extended long play of at least three minutes that I myself could hardly believe. When I finally lost the rhythm, I threw the maracas on the couch across the room and burst out in laughter and amazement. Bébé was so happy that he turned down the music and began to lecture emphatically: "There are very few *animateurs* who can play this instrument correctly. You can't be a real *animateur* if you don't master this instrument. That was great!"

"I'll Be Ready on Tuesday"

After I learned the fundamentals of the maracas (Bébé and I spent very little time on shouts or singing), I decided to start working with the *atalaku* from the Big Stars to learn the particular shouts from our band. Enter Lidjo, the senior of three *atalaku* working in the Big Stars and one of the few members from the band's original formation in the early 1990s. He had a wide face with a gaunt, faraway look that made him seem very serious, the kind of person who often made me wonder what he was thinking. With Bébé, I had started keeping a notebook for my training. During our first meeting Lidjo and I started correcting some of the shouts I had tried to write on my own. I made generous use of liquid paper, blowing, whisking, and dipping again, and I carefully modified incorrect words, highlighting the result with a fat yellow fluorescent marker. Lidjo waited patiently for the liquid paper to dry, sometimes jiggling one leg, sometimes looking around my one-room studio, which probably did not fit his image of American wealth and privilege. Seated next to each other on a small couch, we started to go through the shouts in my book one by one. At first it was a bit awkward. Lidjo was not accustomed to reciting his shouts in isolation, although he did not hesitate when I first asked him to record his shouts on tape so I could listen to them and practice alone.

To facilitate practice I began demarcating the rhythm with a hand clap or by patting on my leg, and before long we were flipping through my notebook and jumping around from page to page, so that the shouts would occur in a more or less random order. Invariably, listening to Lidjo sing the shout would make me aware of imperfections in my notation system. Then, after listening to him for twenty or so minutes, he told me to sing a few. I picked the ones I knew best, and after I started singing, his face lit up. Giddy, happy laughter replaced his indifferent expression, and Lidjo stood up to turn and face me, yelling "Missya Bob!" and offering me a high five. He laughed and worked his faded baggy red jeans up past his belly button, a nervous tic common among musicians in Kinshasa. I do not think it was because my shouts were good; in fact, given my limited experience they were probably not good at all. Rather, it was the novelty of hearing a foreigner singing and shouting phrases that were typically Congolese, typically *kinois*. At the end of a later session, for just a few moments Lidjo closed his eyes to listen to one of my shouts. Just like Bébé in the weeks before, he let himself be carried away by what must have seemed like a strangely familiar sound [audio]:

> Mama tala Makiese, mama yuma yusile
> Mama tala Makiese yeh yeh, mama yuma yusile
> Mai mayema, sango eh mame, pore eh,
> Sango eh mai mayema, pore eh

After Lidjo was sure I had mastered the shout, he started to sing along with me, a teaching technique I found very useful since it gave me the time to assimilate the shout without being constantly corrected. When the harmony was particularly sweet, we would stand up next to each other facing the audience (my couch) and would shake our open hands in the way that singers often do when they perform. A number of people would later tell me that my shouts had a special quality (*quelque chose de spécial*), something "not Zairian" that they could not put their finger on, but something they very much liked. I was personally frustrated by my inability to sound Zairian, but in talking about this with my musician friends, I realized that my difference was useful in stimulating discussion about authenticity and identity (see Heath 1994).[4] People said that imperfections made my shouts good: they were different. They were probably also intrigued by the fact that a singer/guitarist would become an *atalaku*, something surprising since most *atalaku* express secret desires to be singers, although the reverse is rarely true. What I found interesting, however, was that the "not quite Zairian" quality was encouraged in my work as an *atalaku* but proved a handicap in learning the guitar. Did this mean that the performance of the guitar was more sensitive (i.e., more resistant) to variations? If so, what were the implications of such an observation? Lidjo and I continued to practice a few days a week for three or four weeks, eventually mastering more than twenty pages of shouts and almost, but not completely, exhausting the formal animation repertoire of the Big Stars. Lidjo said there were a few I performed particularly well, so I hoped that I had learned the pieces enough to start putting them into context. Very gradually, at first without my noticing, Lidjo had been getting me used to stringing series of shouts together, but we usually never got past two or three before repeating, and as far as I could tell, they did not come in any particular order. When I prepared myself to ask Lidjo the difficult question of how he decided what shouts to put where in a performance situation, I secretly hoped that this was some kind of secret or special knowledge to which I would have access given the extensive nature of my training. But the answer was actually quite simple: "We just follow the record," he said.

Then Lidjo proceeded to tell me, from memory, the order of shouts for each song in the Big Stars repertoire. I stopped him at about twenty songs; almost every song had some series or combination of the shouts we had been learning over the past few weeks. When he wanted to remember the shout order for a particular song, he simply sang the last chorus before the *seben* and stared off into the distance as if looking at something. I am not sure if he was "seeing the song" from the cassette sleeve or if he was imagining the dance steps that corresponded to the shouts, motions he himself had surely gone through hundreds of times in his career as an *atalaku*. Whatever he imagined, it seemed accurate since the shout orders he gave me were consistent over time, and they almost all appeared on the record in exactly the order he had given me in practice. But this did not explain what happened in concert, since very often songs performed live would last twenty-five to thirty-five minutes (compared to six to eight minutes on the records).

"What do you do for the rest of the song?" I asked.

"You just improvise," he said. "After you finish the shouts from the album, you add some of the shouts that are 'in' at that time, and then you just shout whatever comes to your mind." In other words, every song performed live contains a certain number of predetermined core shouts (usually three or four, presumably those judged popular at the time of the recording), followed by a longer series of shouts that although they come from a common shout repertoire, can be arranged and performed in any number of ways. Most often the shouts that fill this free space will be the shouts of the day, while the predetermined shouts are those corresponding to the time period of the song's release. Even very old songs will be performed with the original shouts, although they are then brought up to date by the addition of more recent shouts. Some shouts can be exploited for as long as ten minutes, as long as the shout is new and pleases the audience sufficiently. In this way the innovative impulse of modern, commercial dance music will call up its past while at the same renewing itself through the style of the present.

At one of the first Big Stars shows after their return from Zambia, I sat next to the sound engineer and watched every move of the other two *atalaku* as they performed. My work with Lidjo had made me much more sensitive to what they were doing and saying. I still was not catching everything, but I felt that if I was called onto the stage unannounced (a distinct possibility) I could at least defend myself. But it did not happen during this show. Instead, as I came with my own transportation, I was called on to shuttle Defao back to the practice space after the end of the show. With Defao sitting alone in the front and five band members in the back, most of the conversation happened without me. But at one point Defao turned to me and said, "Why didn't you shout, Monsieur Bob?" I suddenly got nervous because I thought Defao was the person who decided when I was supposed to perform. Thinking quickly, I tried to answer with a convincing tone: "Nako zala prêt mardi"

(I'll be ready on Tuesday), I said, smiling. I hesitated for a moment, wondering if I truly was ready. Just be ready for Tuesday, I told myself. "Just be ready for Tuesday," Defao said, nodding his head up and down and looking out of his window as if all of Kinshasa belonged to him.

On Tuesday afternoon I rushed home, changed my clothes, and started off to practice. After I arrived, there was very little ceremony. Practice started right in, Montana motioned for me to start shouting, and so I began. Hearing my voice inflected through a medium that had become an important part of my everyday practice as a listener was both wonderful and strange. I wanted to be worried for my voice, but the sounds seemed to be floating from my chest. Most of the people in the audience wore an expression somewhere between amusement and amazement, and some were wide-eyed at the novelty of this spectacle. As soon as I finished, one of the singers in the group took the microphone from me and excitedly introduced me to the audience: "Missya Bob, a uti Etats Unis!" (Mr. Bob, direct from the United States!). The band, of course, never missed a beat and continued to play. This experience with the microphone felt different from my experience with the guitar. I could see in the other musicians' faces that they were pleased with my performance. One of the guitarists approached me and said, "That was really good; you have to come every day. I mean it, every day." Even Maneko congratulated me in his own way, with a Fanta orange soda and a small loaf of bread. When Defao showed up for the band meeting he looked at me and asked if I had shouted. I smiled and nodded yes. Then he turned to the junior leaders and asked how I did. They all nodded: "He shouted. He shouted good." Defao laughed in approval. "Missya Bob!" he declared, almost shouting himself. "Good, come to the concerts on Friday and Saturday. You're going to sing, you know? We have one show in Masina and the other one is in Ndjili. We'll give them a great show!"

While waiting for the Friday show to start, the Big Stars huddled into an empty schoolroom nearby the stage on which we would play later that evening. Feeling a bit cramped, I decided to go outside for some fresh air. Ebolo, the chauffeur, asked me to buy him something to drink. After I gave him some money, he said I could sit in his seat in the van parked nearby the schoolroom. I climbed in the van, happy with my new seat, which was more comfortable than the cinder block I had left behind in the schoolroom. Kabosé (one of the front-line singers) was in the passenger's seat, and my arrival woke him up from a light sleep. "Monsieur Bob," he said, stretching his arms and squinting his eyes. "Kabosé," I answered. This was the extent of most conversations between band members. Kabosé turned to look out of his window to see three young men approaching the van. They each greeted him, "Boni massa?" (How's it going, friend?) and shook his hand. Though it was dark, they were wearing cheap sunglasses and garish combinations of oversized mix-matched garments that gave away what they were trying to cover up. Before too long I understood that they wanted Kabosé to "throw them,"—their names, that is—during the performance later that night. I tried not to be too obvious, but I closely watched their interaction.

Kabosé remained very calm, which made me think that this kind of thing probably happened all the time, and this was not even the lead or number-two singer. One by one they slipped a series of bills under his hand, which was open with the palm facing downward. He would close his hand around the money, nod his head in a slight gesture of deference and place the money in his coat pocket before putting up his hand for the next young sponsor. After the transaction was complete, he tried to memorize each of their names. They gave priority to their nicknames: "My name is Dieudonné, but my friends call me 'Ninja Force'" or "'Jackson le Grand Américain,' first name Serge" or "Pompidou, just Pompidou." As Kabosé tried to memorize these self-imposed layers of identity, he looked over at me and started to laugh, suddenly realizing that I was following what was going on. With the three names down pat, Kabosé reached out to shake each of the young men's hands and closed the transaction: "Alright, guys, so thanks, eh?" And they for their part: "Kabosé, you're our favorite singer. We think you're the best, man." He reassured them that the show would be starting soon and they were off, laughing and patting each other on the back. Kabosé let loose a big sigh and turned to me, feeling the need to explain what had just happened:

"Oh Monsieur Bob! [He laughs nervously]. That's the way it works here, you know. People want you to sing their name and you have to do it. It's not easy."
There was a hint of embarrassment in his voice, and I found it interesting that he was aware that this kind of thing may not happen in other countries.
"These are hard times," I offered.
"That's for sure," he answered, still somewhat embarrassed, but proud to be conversing in French.

CHAPTER FIVE

"How much did they give you?" I asked.

"Not that much, but what am I supposed to do? It's the only way I can make a little money." (Field notes, April 11, 1996)

While this transaction was occurring, Defao was seated at a VIP table away from the crowd under a parasol protecting him from a light drizzle. I was walking around to find something to drink when Defao spotted me.

"Monsieur Bob," he motioned for me to join him.

"Fondé," I answered. As I took a seat, I was immediately presented with the ice-cold soda I had been craving just a few minutes before. I asked Defao where the drink came from.

"From the producer" he answered matter-of-factly. A young man approached Defao and discreetly whispered something into his ear. "*Bon, tokeyi.* Monsieur Bob, let's go. We're going to eat." He positioned his sunglasses to where they would be least likely to catch the rain and started off with a very deliberate strut toward the room where we would be eating. As soon as I finished downing my soda, I scurried to catch up with him, bobbing slightly to imitate his walk. We entered a building with a full table setting and plates full of different kinds of food. Two members of the promoter's team pulled back our chairs for us and invited us to sit down. As one of the band's *atalaku*, I was not used to this kind of hospitality; even the singers generally have to sit on cinder blocks without food or drink for hours. For once I was fortunate enough to see how the star was treated by producers, and it differed greatly from the experience of the rest of the band. Even the most senior musicians did not eat with Defao. That night there were two or three people that seemed to be Defao's friends or sponsors. Ebolo the driver was there, but he was not seated. Apart from Defao, I was the only musician in the room. "There's enough for everybody," Defao declared in an affected tone. "Eat to your fill!" I asked a few questions about the producers for the show, and he explained to me that they paid for everything.

In most cases, the producer arranges for the locale, the publicity for the show, and the ticket sales. In addition to VIP freebies for three to five of the artist's personal guests, he gets a prearranged sum of money (*cachet*) that is independent of ticket sales; producers assume most of the risk for live shows. I wanted to ask Defao why he works with so many different producers, but before I was able to get the question out, two members of the production team approached us at the table to make sure everything was all

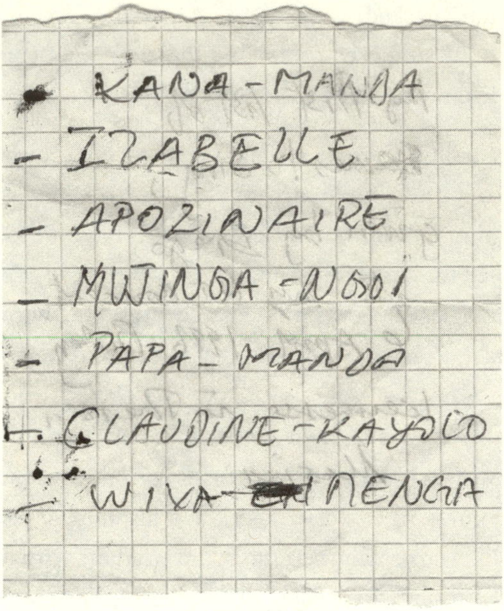

Figure 47. "C'mon Monsieur Bob, you can do it." SOURCE: BOB W. WHITE.

right. After Defao assured them that everyone has had plenty to eat, the two assistants turned to me and handed me a small piece of paper with a list of names that I was expected to shout once I took the microphone (figure 47). I was taken aback at first and tried to explain that I was very nervous because this was to be my first full appearance with the band:

"I don't think I can do that. You see this is my first real show with the band and since I'm new I really have to concentrate on what I'm doing up there. . . ." It was one of those explanations that was going nowhere. One of the assistants looked at me with a blank stare and then looked at the paper again; he was obviously not accustomed to getting this kind of response to his request. I was not accustomed to getting this kind of request.

With all eyes on me, including those of Defao, I decided to take the paper, looking at the names and wondering how I would accomplish what seemed like an impossible task. I had trained to play an instrument and to sing shouts, but none of what I learned had prepared me to do *libanga*. The person who had handed me the piece of paper came close to me and said in a soft, urging tone, "C'mon Monsieur Bob, you can do it." His colleague approached to add titles to his name: "My name is 'Master Dadi, His Excellency the Grand CEO'; it's not hard. Then there's Diego, but you have to say 'Diego Diegoni, the Mega Shege from Oshwe.' And then there's Serge." I cut

Figure 48. Author with the first-string *atalaku* Theo Mbala. PHOTO: JOHN GRINLING.

him off, explaining that I would only be able to take a few names. I promised them that I would at least say their names, in short form, and they both seemed satisfied: "Bon." They leaned back with a huge smile and flipped me a thumbs-up to show their approval. After they were gone, I turned to Defao and said, "I've never done this before." He laughed a hearty laugh and in a loud, congratulatory voice said, "Monsieur Bob!" He licked his fingers and dipped his hands in the bowl of warm, soapy water being held for him beside his seat. I asked him if this happened all the time, and he said he usually got so many requests that he ended up giving most of them to the *atalaku*. On which note he effortlessly pulled out another list of names from the pocket of his jacket and handed it to me: "These have to be thrown." "Merci," I muttered after a brief pause. It was all I could think to say.

At some point during the show I clumsily pronounced the two names I had promised to throw (figure 48). No one onstage or in the audience seemed to notice, perhaps because I was doing it out of obligation instead of as an expression of joy or as a result of an ongoing relationship with the people named. Dadi and Diego, however, sought me out later in the show to thank me for acknowledging their presence, and judging from their reactions, they were both very pleased. In a context such as this, individuals who assert their identity in isolation of social institutions and networks put themselves at risk, primarily because gestures of individualism always run the risk of association with sorcery (White 2004). Acts of social distinction through the performance of popular music are not only socially accessible (anyone can be "thrown" as long as they have money), but they are also socially acceptable since they are spoken through the voice of someone else (Askew 2002; Ebron 2002). This ability to mediate between individual identities and public selves occurs not only through the exchange of money but also through the medium of language, a subject to which I turn in the next chapter.

LIVE TEXTS

IF YOU ASK PEOPLE IN KINSHASA WHY POPULAR
music is important, invariably they will refer to the
music's message: music gives advice or music teaches
something. Even though dancing constitutes a crucial
part of the musical experience and music's performance
(see chapter 4), the music's message is every bit as important as the sound. In this setting, music (much like painting, theater, and oratory) is appreciated to the extent that
it gives people something to reflect on or talk about.[1] A
song that is beautiful (*kitoko*) has pleasant melodies and
rhythms, but it is also valued for telling its listeners something about life in society. As the singer Reddy Amisi explained to me during his first solo tour, "People want to
identify with the singer. A singer-songwriter should do
his own thing, but he should educate. We have to educate young people so they don't make the same mistakes"
(interview, September 27, 1995). But the messages conveyed through popular music are not always simple. In
texts that focus on the desperate nature of romantic love
in Mobutu's Zaire, musicians allude to the ongoing economic crisis that came to characterize life in Kinshasa
during this period. At the same time, their songs are filled

with the names of local urban elites who provide musicians with financial and political support in exchange for being immortalized in song. By playing to both of these phenomena—endemic poverty and public displays of wealth—musicians mediate between two radically different social worlds and their corresponding audiences.

Working with Words

In recent years, a fascinating literature has emerged around the idea that consumption be seen as a form of production (Appadurai and Breckenridge 1995; McCracken 1988; Miller 1994). Retooling or "poaching" the world of goods, "users make innumerable and infinitesimal transformations of and within the dominant cultural economy in order to adapt it to their own interests and their own rules" (Certeau 1984, xiv). Theoretical interest in the study of reception, traditionally the domain of scholars in comparative literature and cultural studies, has been registered more recently in the field of anthropology (Mankekar 1999). A particularly striking example is the recent wave of audience-based research in various parts of Africa (Abu-Lughod 2005; Hunt 2002; Kratz 2002; Larkin 2002; Schulz 1999; Spitulnik 2002; White and Yoka 2006). As Karin Barber (1997) has shown, the emphasis on live performance, as well as the various levels of subtext and self-censorship, makes reading popular culture in an African setting a very complex undertaking. Although relatively little research has been done on exactly *how* African popular texts are interpreted, there is ample evidence to prove that they *are* in fact interpreted: "Such works are made *in order* to be, and *in the expectation* of being, interpreted" (Barber 1997, 8; original emphasis).

An over-reliance on text, clearly a burden during the formative years of popular music studies (see Frith 1996), also provoked much concern for scholars in linguistic anthropology and folklore studies, who beginning in the 1970s drew from their emerging interest in the analysis of performance to show how verbal arts cannot be understood in isolation from their performance context (Duranti and Goodwin 1992). The study of popular music texts from an ethnographic perspective represents real possibilities for the comparative study of popular music since, as Kelly Askew (2002) has shown, song lyrics are often part of how cultural worlds are held together and how social relationships are rearranged, especially in the context of live performance.[2] To the extent that the words of popular music are capable of mobilizing social relations outside of the music, I consider them as examples of what I refer to as "live texts." The thematic approach to the study of lyrics that has dominated popular music studies since its inception gives us some idea of what musicians are singing about, but ultimately it fails to tell us how musicians combine language and sound to create various moods of affect and engagement with the audience.[3] In the spirit of Rob Walser's (1993) suggestion, it is important to see song lyrics as elements of a larger set of communicative practices that go "beyond the vocals" into the realm of oral tradition and performativity.[4]

The particular mood I set out to describe by examining the changes in the content of song lyrics during the Mobutu years must be seen—using the language of the British literary critic Raymond Williams—as "emergent" (1977:123). The analysis of popular song lyrics can benefit from Williams's insights in at least two ways. First, a systematic approach to the analysis of song lyrics reveals a number of words or phrases that recur over time, but that undergo a significant transformation at the level of semantics. These "keywords" (Williams 1976), or clusters of interrelated words and references, can be analyzed to show how language is used in particular historical moments to mobilize power and sentiment, an approach not common in the study of non-Western popular music forms.[5] In the case of Mobutu's Zaire, the keywords *love* and *abandonment* point clearly in the direction of politics, but other words may point elsewhere.[6] Second, Williams' notion of "structures of feeling"—an idea more often cited than articulated—enables us to see how emergent cultural forms such as popular music interact with public discourses about responsibility, affect, and the role of the state.

Like Williams, I have the sense that many aspects of artistic expression are related to something larger than everyday, local experience, but the question of how these aspects are related to a particular moment in history is something that has to be worked out. Williams is somewhat coy with regard to the notion of structures of feeling, but he generally talks about it as "a way of defining forms and conventions in art and literature as inalienable elements of a social material process" (1977, 133). Song lyrics are a valuable source of information about structures of feeling because they circulate so easily and because they tend to resonate across large sectors of any given population (figure 49). When I use the expression "lyrical structures of feeling" below, I refer not only to patterns and structures in the music, but also

Figure 49. Song lyrics often appear in printed form in one of many local music fanzines. SOURCE: *DISCO HIT,* 1999, N.D.

to the structures in political and economic life that make people want to sing in particular ways and write songs about particular things. The lyrics of popular music can be seen as a collective (though not homogeneous) public expression of emotion that links everyday experience to the larger, impersonal structures of political and economic change (Marcus and Fischer 1986). In this sense song lyrics can help us, in methodological terms, bridge the gap between ethnography and political economy.

Drawing from my personal collection of Congolese music (about three hundred CDs and cassettes), I worked primarily with recordings made during the years of Mobutu's career as head of state (1965–97). Arguably, my personal collection of Congolese popular music is not representative of music collections in the homes of Congolese since as a researcher on popular music I tended to buy albums that were either hugely popular or representative of a particular musical generation. In building my collection, I made a conscious effort to achieve equal representation from different schools of

CHAPTER SIX

music and musical generations, and this may introduce a bias (for better or worse) into my analysis. Initially I thought I would choose a certain number of texts widely recognized as hit songs and attempt to identify thematic or linguistic patterns therein. But this idea assumed that hits are representative of popular songs in general and that the category of "hit song" is transparent and unproblematic. Ongoing research with Congolese audiences suggests that people have a hard time distinguishing between hit songs and their favorite songs, something probably common for popular music audiences elsewhere in the world as well (see White and Yoka 2006). In the end I decided to listen to a much larger body of texts, but this meant that I had to divide the listening into two distinct phases. The first phase involved listening to all of the songs of a particular artist, one album at a time, with artists being chosen at random. This made it possible to generate a list of recurring motifs that would serve as the basis for my analysis. During the second phase, using the list of motifs generated in the first listening, I listened to each of the songs again, this time transcribing sections of lyrics and taking more specific notes on particular motifs.

This approach proved time consuming, but it yielded results more revealing than if I had worked with a smaller number of predetermined texts. It also had the fortunate effect of cutting across the material in two completely different directions, one in which I listened to the patterns of a particular artist, and one that juxtaposed the ideas of several artists on a related set of themes. By taking notes on the words, phrases, and expressions that seemed to occur with the most frequency, I was able to get a sense of what Congolese musicians were singing about, in what register, and in some cases with what effect. I also took notes on the figurative language through which these utterances are expressed: metaphor, allegory, subtext, and the like. This approach is based on a particular type of discourse analysis, a content-based method for analyzing speech in oral as well as written texts.[7] What emerged from this analysis was a series of semantic clusters that give some idea about how popular music interacts with and comments on Congolese society, but it may also represent an important methodological advance in the relatively recent field of popular music studies. After explaining the phenomenon of commercialized praise singing known as *libanga* in Congolese popular dance music, I will consider the twin themes of love and abandonment, first in isolation, and then together with *libanga* to describe the mood of insecurity and crisis that characterized life in Kinshasa at the end of the Mobutu regime.

Kobwaka Libanga

Kobwaka libanga (lit., "to throw a stone") is the term most commonly used to describe what musicians do when they cite or sing the names of friends or sponsors either on recordings or in live performance.[8] This expression is also used to describe young children who throw small pebbles at a parent or older relative in an attempt to attract their attention or provoke a response.[9] Throwing pebbles, both literally and figuratively, can be a way of getting attention, affection, or material support; it is meant primarily as a provocation, but it is also, to use an expression from V. N. Volosinov, a "bridge thrown between myself and another" (Volosinov 1973, 86).[10] Any musician with access to the microphone, meaning primarily singers and *atalaku*, has the opportunity to sing someone's name. Names can be sung or shouted, although in concert they are usually shouted. The names "thrown" in a concert performance vary considerably: the promoter, a rich acquaintance, a businessman, a young man who just got paid, a soldier, a political figure, a social club, a group of friends, and so on. It is also common for musicians to throw the names of other musicians and friends present, although this should be seen more as an expression of solidarity than as something related to sponsorship per se.[11]

I use the term *sponsor* in several different ways. For one, it refers to a commercial or corporate entity that offers to assume some of the artist's professional expenses in exchange for the artist's endorsement of a particular service or product.[12] But I also use the term to describe those individuals, often also fans of the artist, who contribute money in exchange for privileged access to the artist's performance and private space and/or for some form of public recognition. I am reluctant to use the word *patron* in this context since conventional discussions of patron-client ties refer to a set of relations between a so-called big man and a series of subordinates at varying levels of dependence over an extended period of time. In the case of Congolese popular music, this model is not a good fit since most musicians have a large number of sponsors, but the majority of these relationships are short-lived or low paying. A large proportion of the people praised by musicians are what I would call onetime sponsors, meaning they support musicians very irregularly.

Individual names can be sung, spoken, or shouted, depending on whether they are inserted in between lines of verses, in between verses and choruses, or fully integrated into the body of the text. In the following example, Super Choc's "Shabani" (1996), the primary sponsor of the song, who also happens to be the producer of the album, is not the sole object of praise, but is woven into a constellation of sponsors (in bold) past and potential:

Shabani (2x)
Many Makiadi Isangala
Ilunga Mwana Boude
Kumbanga na **Super Zaire Papa Mbemba**
Kumbanga na **Air Zaire Papa Kikunda**

Kumbanga na **Air Esperance Saddam**
Ngai na mona Paris, na mona Brussels

Nga na koma na Londres na zonga Kinshasa

Baninga eh **Papy Kintukaho**
Mokolo nini nga na ko mona **Atos Senan?**

Mokolo nini nga na ko mona **Major Jacques?**

Mokolo nini nga na ko mona **Maté ya Air Zaire?**

Mokolo nini nga na ko mona **Papa Wemba Ekumani?**

Mokolo nini nga na ko mona **Ya Lemoso?**

Na tambola na mokili, nanu na mona te
Na tambola na mokili, nanu na mona te
Shabani eh (2x)

Shabani (2x)
Many Makiadi Isangala
Ilunga Mwana Boude
Send me on **Super Zaire Papa Mbemba**

Send me on **Air Zaire Papa Kikunda**

Send me on **Air Esperance Saddam**
So I can see Paris, see Brussels

Set foot in London, and go back to Kinshasa

Oh friends, **Papy Kintukaho**
When will I see **Atos Senan?**

When will I see **Major Jacques?**

When will I see **Maté ya Air Zaire?**

When will I see **Papa Wemba Ekumani?**

When will I see **Ya Lemoso?**

Traveled the world, never seen anything like him
Traveled the world, never seen anything like him
Shabani eh (2x)

This excerpt is interesting because of the way that different sponsors' names are embedded within the text, creating a complex layering of praises and appeals. The subject of the line "Send me on Air Zaire," Shabani, is understood to be the main target of praise. By asking Shabani to send them on an Air Zaire jetliner, however, the singers are in effect addressing two sponsors at the same time. Most *libanga* are found in the dance sequence of songs (*seben*), where the former can take on a special status of its own, sometimes occupying more space than the lyrics or even the shouts. In this example from the Big Stars, the 1995 "Alain Mbiya," once again the names of sponsors are in bold:

Dembi Kwanza, Kwanza Dembi eeh! Dembi!
Violenne, Violenne Pampa, Violenne, Mbiya
Violenne Pampa, Alain Mbiya, Na mputua
Stick your neck out, in Brussels!
José Kasasa . . . Jeancy Feda
Vieux Bolyte Achebo achebo!
Garçon sondage, Hypo! ooh! Hypolite! Achebo, Achebo
Mere Sophie, Papa Do, Papa Do, Mère Sophie
Willy Montand, Mère Godard, Ya Vieux Bakelele
(Shout)
Steve Bimbo, round-trip, **Kinshasa, Paris . . .**
Oh! Sigo Shabani, Alain Shabani
Winetu le Grand, Stone na Swisse!
Didier Somata, Didier Somata na Liège!
Sergosse Edumbi, all over the world
Max Wada, Henriette na fédéraille, Henri Michel
Tired yet? No! Tired yet? Not yet!
Merci Merci Sharufa na Reference Brussels,
Ha ha ha, **Big Stone**

For non-speakers of Lingala, *libanga* often goes unnoticed since names of people and lyrics tend to blend together. Congolese audiences, however—and musicians in particular—pay close attention to the names cited, especially those that occur on a regular basis. Some artists are more active than others in citing peoples' names in their music, and many artists are known to write songs that receive titles only after a potential sponsor agrees to pay for the song. Of the eight songs on 1995 release (*Dernier Album*), seven carry the names of individuals, meaning that most of the songs on the album were purchased or commissioned. Most albums produced in Kinshasa in the past ten years list at least one if not several songs with individuals' names as titles. The money that musicians receive for composing these praise songs depends primarily on the musician's popularity. I have heard of individual songs being purchased for as little as US$100 and as much as US$3,000. When I asked one of my musician friends about the title of a song he had just composed, he responded: "Right now, I just call it 'Leah,' but the title will change as soon as someone buys it." Thus citing peoples' names clearly constitutes a strategy that musicians use to sell more records: "Obviously promoting someone's name is a form of marketing. When I immortalize Mère Malou or Sadara, this means another sales circuit for me. These women have a lot of influence, so that people who know them won't hesitate to buy the album as soon as it is available" (General Defao qtd. in Makobo 1996, 3). By playing on the vanity and the emotions of patrons and fans, musicians can improve their access to various social networks and financial resources. Koffi Olomide prints the names of the people he "throws" in his CD liner notes. With the money earned from these informal agreements, he is usually able to pay a significant portion of the costs associated with producing his albums. The same holds true for the musicians of Wenge Musica BCBG, who during their 1998 tour of North America could be heard soliciting poten-tial sponsors directly in between songs during concerts: "You know we're in the studio and we're going to finish soon, so come by and see us. Our friends know how it operates. Don't miss your chance." The cost: US$1000 a throw.[13]

Unlike the performance of praise in the various griot traditions of West Africa, the singing of praises in Congolese popular dance music rarely slows down long enough to describe with any detail the person being praised.[14] If the musician inserts himself into the text as do the predominantly Mande-speaking *jeliw* of Mali, Senegal, and the Gambia, it is not to show his lin-eage relationship to the family of the person he is praising, but to show that the sponsor is a fan. In reality, *libanga* is more like name dropping than praise singing. The sheer number of names thrown limits musicians' ability to learn anything significant about most of the people giving them money. The most extreme example of this phenomenon I have found occurs in Werra Son's 2001 release "Treize ans," which includes the names of more than 110 different *libanga* [audio]. Beginning in the early 1990s, it was common for songs to cite the names of at least 10–12 sponsors. And given the precarious nature of income and wealth in Mobutu's Zaire, it should come as no surprise that most sponsors will only ever be thrown once. The truly remarkable cases are those names that appear on more than one album by the same group, or on several albums by different groups at roughly the same time.[15]

Fans in Kinshasa have mixed feelings about *libanga*. In general, older people tend to be more critical of this practice, viewing it as a corruption of the music's content and a shameful gesture of upward social mobility. But most people are aware of the extent to which musicians depend on financial support from their fans: "For a musician in Zaire, it is people that are at the center of his preoccupations. What could be more normal than for him to immortalize a brother, a friend, or a benefactor?" (Makobo 1996, 2). This view of commercial praise singing does not go uncontested, but its prevalence among music listeners echoes Arjun Appadurai's observation that "praise is measured by the 'community of sentiment' it evokes and creates, and not by the authenticity of the link between the private (or idiosyncratic) emotions of the praiser and the object of his or her praise" (1990, 107). While it is obviously tempting to see *libanga* as a form of advertising, I think this reading misses the point. Musicians are not just selling a product; they are using language to secure knots in relationships of reciprocity from which they have benefited and on which they will probably need to call in the future.

In this context, praise singing serves various social functions. It is a form of social recognition for those whose deeds or accomplishments stand out in the community, but in many cases it is a form of social distinction, as much for the musicians as for the person praised. At first *libanga* appears completely different from other forms of praise singing in a ritual or ceremonial context, but I would argue that often the results are the same. Individuals in the audience give money and come back with a fragment of prestige (such as a personalized song or a snapshot), just as do those who continue to sponsor musicians outside of the limited context of live performance. Apart from the obvious mutual benefits of the praise-singing arrangement (musicians get financial support and social prestige, sponsors get social prestige), praise for the wealthy and powerful also constitutes a means of activating relations of reciprocity, and as I will argue later, it can also be seen as a way of keeping bad leadership in check.

During a live concert, the singer or *atalaku* will choose the *libanga* according to whom he sees in the audience, but people in positions of high influence are sung even in their absence (especially on albums) since it is rightly assumed that word will get back to them. Mobutu's son Kongolo (alias "Saddam Hussein"), probably the most often-sung figure since the late 1980s, was rumored to have followed very closely the bands that sung his praises and those that did not (see chapter 1). Those that did not sing his name in concert and on recordings would be threatened with physical violence and would often face serious obstacles in their professional activities (having the plug pulled mid-concert, being denied access to promotional networks, etc.). According to one Kinshasa musician, "If you don't sing his name, he'll have your passport!" According to J. P. Busé, members of the military often befriended the musicians of Zaiko Langa Langa because of the young women that flocked around the band, and the musicians cultivated friendships with soldiers as a source of physical protection. Gode Lofombo, the bass player for Empire Bakuba, explained: "I know all the soldiers, and they all know me. I can go anywhere even late at night, and I'll never run into problems. As long as you sing their name they'll protect you; they just want people to hear their name" (personal communication, March 8, 1996).

One *atalaku* I worked with reported that during the peak of his career anywhere from fifteen to twenty people would visit him each day. Fans would each come to give him money so that he would sing their names in concert later that night: "Sometimes if the leader came into a lot of cash, he would give us each a cut, but we made a lot of money on our own: $10 here, $20 there. I would put it in my pockets and it would start to add up" (field notes, February 1, 1996). But much larger sums of money are also offered. The Big Stars van was apparently made possible by a gift from one of Defao's biggest fan-sponsors. Some artists have a reputation for approaching wealthy people and offering to sing their names in exchange for "a little something." One of the *atalaku* I interviewed admitted that he had sought out such arrangements on more than one occasion. I asked him if he thought it was wrong to ask fans for money:

> "No," he said, "if you sing them you can make lots of money. Once I made
> $150, just like that." [He snaps his fingers.]
> "Is it a good way to make money?" I asked.
> "No no, not for the money." He hesitates for a minute. "You see, Bob, the
> important thing is friendship [*barelations*]; these are people you already

know. They help you, like a friend who always buys you beer or helps when you need money for your daughter. Then when I see him I'm happy, and I want to sing his name." (interview, February 21, 1996)

The *atalaku* holds a peculiar moral position vis-à-vis public perceptions of this practice. In a concert setting, the *atalaku* actually spends more time on the microphone than most of the singers, and it would seem that he not only is more likely to throw more different names but also more likely to throw the names of people he does not know (White 1999).

Early examples of citing others' names in Congolese music were idiosyncratic and infrequent. Musicians dedicated songs to beautiful women or the occasional political figure, and made reference in passing to their friends and fellow musicians. Over time, *libanga* became more widespread and formulaic. Since the early 1990s song lyrics commonly include series of repeating lines whose only purpose would seem to be to list the names of people who have in one way or another supported the artist. Here is an example from Viva La Musica's "Sango Pamba" (1990):

Nga nalela nani?	Who can I cry [sing] to?
Nga nalela **Evama Dala**	I'm crying to **Evama Dala**
Nga nalela **Stany ya Tembo**	I'm crying to **Stany ya Tembo**
Nga nalela **Koregiari**	I'm crying to **Koregiari**
Nga nalela **Papa Wemba**	I'm crying to **Papa Wemba**

Other examples show a similar pattern, with repeating expressions containing one element that changes with each iteration:

"I cry for _____" ("Liberation," Wenge Musica)

"The love of _____" ("Charly la suissesse" Delta force)

"I adore _____" ("Kin e bouger," Wenge Musica)

"_____ has turned me away" ("Jeancy," Viva la Musica)

The *libanga* phenomenon often takes the form of substitutable sets of phrases whose exact meaning can vary, but whose semantic contours are constrained by the fact that they seek to engage with particular listeners, that is, with those who have power and money. Through *libanga* musicians are actually citing genres of speech (Bakhtin 1986) that first became common through the mass-mediated idiom of *animation politique et culturelle*, in which traditional forms of praise became fused with the imperative of naming politicians, especially Mobutu (see chapter 3).[16] This ethnographic context shows that it is important to view genre not only as a form of social distinction but also as something that does the work of a particular social relation or cultural encounter (Fabian 1998; Kratz 1994; Seitel 1999). Indeed, if we take *libanga* as a genre of speech, and not simply as a degraded form of repetitive language, the analytical landscape looks considerably more complex. *Libanga* enables musicians to provoke people in positions of power, to seek assistance, to encourage acts of generosity, or simply to demand acknowledgment:

"Come back _____" ("Femme Infidèle," Lofombo)
"_____ where are you?" ("Tu es mon seul problème," Bana O.K.)
"Ask _____" ("Serge Palmi," Wenge Musica)
"Who can I call _____?" ("Papa na Roissy," Koffi Olomide)
"What has _____ done?" ("Persévérer," Zaiko Langa Langa)

Names stand for debts to be incurred, responsibilities to be met, favors to be granted, as in the following example from Super Choc's "Shabani":

Mokolo nini nga na ko mona **Atos Senan?**	When will I see **Atos Senan?**
Mokolo nini nga na ko mona **Major Jacques?**	When will I see **Major Jacques?**
Mokolo nini nga na ko mona **Maté ya Air Zaire?**	When will I see **Maté of Air Zaire?**

This kind of parallelism enables words to function as hooks that lure in listeners with the promise of being publicly named, since as I heard often during my research, "People in Kinshasa love to be sung."[17] People cited are drawn in by the excitement of hearing their name, and because they are named, they in turn draw in others by buying extra copies of the album and playing it for (or giving it to) friends and relatives. A well-known concert promoter based in Pointe-Noire (Congo-Brazzaville) introduced himself to me as someone who had produced "all the big names" in Congolese music. He then proceeded to play a tape in which Papa Wemba mentioned his name in the body of a song text. The cassette was conveniently cued up to the point in the song at which his name was mentioned, and the cassette looked very used, suggesting that I was not the first person to have heard it. After we heard the part of the song with the promoter's name (which I could barely make out) he stopped the cassette, rewound it to the place where it had begun, and proudly concluded: "You see, even Wemba sings my name."

In less than twenty years, *libanga* has become an integral part of the music, not only in the way music is performed but also in the way it is imagined. While this phenomenon often strikes Western observers as morally questionable, from the point of view of many Congolese music fans *libanga* constitutes a normal part of the music's aesthetic. The fact of naming people, whether they are the artist's friends or simply sponsors, gives the music a degree of liveness and warmth by placing musicians (and by extension their fans) in a live network of social reciprocity. In this sense, *libanga* gives people something to listen for, a series of expectations that make listening both predictable and pleasurable. While some fans of popular music express disdain for *libanga*, others listen to it for important social and political cues about their favorite artists. Whom will the artist throw? Where in the song? The idea of Congolese popular music without *libanga*, at least since the early 1990s, is inconceivable for most fans of the music. If you do not throw someone's name, it could be taken to mean that you have no one to throw, and in Kinshasa this would be a kind of musical death.

Fear, Love, and Abandonment

The words of musicians in Kinshasa enable them to mediate between different levels of social and political power. On the one hand, they flatter people with money and power by citing their names in their songs. At the same time, and often in the same line, they sing about the anxiety and feeling of abandonment that characterizes urban experience during the Mobutu era, a theme that has strong resonances with a broad audience in Kinshasa. In the context of Mobutu's Zaire, where musicians are not known for speaking truth to power, this might not seem like a paradox. Indeed, to understand the extent of the political crisis during this period and how it was experienced by everyday people, one should not seek songs of resistance—which are relatively rare—but songs of satire and suffering (Olema 1998).[18] Lyrics about suffering, which generally take the form of plaintive love songs, enable musicians to show sympathy for the situation of the average *kinois* without putting themselves at political risk. As a reflection of musicians' ability to mediate between the people and the state, song texts display a kind of dialogue between *libanga*, which attests to the special arrangements of reciprocity among musicians and local elites, and song lyrics, which use the idiom of romantic love to express emotions of isolation and abandonment.

As an idea that often serves as a vehicle for other ideas, the concept of love in Congolese popular music is difficult to isolate. It is true that love can refer to a feeling of affect between friends and family members (especially parents and children), but the term *bolingo* generally corresponds to what we would call "romantic love," typically heterosexual and not necessarily mutual. Variations on the twinlike terms *bolingo* (love) and *motema* (heart) represent endless possibilities: *bolingo ya motema* (heartfelt love), *bolingo ya sentiment* (intense romantic love), *bolingo ya bomwana* (puppy love), *bolingo pasi* (love with pain), *motema pasi* (heartbreak). Expressions of romantic love are also statements about being modern, and this is part of what makes *bolingo* such an attractive idiom. Love is an object that can be given ("pesa nga bolingo"), taken away ("okimi na bolingo na yo"), hidden ("na kobomba bolingo"), forgotten ("obosana bolingo na biso te"), and cashed in ("compte na bolingo"). The heart is where *bolingo* lives ("ndako na motema na ngai"). It can burst into flames ("motema mopeli moto"), but it will never burn down ("jamais ekozikisa"). It can be closed or locked ("kanga motema"), broken ("motema epasuki"), damaged ("motema ebebi"), and reassured or calmed ("kitisa motema"). *Bolingo* is difficult to separate from marriage (*libala*), which is romantic in its own way, if nothing else as a show of romantic intentions ("Zaniha," Koffi Olomide). Marriage often requires patience, primarily to obtain approval for the union from family members and close friends ("Coupe du monde," O.K. Jazz), but waiting can also make the heart grow fonder. Of course once consummated, marriage is not without its problems ("Libala," Reddy Amisi), and despite the eternal problems of infidelity and jealousy, conjugal relations can still elicit sentiments of deep romantic love ("Phrase," Papa Wemba).

Romantic love, however, increasingly reflects the effects of the economic and political crisis of the Mobutu years. The heartbreak of the 1950s and 1960s becomes a series of illness and disease ("maladie ya motema") resulting in death, both symbolic ("na kokufa pona bolingo") and real ("maladie yango") in reference to the AIDS epidemic. Romantic love becomes a drunken disorientation ("bolingo ya kwiti"), a childish state of idiocy ("na komi zoba," "na komi dingue"), even madness ("bolingo oyo ezwi nga folie"). The sources of love-related problems seemed clearer in song lyrics before and around independence: girl leaves boy, boy feels sad, boy cries for her to return. In the 1990s songs that speak to problems of romantic love ask angst-ridden questions about abandonment. They seem to have no answer and are addressed to no one in particular: "Who will console me?" "Who will take care of me?" "Who will I cry to?" Whereas crying in song lyrics of the past was primarily associated with heartbreak, in today's song lyrics it is linked with hunger, uncertainty, and isolation. I am interested in working through this idiom of abandonment, primarily because it can be seen as an expression of the way that it felt to live and survive in Mobutu's Zaire. The story of abandonment begins with one person being left behind, as in General Defao's song "Gégé":

Nani akopesa ngai loboko Kalonda?	Who will help me, Kalonda?
Mwa o pesi mokongo okeyi na yo eh	You turned your back on me, you left
Okopesi mokongo Kalonda	You turned your back on me, Kalonda
Butu na ngai ekoma kaka ya basouci	My nights are filled with worries
Y'otikeli ngai mokuya ya yo, okeyi na bisengo	You left me with sadness, you took away my joy

The abandoned person is reduced to nothing, as in Koffi's Olomide's 1995 hit "Fouta Djallon":

Amour, amour, amour, amour	Love, love, love, love
Po nini ozongisi nga a zero?	Why did you reduce me to nothing?
Nazalaki muhumbu na yo	I was your slave
Po nini okomi opesa nga liwa avant l'heure?	Why did you decide to kill me before my time?

And unsure how he or she will make ends meet ("Famille Kikuta," General Defao, 1995):

Libala a pesi ngai deception	Marriage has been a huge disappointment
Bana na maboko, yaya pe ba boloko	Kids in my arms, my big brother in prison
Famille ya bobola	A family with no means
Nani a kopesa ngai maboko?	Who is going to help me?

The jilted lover looks everywhere to recover what he or she has lost ("Perdue de vue," Viva La Musica, 1996):

Ah ngai naluka luka zamba nyoso	I looked everywhere
Epayi yo okende na yebaka te	I have no idea where you went
Okima, okima nga, osundola nga,	You ran from me, abandoned me
Nakati ya esanga	I am completely lost

Fear turns to panic and anxiety as in "Dieu seul sait" by Empire Bakuba (1993) and "Chef de quartier" by Pépé Kallé (1996):

Ngai moko, mawa trop	All alone, I am so sad
Londende ezingi motema	My heart is overrun with worries
Nani a koconsoler?	Who will make me feel better?
Esika nini na kenda oboma nzoto na ngai?	Where can I go to protect myself?
Nani a kosunga ngai ndenge osalaki?	Who will take care of me like you do?
Nani a kofutela ngai minerval?	Who will pay my school fees?

The search for a solution begins with a series of questions ("Papa na Roissy," Koffi Olomide, 1998):

Na benga nani? Na tuna **Tutu Kukoba**	Who can I call? I'll ask **Tutu Kukoba**
Na benga nani? Na tuna **Guy Komo**	Who can I call? I'll ask **Guy Kono**
Na benga nani? Na tuna **Papa Roger**	Who can I call? I'll ask **Papa Roger**

The only solution involves a proposition for the loved one to return as quickly as possible ("Reviens Shaaly," Zaiko Langa Langa, 1998):

J'aime **Shaaly, Shaaly** mon préféré	I love **Shaaly,** he's my favorite
Zonga noki, papa o consoler nga	Come back soon, to make me feel better

Epayi nazali, posa la vie esili	From where I stand, it looks like my life is over
Na komi na ngai lokola mwa kizengi	I have become like an idiot in the face of love

Through the lens of a highly flexible theme such as bolingo, a wide variety of themes come together under the roof of a song. Magic (nkisi) is used to win someone's heart or to defend oneself against a romantic rival. Life in the city is both desired and feared because in the city love is free of the constraints of village life, but love can also lead to a death caused by careless sexual or financial behavior. Money is seen as a problem in itself, but it is most often presented as a prerequisite for love. For some critics the music's over-reliance on lyrics about love evidences musicians' loss of the creativity or determination required to write meaningful lyrics (Nkashama 1992); for others it reflects a deeply romantic, modern sensibility capable of articulating something unique about Congolese popular music and national identity (Tchebwa 1996). Both of these readings have some element of truth, but I tend to see songs about love more as part of the music's method than its essence. In this context, lyrics about love serve as a metaphorical playground on which people play with meaning and wait to see the effect it may have on those around them. If this playground continues to be a place where people want to play, there are good reasons. More so than songs with a "message," songs about love are extremely effective at holding the interest of audiences. Yet the way in which songs achieve this effect is not immediately obvious.

Lyrical Structures of Feeling

To understand how different themes and speech genres are employed within the context of a single song, it is important to examine a smaller number of song texts in greater depth. In many of the song lyrics cited below, for example, the reader will notice complex linkages between romantic love and poverty, and how this hardship appears alongside musician's strategic use of libanga, which can be seen both as a plea for support and as evidence of musicians' decadent lifestyle. In an effort to examine these aspects of song lyrics in interaction with each other, I have retained as much of the original song as possible. Each of the texts I have chosen enjoyed a significant amount of popularity leading up to or immediately following the end of Mobutu's rule in the second half of the 1990s.[19] The song texts come from different artists, and though they all touch on the themes of love and abandonment, they do so with different narrative angles: J. B. M'piana's story of class-based discrimination and social isolation ("Feux de l'amour"), Werra Son's text about the innocence and disillusionment of first love ("Treize ans"), General Defao's desperate plea from a woman to her absent husband ("Famille Kikuta"), and Koffi Olomide's chilling account of indifference and unrequited love ("Ko ko ko ko"). Following excerpts and a short discussion of each text, I will analyze the themes that cut across these lyrics and how they relate to the structures of feeling that came to characterize popular music and social experience in Mobutu's Zaire.

"Feux de l'amour" (J. B. M'piana, 1996)

. . . .

Nakini liboso ya kolinga moto	In Kinshasa before loving someone
Bakoma kotuna "ofandaka wapi?"	The question they ask is: "Where do you live?"
Biso tovandi na Malweka	We live in Malweka
Nani a kolinga biso?	Who will love us?
Mingi baboya bango se bongo	So many have been rejected for this reason
Mosika eleki, bangungi baleki	It's so far away, filled with mosquitoes
Taxi kutu baboya kokoma	Taxis even refuse to go there
Basusu liboso ya koloba oui	Others before saying yes
Bakoma kotuna "otangaka wapi?"	They have to ask, "Where do you study?"
Biso to buka biki mwa kala	We didn't go very far in our studies
Nani a kolinga biso?	Who will love us?
Tika tokosa ata kokosa	Let us lie, we just want to lie
Ngai nazali gradué, Ngai nazali licencié	"I graduated from college," "I've been to grad school"
Ngai nazali ingénieur, mpo balinga nga	"I'm an engineer," just to be loved
Mosusu liboso ya kolinga moto	Others before they love someone
Bakoma kotuna de quelle famille es-tu?	They have to ask, "Who is your family?"

Biso famille ezanga griffe, nani a kolinga biso?
Nzambe ya mpungu bandela mokili oyo
Otunaka moko moko soki nani a kolinga
Ko botama lisusu na famille ya pauvres
Ngai te, nga obele na famille ya
Adam Bombole, le grand Saoudien
Po ba melaka ti tongo nionso, na miliki, na manteka, na saucisson

Our family doesn't have a designer name, who will love us?
God, you who created this world
Ask the people one by one who would want
To be born again poor
Not me, I just want the family of
Adam Bombole, the Grand Saoudien
Because they drink tea every morning
With milk, butter, and sausage

.   .   .   .

Suka wapi, eh?
Kolinga kolinga suka wapi, **Ruphin Makengo?**
Ba banda yango ba tika yango, **Jean Ngandu**
Koluka lokumu to pe nini, **Lidi Ebondja?**
Ba susu kutu ba zonga sima, **Sami Mikobi.**
Mingi kutu ba senga la paix
Koluka lokumu to pe nini mama, **Ambroise na biso?**

Where does [love] end?
Love, love, where does love get you, **Ruphin Makengo?**
They started with love, they left with love, **Jean Ngandu**
Is it just a question of pride or what, **Lidi Ebondja?**
Others lost everything because of love, **Sami Mikobi**
And many just gave up
Is it just a question of pride or what, **Ambroise na biso?**

[seben]
Oh ho ya **Mado**, yaya na **Daida**
Ya **Michel Miche k. Kabeya**
Ya **Zeze Zebra-Force**
G. G. Fula Mambu hein
Papa leki Mbayo
Nous devons respecter les gars qui ont vécu

Oh ho ya **Mado**, yaya na **Daida**
Ya **Michel Miche k. Kabeya**
Ya **Zeze Zebra-Force**
G. G. Fula Mambu hein
Papa leki Mbayo
You have to respect those who have been around the block

Atomisi Lenga-Lenga Maître Mado, Gino	Atomisi Lenga-Lenga Maître Mado, Gino
Le haut sommet **André Kimbuta** (rire)	The high summit **André Kimbuta** (laughs)
Femme d'affaire, **Nancy** ndeko ya **Elisée**	Business woman, **Nancy** sister of **Elisée**

In this song, romantic love is mapped onto a social geography of inequality [video]. Those who live in peripheral, poverty-stricken neighborhoods have limited access to public facilities (transport, sanitation, education), but they are also limited in terms of who they can know and love. Neighborhoods are thus markers of class-based social difference. Those who come from families with no name (the term *griffe* is generally used to refer to the brand names of international designer fashions) are driven to lie about their status to find love. The recurring question "Who will love us?" refers to the social stigma inherent in romantic relations across class lines, but it also references the recurring anxiety of being abandoned by the state. The text reminds us that people do not choose poverty, restoring momentarily the dignity of those who are otherwise seen as poor and uneducated. Then in a complex change of register, M'piana plays on the notion of abundance to flatter his sponsor (Adam Bombole), creating a tension between the socially marginal who he claims to represent in the first part of the song and the elites who he publicly acknowledges during a long list of *libanga* at the end. When M'piana expresses his respect for those who have been around the block ("les gars qui ont vécu"), it is not clear if the block he is referring to is in Malueka or in a wealthy area of Kinshasa known as Macampagne. Thus the dialogue between the lyrics and the *libanga* creates a structural ambiguity that enables the musician to mediate between two completely different social worlds.

"Treize ans" (Werra Son, 2001)

. . . .

Nazela ye asilisa kelasi aya kobala nga	After his studies we were going to get married
Cartier Rita Omanga	**Cartier Rita Omanga**
Tongo nionso akendeke kelasi ayaka na ndako	Every day after school he would come to my house

Ngai ko nafutelaka ye batike yeye, **Nathalie Putu**

I used to pay for his bus ticket, **Nathalie Putu**

Ngai ko nasombelaka ye ba syllabus

I used to pay for his notebooks

Nga **Nanette** nafutelaka ye ba minervals

Me, Nanette, I used to pay his school fees

Ah **Dorothé Ferre**

Ah **Dorothé Ferre**

Ba parents na nga babengani nga na ndako pona yo

My parents kicked me out because of you

Babalisi nga na mibali ya mbongo nalingaki te

They wanted me to marry a rich boy but I refused

Bolingo ekomisa nga zoba kolandaka yo, **Claudine Dakosta**

Love has made me stupid, **Claudine Dakosta**

Anzulusi nga lelo asundoli nga vraiment, **Lili Debora**

You made me old and then left me, **Lili Debora**

Soki nakinisi nakolela **Jolie Mayala**, Wapi **Willy Mayanvu**

When I think about it I just cry, **Jolie Mayala**

Soki nabanzi nakomiboma nzoto

When I think about it I just want to die

Nakufa na nga martyre ya bolingo na me

I'm dying here, a martyr of love

Rochide bolingo ezang'assurance nakosuka wapi?

Rochide, love has no insurance, where will I end up?

. . . .

Tango asilisi kelasi alobi akobala na ye lisusu nga te

When he finished his studies, he changed his mind

Po nazali mwasi ya niveau na ye te, **Guy Boston**

He said I wasn't at his level, **Guy Boston**

Soki oyebaki que naza mwasi ya niveau na yo te

If you knew that I wasn't at your level

Ebongaki oyebisa nga avant nabenda nzoto, **Hugues Kashala**

You should have told me earlier, **Hugues Kashala**

Tala lelo olekisi nga batango na nga ya pamba

You made me waste all this time

Baninga nionso tokola babali, **Chibebi Kangala**	All of my friends are married, **Chibebi Kangala**
Baleki pe na sima bakomi kobala	Even my younger sisters are already married
Claudine Kinua asiliki	**Claudine Kinua** is angry

. . . .

José Kongolo na **Dalida**	**José Kongolo** na **Dalida**
Ima ole oh nga nazui ba idées, **Robert** le français	I was so naive, **Robert** le français
Nabanzaki tokovand'éternelle-ment, **Roi David**	I thought we would be together forever, **Roi David**
Tala lelo otiki nga moko na pasi, nakolela epai ya nani?	And today look at me, who can I cry to?
Godar Kidina	**Godar Kidina**

. . . .

Oyo nionso se ba souffrances, **Annie Dembo**	All this is only suffering, **Annie Dembo**
Charlotte Chalamama, mama na **Eder, Mosi Singi**	Charlotte Chalamama, mama na **Eder**'s mother, **Mosi Singi**
Awa bolingo ekeyi	Here love is gone
Nakokota na ngai ata losambo, **Tabu Fatu**	I will devote my life to prayer, **Tabu Fatu**
Nzambe ye mei ako soulager nga	God himself will make me feel better
Mateya nakoyokaka na ba louanges yango	I will hear the scripture and praise
Ebikisaka **Nono Lomboto**	It heals, **Nono Lomboto**

Like "Feux de l'amour," this song references the difficulties of class-based social difference through an idiom of love [video]. The protagonist turns away a potential husband from a wealthy family, preferring instead to use her meager resources to help her first love finish his studies. She is shocked to learn that after all her devotion and sacrifice, the beneficiary of her generosity turns his back on her, saying that she is no longer at his level. She begs him to reconsider: "What will become of me? Whose shoulder will I cry on?" She is no longer able to provide for herself, especially given the stigma that accompanies her fiancé's change of heart, and through libanga the voice of the musician appeals to a series of people to witness her hardship (José Kongolo, Roi David, Godar Kidina). With all hope of love gone, she turns to prayer to calm the pain and heal her wounds. There is a structural tension in this song between the feeling of helplessness given off by the lyrics and the astounding presence of *libanga*. The complete version of this song mentions more than 110 names, a large number of them those of women. Given the subject matter of the song (a young woman driven to prayer by the disillusionment of love), it seems unsurprising that the *libanga* include an important number of women relative to men. This text illustrates the importance of Kinshasa's burgeoning evangelical movement, a phenomenon often explained as a response to the economic crisis of the 1990s. For some women, going to church represents a means of reconstructing an image of piety and female honor while still maintaining a presence in public with the hope of meeting someone new. For other women, however, the pain of being abandoned proves too great, and prayer becomes a place of permanent refuge and emotional safety. (For more on women's strategies see Vansina 1982, Walu 1999.)

"Famille Kikuta" (General Defao, 1995)

Papa ye, po nini okimi ndako?	Oh husband, why did you leave home?
Papa ye, po nini okimi ndako ?	Oh husband, why did you leave home?
Likambo overifier te po nini okimi ya **Kaliba?**	You didn't check the story, why did you leave **Kaliba?**
Didi aye obala nga na mbongo	When Didier came to marry me, he had money
Soki mabe benga bafamille bosolola	If there is something wrong, let's talk to our families
Okimi ndako na yo	You left your home
Okimi bana ba yo	You left your children
Nani a kobokolo bango?	Who will take care of them?
Papa ya bana eh	Father of your children
Zonga ndako, tobongisa na malembe	Come back home so we can work it out
Papa ye, a yo leli	Husband, they are crying for you
Oh papa yeye, eza nde likambo	Husband, this is really a problem.

. . . .

Libala a pesi ngai déception	Marriage has been a huge disappointment
Bana na maboko, yaya pe ba boloko	Responsible for the kids, my big brother in prison
Famille ya bobola	A family with no means
Nani a kopesa ngai maboko?	Who is going to help me?
Na mokumba na za nango	The burden is all mine
Papa eh, a yo leli	Husband, oh they miss you
Oh **Bruno Sanda**, eza nde likambo, **Damien Kikuta**	Oh **Bruno Sanda**, what a problem, **Damien Kikuta**
Na zuwa baku ya lelo eleki pasi	I have known bad situations, but this is the worst
Kimbunzi nyoso esila nateka na bwaka nzoto	All of my wares are sold, I give up
Mobongo ekweya na kota faillite	My commerce fell apart, I am going bankrupt
Oh papa, na kota kelo	Oh husband, this is hell
Bamoyen nyoso esila na dépenses ya bana	Providing for the children has depleted my resources
Koliya ya bana	The children's food
Pona na kelasi ya bana	The children's school fees
Ba soins médicaux yo ya bana	The children's medical bills

. . . .

Inspecteur Konde, Denis Konde	**Inspecteur Konde, Denis Konde**
Guy Guy de Paris	**Guy Guy de Paris**
Nasolo, Sele Mokwangu	**Nasolo, Sele Mokwangu**
Dans la scène **Roger Mayemba**, ozongi Paris?	On stage **Roger Mayemba**, are you back in Paris?
Oh le boss **J. P. Kamanshito, Guy Mayangi**	Oh le boss **J. P. Kamanshito, Guy Mayangi**

Families are torn apart by the effects of the crisis, here, as in the two previous examples, explained from a female point of view [video]. The response of the jilted lover is focused primarily on how the husband's departure has affected the children, a socially acceptable response in a context in which the relationship between a man and his wife ("mama ya bana") represents the future of a lineage and not just an expression of conjugal love. Thus the protagonist appeals not to her husband's sense of romance, but to his sense of duty, arguing that the burden of caring for their children in his absence will be too much for her to handle.[20] She begs him to return, even if it means getting other members of the family involved to find a solution. As a commissioned piece of music, this song represents a fascinating form of connection with audiences. Through Defao's words, we hear the pain and anxiety experienced by a woman who is helpless following her husband's departure. Yet the fact that she commissioned an entire song to convince her husband to return home suggests that her financial situation is not so precarious. The musician's words can be imagined as an act of mediation intended to bring the husband back to his senses, but the song text remains silent with respect to why he left in the first place. Thus the song acts in real terms, using *libanga* to provoke a change of heart in a man that decided to abandon his wife and children. By extension it is possible to see how the message intended for Kikuta can be interpreted as referring to a much larger category of *responsables*, those seen as having taken on the responsibility of providing for the children of the nation.

"Ko ko ko ko" (Koffi Olomide/Fally Ipupa, 2003)

Ko ko ko ko ko ko, Fungola ndako nga na batama	Knock knock knock, open the door and let me in
Ko ko ko ko ko ko, Fungola ndako po nga na batama	Knock knock knock, open the door to let me in
Awa libanda ba nzoko ba nkoi bakomekana	Here outside the elephant and the leopard are restless
Bipayi oyo kuna batondi meke ya ba metiola pe bayindo	Everywhere there are light and dark-skinned people
Alain Barakuda	**Alain Barakuda**
Eh muindo pe ya pamba pamba te, obe muindo ya ngolo	But not just any dark-skinned people, beautiful ones
Ngai ekelamu ya Nzambe oyo	I am nothing but a creature of God here
O'ya lekela vraiment ntango	A creature of God who is beyond his prime

. . . .

Est-ce que c'est vraiment toi,
    mon amour?
Okangi na yo matoyi **Charly**
    y'oboyi ata koyoka kolela
    na nga
Honoré Buze, Ado Transpar
Y'otika nga na songe ya mboka
    matanga **Josée Lukote**
Mongongo na nga nani ayoka
    Charly
Kingo na yo na lipeka ya moto
    mosusu
Te, topakola vérité maquillage te
Ata miso eboyi kotala permettre
    matoyi eyoka
Quartier Latin pe he
Kolela na ngai ya suka ai pitié
    Pitchoko
Alain Barakuda demi-dieu
Ezui ngulu'a zamba ngulu'a
    mokili koseka te
Ezui le **Grand Mopao** ba
    nguandi boseka te
Ezui Fally Ipupa mère **Fim-
    bongo, Lorise la congolaise**
Nazui ferié na motema faute
    ewuti epai ya **Washington**
Monoko ezui congé ya kobenga
    kombo ya **Charly**
Ibrahim Shako
Na suspendre matoyi koyoka ba
    "je t'aime" na yo
Motem'etikala se na stock ya
    kal'a provision'a bolingu'a
Bébé Nakukuenda, oh **James
    Charly**

Is it really you, my love?

You won't listen **Charly**, not even to
    my tears

Honoré Buze, Ado Transpar
You left me in a faraway village, **Josée
    Lukote**
Who will listen to my voice, **Charly**

Your neck resting on someone else's
    shoulder
No, let's not try to hide the truth
Even if your eyes won't look, let your
    ears listen
Quartier Latin too
These are my final cries, have pity
    Pitchoko
Alain Barakuda demi-God
What happens to a boar doesn't
    make a pig laugh
What happens to **Mopao** shouldn't
    amuse his enemies
It's got Fally Ipupa **Mère Fimbongo,
    Lorise**
I took a break for my heart,
    Washington is to blame
A vacation for my mouth, calling
    Charly's name
Ibrahim Shako
I closed my ears to avoid hearing
    "I love you"
My heart is left with old memories

Bébé Nakukuenda, oh **James Charly**

Ah eh **James** kokenda te Olelisi moto lokola Bakandja	Oh **James** don't go, you made me cry like Bakandja
Ah he eh, ah he Zonga zonga oh oh	Oh woah, woah, come back, oh woah
Beethoven Yoko Germaim	**Beethoven Yoko Germain**
Junior Okita na **François Babaki Modogo**	**Junior Okita** and **François Babaki Modogo**
Le groupe Christian Peugeot Investissements	**Christian Peugeot Investments Group**

The most striking element of this song is the feeling of indifference conveyed by the song's central metaphor "ko ko ko ko," an onomatopoeic expression for the sound of knocking on a door [video]. The protagonist tries desperately to provoke a response to his heartfelt declaration of love, but to no avail; she has closed her eyes, her heart, and worst of all her ears. She will not even talk to his friends. Her refusal to answer his call drives him to the limits of his patience and shakes his will to go on ("I am dying for you"). The cyclical nature of the music (a single, repeating partition) reinforces the feeling that his suffering will never end, creating a trancelike sound similar to the music associated with the practice of mourning. The unpredictable placement of the chorus ("ko ko ko ko") reinforces the general feeling of disorientation created by the lyrics. It is interesting to note the degree to which *libanga* are integrated into the body of the lyrics ("James don't go"; "Who will listen to me, Charly?"; "I am losing it for Pastor Miba").

As Steve Feld has shown in his research on music among the Bosavi (1982), the emotional register of song references historical relationships with space and time. Song lyrics in Kinshasa evoke deep melancholy and tears, but more and more the tears they reference are those of economic difficulties ("Famille Kikuta"), injustice ("Feux de l'amour"), and disorientation ("Ko ko ko ko"). They try in vein to return to a time when things were simple ("Treize ans"), but the temporality of the crisis is never far away. In the context of Mobutu's Zaire, this crisis took on epic proportions, and at each of its stages people wondered how they would continue to survive. The real crisis, however, is one of political culture, since in many ways the words of musicians reverberate within a system of rule based not on law but on connections. Musicians' criticisms of people in positions of power take the form of requests for political and financial protection, but never

Figure 50. Werra Son posing with a female fan as young male fans look on.
PHOTO: SERGE MAKOBO.

of political reform. It is in this sense that musicians have assimilated the political culture of the Mobutu years, relying on the clichés of praise and of public displays of submission through what Crawford Young and Thomas Turner describe as a "thick layer of fawning sycophancy" (1985, 171). The *libanga* phenomenon takes the logic of praise singing promoted during Mobutu's authenticity politics and pushes it to unimaginable extremes, with individual songs sometimes citing the names of more than one hundred people; one song even begins its *libanga* by throwing the name of Jesus Christ ("Feux de l'amour").

Much of the participation in this phenomenon is not wholly conscious now that these learned behaviors have become part of a formulaic reproduction of sound already invested with power, a *kind of rumba habitus*. As Ngandu Nkashama observed more than ten years ago, the lyrical strategies of young musicians during the Mobutu years reinforce a feeling of "sudden panic," and "there no longer exists a text that is constructed in narrative sequences or recitative parts" (1992, 481). This does not mean, however, that the music no longer has any meaning, since as I have attempted to show, popular music continues to exist as a source of joy and wonder for hundreds of thousands of young people in the Congolese capital, especially young women who, as this chapter has shown, are an essential part of how male songwriters imagine and organize lyrical narratives (figure 50). In my ongoing research with audiences in Kinshasa, there is anecdotal evidence to suggest that women are more likely to listen to and memorize song lyrics, but further investigation is required to confirm or explain this phenomenon.[21]

Given the dramatic changes in the content of popular song lyrics, what about the music continues to be compelling? On the one hand, the words of popular music in Kinshasa reflect the hardships of life in an economy of crisis. They address the questions of betrayal, financial insecurity, social inequality, and endemic poverty, but they do so primarily through an idiom of romantic love and release. The growing importance of the *libanga* phenomenon alludes to changes in the lyrical structures of feeling I have set out to describe. In most songs, *libanga* begins gently during the main body of lyrics and then gradually takes over the song, until finally in the *seben* it takes the form of a listing of names. This praise-singing frenzy reflects a growing sense of social and political urgency that certain observers have characterized as apocalyptic (De Boeck 2005), and the very presence of *libanga* in popular music suggests that traditional networks of social reciprocity are not as reliable or as desirable as in the past. At the same time, however, there is something about the lyrics of popular music that echoes Kinshasa's long-standing tradition of *débrouillardise* (Trefon 2004), which must be seen more as an expression of people's dignity than of their survival instinct. From this point of view, *libanga* appears not as a corrupted form of language, but as proof of the music's social relevance and potency. Through the words and gestures of popular musicians, and despite the growing sense of desperate insecurity, it may be argued that generations of young people in Kinshasa have looked to popular music as an opportunity to shine (Gondola 1999; MacGaffey and Bazenguissa-Ganga 2000).

7

THE POLITICAL LIFE OF DANCE BANDS

THROUGH THE PLATFORM OF SELF-PROMOTION known as *libanga*, popular music in Kinshasa reinforces not only the idea that political power can be purchased but also that it must be made manifest through performance. The ubiquity of this phenomenon in Kinshasa adds to the impression that there are important people everywhere, or as my research assistant Serge Makobo used to say, "Il y a trop de chefs dans ce pays" (There are too many chiefs in this country).[1] This phrase quickly became a running joke between us, but it also illustrates an important characteristic of the political culture in Mobutu's Zaire, namely, that bad leadership encourages people to strike out and form structures they can call their own, a form of organizational dislocation I will refer to as "splintering." The domain of popular music, though by far not the only domain affected by this phenomenon, offers a particularly good example of splintering. As a central dynamic in Congolese popular music, splintering occurs for multiple reasons, but mainly because it represents a means of gaining access to financial and political resources. Thus the tendency toward splintering is inseparable from the desire to become a *chef*. A closer examination of splintering is important not only because the phenomenon characterizes a good part of the music scene but also because it usually occurs at moments when agreed-on notions of leadership and authority break down.

I am interested in the notion of micropolitics, a concept often used but rarely problematized.[2] David Hecht and Maliqalim Simone (1994) define micropolitics as a set of local cultural/political responses to an absence of government. Micropolitical activities, they argue, undermine the process of development, but they also point to a unique African ability to survive in and adapt to an increasingly globalizing world. I find this definition interesting, especially for the case of the Congo where survival has become a high art (MacGaffey 1991; Trefon 2004), but also problematic because it tends to view the state as the primary determinant of culture and cultural change. I use the term *micropolitics* to mean the diffuse set of political structures and practices that operate among individuals or among individuals and institutions, primarily those outside the conventional units of macropolitical analysis (e.g., the Western nation-state).[3] Following Achille Mbembe, I argue that "to account for postcolonial relations is thus to pay attention to the workings of power in its minute details, and to the principles of assemblage which give rise to its efficacy" (1992a, 4). Antonio Gramsci's theory of hegemony (1971), which makes the crucial distinction between power and force, has enabled cultural analysis to move away from the dichotomy of domination and resistance implied in much of the anthropological literature. Thus micropolitics in Gramscian terms (a "moving equilibrium") is interested not in the "ruler" or the "ruled" per se, but in the complex interaction that enables a relation of power to be reproduced and sustained.[4]

This chapter attempts to make a more explicit link between the study of micropolitics and ethnographic discussions of power. Johannes Fabian's *Power and Performance* (1990) provides an excellent example of this approach. The theatrical rendering of the Luba axiom "power is eaten whole" exposes the connection between power and eating in many African societies and suggests a cultural idiom in which power is conceived of as whole and embodied in persons (Fabian 1990, 25).[5] In his study Fabian explains not only how artists fix into place and subvert hierarchical social formations but also looks at how their decisions about content are influenced (and co-opted) by local and national political interests. Each of these approaches challenges us to view power as a set of social relations grounded in history and culture, and not simply a "thing" possessed or wielded.[6] Combining the insights of Gramsci with the methodological approach of Fabian, I will describe various fields of action in which superiors and subordinates—musicians and band-leaders, female musicians and male musicians, musicians and sponsors— are tied up in plays of power that are simultaneously antagonistic and self-perpetuating.

A Band Is a Hierarchy

Given the size of most professional musical groups in Kinshasa (usually between fifteen and twenty-five members), some form of hierarchy within groups hardly seems surprising.[7] Hierarchy in this setting is usually ex-pressed through an idiom of seniority that conflates age and size: "C'est un petit, il ne connait rien" (He's a kid; he doesn't know anything). The use of the term *petit*, condescending to a North American ear, occurs with astounding frequency in discussions about the life history of musicians and musical groups. The term refers more often to age than to size, although size (meaning "popularity") is also important given the fact that hierarchies of success can operate independent of age or generational order. Through the utterance of such a commonly heard phrase the speaker places himself within a group of *bavieux* ("elders" or "people with experience") and opposes himself to the unrefined state of youth and inexperience. Another common formula uses the name of one musician to refer to a group of musicians or generation (e.g., "Les Reddy," referring to a singer named Reddy and those with whom he began playing music). Statements using this form usually serve the purpose of locating individual band members within a genera-tional or professional hierarchy.

Seniority is also expressed through the metaphors of space and time: "Bavon was later. When he started I was already here." By virtue of the fact that the speaker was already present when the new artist began or arrived ("he found me here"), the speaker can make special claims on knowledge or seniority based on prior physical presence. This kind of preemptive claim is very common in discussions about musical innovations, especially those related to new forms of musical technology. Different musicians take credit for having introduced new instruments, such as the electric guitar or the jazz drum kit, and the matter never seems resolved. There is always someone else laying claim to priority: "I was the first." Statements such as this express the speaker's prior access to cultural and social knowledge (links with the past), but also his or her influence on the generations of ideas to come (links with the future).

When musicians speak about their trajectories as stars, they reinforce this hierarchy by resituating their success in relation to their musical mentors and idols. Musicians talk about their "spiritual ancestors" (Tchebwa 1996) not only to appease them but also because creating a sense of intimacy with *les grands* (the big ones) effectively makes oneself a future *grand*. In television and press interviews, musicians commonly discuss their position vis-à-vis their mentors and musical influences. Sam Mangwana articulates his identity as a Central African and as a product of those musicians that came before him:

> For me it is a great joy to accept the invitation [he is referring to the interview]. You know, brother, I'm part of this Central African culture and in some ways we are unstoppable because we have brought so much [to African music] with our know-how. Myself, I was initiated by the big names in Zairian music: Tabu Ley put me on the right track, and I always had the late Kabasele Tshamala "Grand Kallé"; Nico, I got advice from him too, and especially Vicky Longomba is a singer that I like very much. . . . Mujos, Kwamy, and many others. I was taught by them, and that's why I agreed to be here today. (qtd. in Ntondo 1997–98, 44)

Musicians' comments show that the force of the individual is rarely asserted on its own or of its own merit. Here is Reddy Amisi on the subject of his bandleader Papa Wemba:

> Reddy is Papa Wemba's son. Everything that I do amounts to nothing more than the work of those that have come before me in Viva La Musica. I respect Papa Wemba, my boss, as well as the values of our group. Just between you and me, Papa Wemba can't always give us everything. At our age, with the responsibility that we have, I think it's important that we be able to take care of our own needs. We can't depend on him for everything. He has his own problems to take care of. And so, it's up to us to play the game. He has brought us all over: to the States, in Africa, to Japan, and so on. So if you see me playing concerts in my own name, understand that this is the reason why. I will always be loyal to Papa Wemba. I am not

the master of my destiny. Everything that I do is blessed by him. (qtd. in Prezio 1996, 2)

In his attempt to make a claim about his artistic authority, the musician inserts himself into a specific artistic lineage. This claim to belonging also legitimates the value of the musical secrets presumably entrusted to him. Important are not the artist's musical influences per se, but his position relative to those who came before him. If a musician cites the names of his *grands*, it must be seen as an attempt to assert his individuality without falling victim to the narcissistic self-promotion increasingly required of musicians who need to groom their image as stars. Thus the paradox of social eminence in the Congolese setting is not simply that acts of distinction are embedded in culture and society—for this holds true in all cultures—but rather that they assert individuality by association with a group, a phenomenon that Ellen Corin has referred to as "anchoring" (1998).

Most working musical groups in Kinshasa are formed around a charismatic leader-virtuoso, often a lead singer whose band carries his name: Nico et l'African Fiesta, Franco et Son Tout Puissant O.K. Jazz, Bozi Boziana et Anti-Choc, Les Big Stars de General Defao, Koffi Olomide et Quartier Latin, Wenge Musica de Werra Son, and so on. The charismatic leader, usually having separated from a previous group to form his own, surrounds himself with younger, less well-known musicians unlikely to question his authority and willing to work for little money in hopes of getting some exposure to the music business. The bandleader's status is contingent on the presence of a certain number of followers, and the longevity of the group is generally limited to the leader's lifespan. He may have the objective of identifying and training up-and-coming artists, but in Kinshasa this approach is the exception to the rule. Charismatic leaders in the music scene tend to hold on as long as they can in the same role as singer/bandleader (e.g., Wendo Kolosoy, Tabu Ley Rochereau, Nyoka Longo).

The band with which I conducted the majority of my research offers a good example of charismatic leadership. Defao himself was more than just the band's leader; he was its founder, and most members of the band addressed him as "Fondateur," or "Fondé" for short. He lived, ate, and slept apart from the rest of the band. He consulted regularly with the senior members of the band, but he rarely traveled with them and never socialized with them outside the work context. These senior members, or *batêtes* (heads) as he called them, were not his friends; they were his most loyal and skilled workers, and they were a buffer between him and the everyday problems of the rest of the band. The *batêtes* included the band president, the band manager, the practice manager, the head doorman-bodyguard, and two of the front-line singers. The leader's authority, based not only on his skill as a gifted singer and dancer but also on his ability to provide for his musicians, was reinforced by the very careful distance he kept between himself and the almost forty official members of his band. The picture reproduced here of Defao having fun with the musicians was taken in the lobby of Defao's hotel during our tour in Matadi (figure 51). It captures the only time I saw Defao interacting with the musicians offstage during the tour.

Nonetheless, the *batêtes* had considerable control over daily operations, especially over the administration of band practice, personnel decisions, and disciplinary measures. Defao himself usually showed up at concerts well after the band had started playing, and he would often miss practices all together. This gave the *batêtes* quite a bit of artistic and administrative responsibility and freedom. The most important of these junior leaders was the second lead singer, the person who became the lead singer in Defao's absence. Soon after Defao returned from Europe (following a large turnover in musicians), Montana obtained the title of *président d'orchestre*. In a special inaugural ceremony, he was presented to the public and from then on was simply known as "Président." As president, Montana had the authority to make decisions regarding the choice of musicians, onstage activity in Defao's absence (the movement of *danseuses*, the length and order of songs and dance sequences, choices with respect to who would play at any given time, and start/end times), and certain other high-level concerns. Special requests from musicians for money, medical leave, and medical expenses were considered by the president (usually in conjunction with the *chef d'orchestre*, or band manager), unless they were serious enough for the bandleader to intervene. Defao nonetheless required periodic reports from the president and the *chef d'orchestre*, especially in the case of any disciplinary actions.

The *chef d'orchestre*, in this case also the first lead guitarist, acted mostly as an administrator. This role is not to be confused with managers in the North American music industries, who are not members of the band but act as commercial agents or brokers for it. The duties of the Big Stars band

Figure 51. Defao with musicians in the lobby of his hotel. PHOTO: BOB W. WHITE.

manager included maintaining an inventory of the equipment, monitoring band members' progress and attendance, arranging logistics for concert and touring engagements, distributing money earned at the door during band practice, and putting into writing any official decisions and correspondence concerning the band (disciplinary actions, contracts, travel arrangements, etc.). The band manager is by far the busiest member of the band and is free to make most decisions concerning administrative issues. High-level decisions (such as suspensions or the choice of musicians for important shows or tours) are made together by the band manager and the band president, although it seems that the band president has the final say between the two. Ultimate veto power lies with the bandleader, who always reserves the right to intervene.

Below the president and the manager exists a third level of authority: the practice manager (*chef de répétition*), who often decides the song order and listens for musical mistakes during practice. In this particular case the first rhythm guitarist occupied this position. In addition to managing public practices, he also oversees private band practices, which are usually devoted to the composition of songs or musical arrangements. As a rhythm guitarist, he is the musician most keenly aware of the structural aspects of the music, especially song structure, the relative volume of instruments, tuning, and arrangements. The practice manager reports to the band manager and sometimes makes decisions for the band manager in his absence. After the practice manager comes the dance manager (*cheftaine des danseuses*), who reports directly to the band president. Since most dancers are female, this position is usually filled by a woman.[8] She is usually one of the senior dancers, but is also chosen on the basis of her reliability and discretion. The dance manager is responsible for choreography and dance practice, only some of which happens outside band practice, and basically enacts the decisions made by the band president or bandleader with regards to who will dance, when, and what they will wear. Dancers and musicians interact freely, but dancers usually stay together in groups of two or three. Later in this chapter I will discuss the *danseuses'* marginalization in male-run bands and how they often become scapegoats in the resolution of conflicts between band members.

A fourth layer of hierarchy exists at the level of the musician members of the band. At each musical post (lead guitar, drums, tenor voice, etc.) there are anywhere from two to four qualified musicians whose skill level or seniority dictates who will play and how often. The most senior or most skilled musician has the status of *titulaire* (first-string or permanent) musician and because of this status will have more time onstage than the other musicians in his category. For high-profile concert appearances such as TV shows, political rallies, and wedding or funeral ceremonies, the *titulaire* generally plays the entire engagement. The backup musicians for any given post, usually referred to as *doublures* (second-string), are completely at the mercy of decisions made by the president and the bandleader and feel extra pressure when called on to play, since they only have limited opportunities to practice in a full performance situation. They must remain on standby at all times, and they usually stay close to the *titulaire* to gain his respect and learn from his experience.

The rest of the group is made up of nonartists. The sound engineer usually has two assistants and in most cases reports directly to the band manager, but in his absence can also take orders from the practice manager. The sound team is responsible for moving, setting up, and operating all sound equipment (sound board, amplifiers, microphones, speakers, cabling, etc.). As the only band members with any knowledge about operating unreliable equipment, they are present at all live engagements and most (if not all) band meetings. They sometimes receive the assistance of the two doormen, whose main responsibility is to control fans' movement before and during the concert. As full-fledged members of the band, they receive small regular salaries and transport, although before and after shows they are required to travel with the equipment. The senior doorman, in this case a former soldier in the Zairian army, often acted as a personal bodyguard to Defao, and in some circumstances was consulted as a member of the *batêtes*. Apart from the bodyguard, the only nonartists that mingle with the senior members are the band doctor (actually a male nurse) and the band driver, who both enjoy a privileged position close to senior band members during concerts and tours. Some bandleaders also have a public relations specialist (*attaché de presse*), who facilitates relations with members of the press, or a personal assistant (*secrétaire personnel*), who also enjoys close contact with the upper end of the band hierarchy.

This brief description of the band structure illustrates the extent to which hierarchy and discipline order the activities of musicians and musical groups (table 1). Defao's stage name ("Le Général") and the common use of the Lingala term *soda* (soldier) to describe musicians suggest an organizational framework based on a military metaphor, but the band structure is often described in terms of a sports organization. *Titulaires* dominate show time, while *doublures* wait for a chance to play. The singers, occupying the front part of the stage, are referred to as the *attaque-chant* (offense) and the instrumentalists, situated behind the singers, are called the defense. Band members address the leaders of the group with terms of respect such as "Président" or "Chef." Sometimes they combine these terms with the person's first name, such as "Chef Maneko," which is also used in the leader's absence. Metaphoric language reflects an organizational logic based on a strict hierarchy, but language also helps keep this hierarchy in place.

Hierarchy Is Elastic

Although the *batêtes* have considerable control over artistic and administrative matters, many decisions remain clearly within the control of the bandleader. Decisions of this type tend to be long-term or strategic in nature. Defao, for example, maintained a busy working schedule for the band by booking concerts in low-profile events and densely populated, low-income neighborhoods (*quartiers populaires*). The Big Stars often played at local bars

```
                    Bandleader
              (founder of group and lead singer)

                    President
                    (#2 singer)

                  Band Manager
                   (lead guitarist)

         Driver    Bodyguard    Doctor

       #3 Singer    #4 Singer    #5 Singer

                 Practice Manager
                  (rhythm guitarist)

      Bass Player                Keyboard Player
  Second-String Singers      Second-String Guitarists

                     Atalaku
                    (first string)

                     Dancers

                     Atalaku
                   (second string)
                   Percussionist

        Sound Engineer    Doormen
```

in Bumbu, Masina, Ndjili, and other neighborhoods with high percentages of unemployed young men. When I asked Defao why he tended to favor certain neighborhoods in scheduling concerts, he answered that it was not necessarily a matter of choice. Because of the lack of producers, he explained, he was forced to play where demand was the greatest. Financial matters for the most part rest with the bandleader. In Defao's case, instead of buying a house or an expensive car, as most well-known musicians do, he decided to invest his money in a band vehicle, a red Toyota Hiace minivan, which could transport both band equipment and musicians whenever the band played and which was the envy of many groups in Kinshasa in the mid- and late 1990s.

Decisions regarding band size and the number of musicians in training ultimately lie with the bandleader. Most bandleaders judge it necessary to keep a large number of musicians on call in case of sickness, absence, or suspension. Keeping two to three active musicians per post is a constant reminder to the *titulaire* that he is not irreplaceable, and to the *doublures* that they have a long way to go before being able to play on a regular basis. Second- and third-string musicians, as full members of the band, are expected to be present at all times. Since they pick up band-specific songs and techniques as they go along, the need for special training time is almost eliminated. To even gain acceptance as a second- or third-string musician, it is necessary to learn some part of the band's repertoire in advance, usually five to ten songs. With respect to auditioning and selecting musicians for certain key posts (especially singers and lead guitarists), the bandleader plays a more important role. From my notes:

> At a band meeting I recently attended, I noticed that one of the singers who had just auditioned was sitting in the back of the room.
> "What are you doing here?" the bandleader asked in a strong tone.
> "Sorry, Chef, I thought I was in the group."
> "No," he said, "you haven't even presented your credentials yet. When you can sing six or seven songs perfectly you come and see me. You're just sitting there listening to everything we say. This is a private meeting you know." He stood up and the bodyguard motioned him to leave with a gesture of very fragile authority. As the embarrassed singer moved toward the door, the bandleader repeated what he had said, half smiling:
> "If you know seven or eight songs to the note, then you come see me . . . before you know nine songs don't come to see me, do you hear me? And come looking nice, good and yellow!" [a reference to the recruit's dark complexion] (November 17, 1995)

Under certain exceptional circumstances, the bandleader will intervene to fine-tune technical aspects of the music. During one practice, the bandleader called his first and second singers to the microphone to fix (*kobongisa*) one part of a particular song. This type of correction would always occur in a scolding tone and was most likely intended to embarrass the musician since it tended to happen in the presence of the entire band. When one day I witnessed the first and second singer of a group being corrected, it became very clear that no one was safe from reprimand. On another occasion, one bandleader ordered the new drummer to sit behind his set where he was instructed to play several variations of the dance rhythm he used during the fast part of each song. "Trop de fantaisies" (Too many frills), the bandleader said. After identifying the rhythm he was looking for, the bandleader instructed the drummer to play that rhythm *and that rhythm only* for the dance sections (*seben*) of the entire repertoire. The correction of musicians in this way rarely happens outside a private band meeting. During practice, a poorly executed song can be started over after discreet comments to the musician(s) at fault. Musicians making mistakes during concerts can be reprimanded in between songs with backs to the audience, but also sometimes during the song itself if the mistake is considered serious enough (an out-of-tune guitar, a rhythm too fast, etc.).

After practice, a short period of milling around and cooling down (fifteen to forty-five minutes) usually ensues. Then when either the junior leaders or the bandleader see fit, they call all the musicians back into the practice room. If the bandleader attends, the junior leaders call the meeting to order first, and the bandleader will enter after everyone is seated and quiet. As he enters, usually with some degree of ceremony, members of the band stand up, and after he has taken his seat, band members can once again sit down. Meetings usually last from one to three hours and cover a variety of topics. Most meeting time is taken up with assessments of individual performance during practice or concerts. From my notes:

> That meeting was unbearable. Two hours of reprimanding and in-house matters: the guitarist was out of tune. If it continues, one-month suspension. The singer out of tune; if it continues, one-month suspension. The *atalaku*, you talk too much. The other *atalaku*, if you can't sing the shout, leave it for someone else. The new singer, not bad, but not there yet. Band manager, get the dancers in order, redo the last song, it's too messy. Bass player, play bass with some guts, vary your lines more, and so forth and so on. (April 11, 1996)

Every time a musician is called on, he or she stands up and removes any headgear. Musicians rarely respond to criticisms from the bandleaders. They are supposed to listen, express a healthy dosage of humility, and promise to fix their mistakes (*bongisa mabe*). It is not uncommon for the bandleader to use humor to humiliate or embarrass band members. "Fany!" one bandleader addressed his favorite dancer. "Stand up. You've been dancing very well, but everyone in the band is dying to know why you haven't slept at home for the past three nights." Laughter erupts in the room. She gives a coy response, and the bandleader goes on to one of the front-line singers, who came to practice wearing American-style whitewater rafting sandals. "What are you wearing on your feet? What? Shoes?! Those aren't shoes; those are for tourists!" The singer tries to interject shyly: "It's a new thing in the States . . . ," but the bandleader is not buying it: "I don't care if they look American, I don't want to see them again."

After all individual feedback has been given, and before moving on to administrative matters, the leader of the meeting usually asks if anyone in the room has any questions or concerns. This part of the meeting, usually near the end, can sometimes seem the longest, because it is the only chance that musicians have to comment on band policy, intraband conflict, or musical aspects when they have the full attention of the bandleader and the other members of the band. Questions range from scheduling clarifications to comments on equipment to special requests for medicine or sick leave. Afterwards upcoming schedules are announced, as well as the lineups for certain shows (e.g., for a wedding that does not require the full band). Then comes the time to distribute transport money and sometimes salaries. At the end of every meeting the band president claps his hands twice to signal the meeting's end.

One day while I was sitting talking with the band manager of a well-known local dance band, one of his singers approached us and said: "Listen, I was talking with the leader, and he said 'I'm asking you all to leave Shako behind. Leave him behind.'" His voice was determined and he had an out-of-breath look on his face, just having been entrusted with the transmission of this very important information. Shako was one of the first-string singers often positioned next to the leader in concert. The person who brought the problem to the junior leaders' attention, a talented young singer by the name of Doudou, seemed to enjoy considerable favor from the leader for his focused vocal energy and strong stage presence. Shako was the loudest of the lead singers, known mostly for his acrobatic skills as a dancer and his outrageous outfits and hairdos. This most likely constituted a source of tension between the lead singers, who competed among themselves for the attention of fans and supporters.

Apparently Shako had undermined band protocol by bringing an auditioning singer directly to the leader instead of first going to the *batêtes*, all of whom agreed that this behavior was unacceptable. Doudou appeared especially insistent that this transgression should not be tolerated. After a short consultation among themselves and a quick visit to the leader to confirm what he had said to Doudou, it was decided that Shako would not be allowed to travel on the next tour, a two-week trip to Kenya. Not only was the severity of the punishment striking (touring is a true privilege because of the status and access to new social and financial networks that it offers); also interesting was the fact that the bandleader had requested that a relatively high-level decision be taken by someone other than himself.

Following a recently completed tour in Congo-Brazzaville, another group I worked with was having personnel problems of a different order. There were rumors that the leader had suspended an important number of musicians for a period of two weeks due to what he called "lack of discipline." Apparently one of the dancers was sleeping with a producer, and this had led to a series of brawls among several band members. After the suspensions' announcement, the leader refused to discuss the matter any further, and band practice was temporarily suspended. When he finally decided to discuss what had happened, he called a special meeting with the junior leaders. His primary concern seemed to center around the band's size:

> "We need to clean up the band. It's so big it's starting to look like a born-again church," he said. "We need to cut some people from the list." This prompted the band manager to speak:
>
> "Président," he began, "I have been with you for a long time, I have been with you since nineteen eighty . . . ," he tried to calculate the exact year.
>
> "Eighty-three," the bandleader added, growing visibly impatient.
>
> "That's right, 1983. Ever since 1983 I have been with you and since then it seems like things have changed. When I say things have changed I mean that . . . well . . ."
>
> "If you want to play," the leader cut in, "then we just start playing. You guys go and make a list and when the list is finished, then we start practice. All you have to do is choose the musicians that you want to keep and get rid of the rest."
>
> "I don't know, excuse me, Président," started the bodyguard, "if you ask my opinion, I don't know, to me it just seems like . . . if you have to

cut certain people . . . there are some people that. . . ." The leader cuts
in again:

"Fine, so give me another idea," shot back the leader. The junior leaders
all had a blank stare on their faces. The usual stern expression of the
most senior singer became nervous and childlike as he tried in a last-
ditch effort to explain what the others weren't able to.

"Président, excuse me, only you know what is best for the group, but
some musicians have been with us for a long time." They all agreed
that it was important to get rid of some dead weight, but at the same
time it was difficult to exclude certain members of the band, some
of whom had been personally involved in the conflict. By this time
the bandleader was becoming frustrated with the timid stance of his
junior leaders.

"Look," he said, "you have to change something in what you're saying.
You say this is my band, but it's not my band, it's our band. I can't fix
things by myself. We have to fix things together. It's not my band."

And with that he got up and exited the room, leaving everyone speechless.
The musicians stood up and started out of the room after a brief pause, as
if by moving they could somehow shake it off. They all knew it was his band.
He formed the band. He was the star. It seemed that he was either trying to
give the impression that his band was organized in a democratic fashion or
that he was unwilling to take the responsibility of downsizing a band that
everyone realized was getting much too large to manage. The way the bandleader explained it to me was this: "I choose the junior leaders; the rest is
their responsibility." The junior leaders, however, seemed truly uncomfortable with this responsibility. They all knew that the leader had certain people
in mind, and they knew who those people were; it seemed that they had no
choice but to eliminate them from the band. After the meeting, the band
manager wore a worried look on his face, and it was not because of the malaria attack he felt coming on. He expressed his frustration with what they
had been asked to do. "How can we make a decision like this?" Apparently
they had already been threatened by one of the dancer's brothers (a soldier)
who was upset because he had heard rumors that his little sister was going
to be kicked out of the band. And some of the people to be cut were longtime
personal friends.

The band meeting the next day had a heavy air. It had been almost two weeks since the band had practiced, and no one quite knew what to expect. The musicians were called into the practice room, and the band manager, taking over in the absence of the bandleader, was nervously curling a piece of paper in his hand as he started to speak. He began by talking about what had happened during the tour, saying that music required a certain amount of discipline. Not just on stage, but all the time: "You have to have *maîtrise* [self-control], and too many people in the band have lost their *maîtrise*. Those of you who are having problems with your position, go and fix it, he said, and when you have your *maîtrise*, then come back, but first you need your *maîtrise*." Without addressing them directly, he was speaking to the people about to be cut. He handed the paper to the bodyguard who uncurled it and began to read it aloud: Kasongo . . . Jose . . . Yaya . . . Didier . . . Kanza . . . Ouivine . . . and so on until the end of the list. After a few moments of silence, he curled up the paper. Trying to look tough through a cold sweat he said: "If your name is not on the list, the meeting is over." Those whose names had been called smiled nervously and looked around; the others gathered their belongings and left the room, some scurrying, others sauntering defiantly.

One by one each of the musicians that had made the cut were called up to see his or her new monthly salary, presumably more money than before, for most probably somewhere around $20. This salary did not amount to very much, but most musicians saw their position in the band as a source of wealth, not only for the prestige associated with playing in a successful group but also for the possibility of one day being recognized as a famous performer in his or her own right.[9] As a part of his concluding words, the band manager gave advice to the remaining members that they should not let this go to their heads. They still had to prove themselves worthy and capable, especially since some of the remaining musicians were second string and thus had just been promoted. Then he began to reprimand the *danseuses* for being the root cause of the indiscipline. "Their presence only causes problems [*batiaka desordre*]," he said, not addressing them directly. "First they have their little conflicts between themselves, and then before you know it's affecting the whole band. They will have to be very careful if they want to hold on to their jobs." The three remaining dancers held their heads down. One of them was fighting back a smile and received an elbow jab from her neighbor.

After the meeting, the *batêtes* had different perspectives on the situation. One junior leader expressed fear that angry family members of the dismissed musicians would attack him. He was convinced this was some kind of strategy on the part of the bandleader, a way to scare people into shaping up, and he felt sure that most of the musicians could eventually return. The band manager still seemed unresolved on the issue. "It's very difficult," he told me. "We tried everything to change his mind." This certainly was not the first time that the bandleader had enforced disciplinary measures. In fact, he was beginning to get a reputation for imposing excessive suspensions on members of the band.[10] This time, however, it was different; people were not being suspended, they were being fired. None of the excluded musicians were prohibited from approaching the bandleader for a chance to return to the band, but to be successful, they would have to appeal through well-chosen intermediaries on several occasions, and apart from expressing remorse, they would have to find some way to convince him of their commitment to his authority.[11]

And so it seemed that the bandleader had imposed his will without ever asserting his power. At first I saw his position as a way of trying to seem more fair or democratic, but the more I thought about it, the more this explanation seemed unsatisfactory. Clearly, the band had gotten out of hand. It was too large to transport, feed, and organize, but most important it was too large to trust. From the bandleader's point of view, the musicians were out of control (i.e., they no longer had maîtrise), and they were disrespecting his authority by causing public disorder. Something had to be done, but drastic cuts made by the leader himself would make him look cruel, so he had delegated this responsibility to his junior leaders. He tried to give the impression that they could choose freely, but in fact they had very limited choices: they were expected to eliminate certain undesirable elements of the band. By forcing the junior leaders to take action, the bandleader downplayed his own role in the decision to clean things up.

The bandleader's strategy, however, did not only involve displacing blame. Strategically speaking, it also involved testing the loyalty of his musicians. Several days after the dismissals, the bandleader appeared at practice to discuss the rumors he had begun to hear that many people felt unhappy with the recent changes.

> "This band," he said, "is like a business. We are not friends or brothers; we are musicians in a band. And in a band, just like in a business, work is work. That's just the way it is. I understand there are some people who

are not very happy with the changes that have been made, so I wanted to hear what you all have to say on this matter. One by one. Do you think the band should stay like it is, or do you think we should bring back the people who were cut? That is the question I want to ask you today."

The musicians began to wriggle in their seats. Everyone most likely had their own thoughts on the subject, but to express them like this, in front of the bandleader, made them visibly uncomfortable. The bandleader went around the circle:

"Ouivine? Stay like it is or bring them back?" She did not respond. She was looking at the ground.

"Didier? Stay like it is or bring them back?" Didier was one of the newest members in the band. He looked as if he would not be able to answer, then he said:

"I think the band is better the way it is now." The bandleader seemed happy; he went on to the next person.

"Max? Like it is or bring them back?" Max was obviously nervous. He is playing with his hat.

"I don't think everyone should come back, just certain people."

"Just certain people?!" the bandleader's tone rose. "Which people?" A long pause and no answer.

"You see? Do you see how hypocritical these people are?! Look at this!" the bandleader continued. "Why are you people afraid to say what you really think? Who do you think you're going to offend?"

The following answers were even less elaborate than those before; increasingly musicians uttered, "stay like it is." The bandleader continued going around the circle, but his point had already been made. By forcing each member of the band to state his or her position, he was able to publicly flush out those members of the band that valued their friendship with excluded band members more than his authority. These members, along with those that had been cut, threatened his authority since their loyalty obviously lay elsewhere. Once the leader had made his point, life in the band continued as usual, and eventually most of the dismissed musicians found their way back to the band. Perhaps this process constituted an exercise in reasserting the bandleader's authority.

Loyalty tests reinforce relations of power and structures of hierarchy.

Given the opportunity, most people in organizational hierarchies will exercise power passed their way, although not in the same way or for the same reasons. Some individuals will exercise power with a certain sense of satisfaction as they begin to visualize themselves occupying positions of increased importance in the hierarchy. Others, less ambitious and perhaps less confident, will simply follow orders for fear of losing their current place in the social-professional order, even if it means sacrificing personal or social ties. In the context of band structures in Kinshasa, hierarchies maintain a certain elasticity since superiors place a semblance of power in the hands of subordinates who pull the hierarchy back into place, some because they enjoy the feeling of power, and others because they want to protect their place in the hierarchy. This extension of power serves the leader by helping him distinguish between the loyal and the nonloyal, but it also gives the general impression of a diffuse, omnipresent authority, the kind that proves the most effective at curbing dissent, and the very type of authority that Mobutu enacted through propaganda mechanisms such as *animation politique et culturelle* and through his secret service networks, supposedly the most elaborate anywhere on the continent.

La Dislocation

When pressure on the hierarchy's elasticity becomes too great, or when the hierarchy is no longer elastic, the organizational structure breaks down and splintering occurs. Splintering ("dislocation") happens when one or more members of a band decide to leave the leader and to strike out with a band of their own. Splintering as a general aspect of African social organization is often invoked in the early social anthropological literature on political organization in lineage-based societies (Evans-Pritchard 1940; Turner 1957). Godfrey Lienhardt, writing on social structure in Dinka society, explains the phenomenon of segmentation in terms of group size: "It became so big, so it separated" (1958, 116).[12] While Marshall Sahlins (1961) has argued that the idea of segmentary lineages should be used to describe only particular lineage-based societies (especially the Tiv and the Nuer), Igor Kopytoff has put forth an argument that suggests political segmentation as an important part of cultural principles in various parts of the continent (1987, 15). In an edited volume of works on what he refers to as the "African frontier," Kopytoff speaks in much more general terms:

Anyone familiar with the routine workings of African social organization will recognize these events. An elder is accused of witchcraft, a disgruntled group of siblings feels mistreated by their deceased parent's successors, a chief's son loses the struggle over succession, an adventurous hunter or trader goes out in search of new game or profits — such people are forever leaving their settlement, accompanied by their brothers, sons, nephews, other relatives, retainers, and adherents. They move beyond the edge of the village, "into the bush." . . . Here, they set up a compound, or a hamlet, or a mini-chieftancy of uncertain autonomy, or join a settlement already established by others like them. (6)

Jean-François Bayart, in his discussion of the "exit option," has argued that this "logic of schism" is fueled by the perceived abundance in land (1993, 22). But Kopytoff's analysis refers to the "general value of 'being first'" (1987, 22), which is linked to long-standing traditions placing a high value on wealth-in-people (Vansina 1990). Similarly, Lienhardt writes that "each man wants to found his own descent group, a formal segment of the subclan which will for long be remembered by his name" (1958, 118).

Several terms (mostly French) are used in Kinshasa to describe the phenomenon of splintering: *dislocation*, *scission*, and *déstabilisation* are the most common. Most of Kinshasa's well-known bands have either resulted from or been victims of splintering. Some bands, such as the early rumba orchestras (O.K. Jazz and African Jazz) and later groups formed since the new wave period (Empire Bakuba, Zaiko Langa Langa, and Wenge Musica BCBG) were created independently of already existing groups, though this type of formation is not as common as those formed by splintering. The trend of splintering is explainable in part by the fact that musicians usually prefer to depend on the reputation of already established musicians to make a name on their own merit. But it is also true that older, well-established musicians maintain an authoritative grip on the music scene that makes it exceedingly difficult for musicians to form independent groups.[13]

Zaiko Langa Langa, the flagship group of the Zairian new wave in the 1970s, has undergone enough splintering to be considered a true clan. Originally formed in 1969, Zaiko's first lineup remained stable until 1973, when its first offshoot (Isifi Lokole) separated with a substantial number of its singers and musicians. Six years later (1979) a similar event occurred, but this time the splinter group retained part of the original group's name, calling itself Grand Zaiko Wawa. Two years later (1981) another large departure of musicians (together with a series of musicians from the 1974 split) formed one of the Kinshasa's most prolific splinter groups ever, Langa Langa Stars, otherwise known as Les Sept Patrons. At this point the original group remained intact despite the numerous changes in personnel and structure. Each splintering led the original group to recruit new musicians and personalities, and by the mid-1980s, Zaiko had again gotten large enough to merit another full-scale *dislocation*.

In the early 1980s Zaiko Langa Langa recruited J. P. Busé in an effort to compete with various rival splinter groups challenging Zaiko's dominance at the time. According to Busé, the leaders of Zaiko selected him to gradually replace Likinga, a singer who had been very important in the band's early years but who had become less reliable due to his involvement in various illegal activities and his subsequent imprisonment. When Busé approached the bandleaders to propose a song for an upcoming album, he was refused on the grounds that he was not yet an official member of the group. This response came as a great surprise to him since he had already been singing and touring with the band for quite some time. He says that this incident led him to pursue a solo career: "I saved up all the money I could, never spending it on cars and clothes like most musicians did, and when my album was finished, I took a picture of me and Nyoka taken during a Zaiko concert and I put it on the cover of the album with the title *J. P. Buse and Popolipo [the guitarist] of Zaiko*" (interview, August 25, 1997). Busé's tone in telling this story suggests a certain sense of satisfaction with having used Zaiko's name and image to his own advantage. Within a few months, he decided to leave the band and use his savings to start his own group abroad.

Musicians later discovered that Zaiko's leaders were hiding information from them with respect to earnings (primarily through copyrights) and concerning the fact that one of the band's leaders had registered the group as a private enterprise under his own name. When the musicians in Zaiko tried to call a general meeting to clarify matters, the bandleaders refused, fearing the full "uncovering" of their mismanagement, in the words of Busé. After numerous failed attempts at dialogue with the leaders, many musicians stopped attending practices and performances in protest. In response, the leaders called a general meeting, and all members absent were publicly fired from the group. This, as Busé explained, meant "war" ("c'était la guerre").

With financial help from various sources, several members of the band (Ilo Pablo, Lengi Lenga, Bimi Ombale, and Mazaza) rounded up a number of dissatisfied Zaiko musicians and left the group to form their own band: Zaiko Langa Langa Familia Dei.[14] Busé put off his plans to form his own group to join Familia Dei, but he eventually also became discouraged with the management in the splinter group. During a Familia Dei tour to Canada in the early 1990s, he left the group and decided to stay in Montreal to pursue further studies and a solo career in music.

Defao is himself a distant member of the Zaiko clan. He was first discovered by Mwanaku Felix, the wizard guitarist and cofounder of Zaiko Langa Langa who splintered from Zaiko to form Grand Zaiko Wawa in 1979. Defao remained with Mwanaku until 1983, when he decided to join forces with the newly formed Choc Stars, a splinter of Langa Langa Stars (itself a splinter of Zaiko). Ben Nyamabo, the cofounder of Choc Stars, explained that Langa Langa Stars basically had two cliques, a division caused by opposing views about the role of Kiamanguana Verckys, a well-known producer and musician involved with the group in some capacity as a producer (interview, May 21, 1996). After leaving the group and later returning from abroad, Nyamabo joined with the anti-Verckys clique to form the Choc Stars. After some years as a member of Choc Stars, Defao moved to make a group of his own, the Big Stars. According to Nyamabo, Defao left not only because he wanted to be a *chef* but also because, like many other musicians, "they always think we're taking their money."

Manda Tchebwa has suggested a number of reasons for the phenomenon of splintering in Congolese popular music: the desire for individual recognition as a star, the absence of fair and transparent financial management, the need for artistic renewal, and the deliberate destabilization of groups by older musicians who feel threatened by up-and-coming stars (1996, 173–75) [video]. As discussed earlier in this chapter, conflicts between women and men are often at the root of various types of tension between musicians. Most women in the music industry participate as dancers, and despite this subordinate position in the band hierarchy, they receive special treatment in some situations. This takes the form of preferred seating on buses and trains or of more desirable accommodations (i.e., cleaner or closer to the site of performance). This preferential treatment is often based on the woman's ability to "charm" those that provide for her: members of the promotion team, senior band members, or the bandleader himself. One band manager I interviewed stated very clearly that any woman who wanted to dance with their band had to "pass through him first," meaning that she must provide sexual favors to get the job. He explained that most new dancers were required to pass through not only him but also several other junior bandleaders, each threatening her with expulsion and public embarrassment if she refused to comply. Stories about conflicts among famous musicians over dancers abound in the popular press and in rumors.

Because such incidents are relatively common, bandleaders often warn musicians against getting involved with dancers.[15] Musicians themselves say, "Oh no! Dancers are dangerous" or "Watch out for AIDS!" an expression that musicians use in a joking tone when dancers walk by or leave the room. Not only are dancers perceived as "loose" or "easy" (Makobo 1996, 17), making them prime candidates for sexually transmitted diseases but they also often have to take the blame for being at the origin of conflicts between men. Bandleaders claim that female dancers "only cause trouble." They rarely explain exactly what dancers do, but imply that their capricious nature creates a general atmosphere of indiscipline difficult to control. In the case of the group touring in Congo-Brazzaville, the band manager's assessment of the situation highlighted the dancers' role in the conflict: "It's a mess," he said. "Everything's a mess, and it's all because of the dancers. The dancers have to understand that they are not musicians, they are dancers, and if they don't start to act like it, they'll have to look for work somewhere else."

Musicians, unlike dancers, can supplement their income by working elsewhere, but this must be done discreetly so as not to cause tension among the musician and his fellow band members or the bandleader. In Lingala, this work is known as zonzing (roughly equivalent to the English moonlighting) and usually refers to short-term contractual agreements made between already established professional musicians, most often for studio recording sessions. Zonzing opportunities are much sought after, not only for the money but also for the prestige associated with solicitation as an individual performer. Listening to the way musicians talk about zonzing, one is impressed with the sense of adventure associated with this kind of work. Zonzing is prestigious because the best musicians are solicited this way, and it is also viewed as a type of "coup" (MacGaffey and Bazenguissa-Ganga 2000) that enables the musician to work around the structures of power within a band hierarchy. One musician explained to me that the only way he could make a living was by *zonzing*, but he said that if his bandleader found out, he would probably face suspension or dismissal from the band. In some cases *zonzing* marks an effort to secure additional income, but it can also constitute an attempt to forge new working relationships so that one day the musician in question might start a band of his own.

By far the most common reason cited for splintering is some sort of conflict over the management (or mismanagement) of funds.[16] Musicians dissatisfied with their leader will say, "He doesn't pay well" or "He doesn't do anything for us" or "We get nothing!" And they cannot help but note the high level of comfort and the material goods enjoyed by their leader: "He's got tons of money, but we never see a cent." Defao explained his relationship with his then bandleader, Ben Nyamabo: "I should let you know that as long as Ben doesn't pay me my copyrights all at once, I will never stop doing *zonzing*. If I continue to get them in small amounts, long live *zonzing*" (qtd. in Makobo 1996). In many cases, the bandleader puts the band charter and the band's original compositions in his name, in effect making himself the sole beneficiary of the musicians' creative efforts. Because of bandleaders' secrecy with regard to such questions, musicians cannot know for certain if their incomes represent a fair percentage of the band's total earnings. Clearly these problems have as much to do with trust as they do money.

There are a number of reasons why bandleaders fail to provide for their musicians. For one, they rarely have enough money to pay everyone in the band, especially when the average professional band employs more than twenty-five people and a significant part of a bandleader's wealth is tied up in social and political relations. Furthermore, paying musicians a regular salary does not provide the bandleader with as much prestige as spending the money on other, more conspicuous forms of consumption (clothing, transportation, cell phones, travel, etc.). Finally, there is an unwritten agreement in the music scene in Kinshasa that the real compensation for musicians' efforts lies in the access they enjoy to bandleaders' social and political networks. Being part of a visible organization, such as Defao's group during the 1990s, ensures visibility for the members of the group, and this visibility enables them to tap into the leader's networks of fans and patrons, which in turn increases their chances of starting a successful group of their own. The former Zaiko member and now the leader of at least three full-time pro-

CHAPTER SEVEN

fessional bands, Papa Wemba talks about these relations with great candor: "I am a star maker, and that is what I give my musicians. I don't have to give them anything else" (interview, January 15, 1996). Much as in the world of Congolese politics, what attracts people to positions of power and visibility is not the position itself, but what the position represents in terms of access to various types of social networks and cultural capital.

Behaving like a Big Man

In a thought-provoking collection of essays about the politics of postcolonialism in contemporary Africa, Achille Mbembe argues that "the subjects of the *commandement* have internalized authoritarian epistemology to the point where they reproduce it themselves in all the minor circumstances of daily life" (2001, 128). The common desire to become a *chef* is evident not only in music but also in churches, businesses, schools, sports organizations, and of course in politics. In Kinshasa one often has the impression that there are *chefs* everywhere: *chef de répétition, chef d'orchestre, chef de service,* and outside the music world just as many *directeurs, présidents, chefs de protocol,* and *sous-chefs.* When I commented on this phenomenon to close friends, they would usually react with a mixture of laughter and embarrassment, and in most cases they would say "Zairians love titles" or "Zairians are like that." Then they would proceed to explain that the Mobutu system was in large part responsible for this phenomenon. They would refer to Mobutu's practice of regularly rotating civil servants and political appointees, and how this contributed not only to the consolidation of his authority but also to a greater degree of anxiety and inefficiency among appointees, who in reality could be moved or suspended without any reason or notice. Being put in a position of power could be seen as a reward, but also as a test of loyalty, and to have this position taken away was seen as more than a form of punishment; it was seen as a life-threatening development. Given the constant threat of removal, demotion, suspension, imprisonment, or even "disappearance," appointees in the Mobutu system tended to divide their time between covering their tracks, proving their loyalty, and taking advantage of their position for as long as it lasted. As Johannes Fabian has written, power in Mobutu's Zaire is "constantly to be acquired because it is always in danger of being lost" (1990, 66). Or in the words of the Congolese hip-hop collective Bisso na Bisso: "Time is so brief, in the skin of a chief" [video].

If there is a self-perpetuating tendency toward splintering in the Kinshasa music scene, it is because splintering suggests the possibility of becoming a *chef*, and one of the most important forms of prestige in the Congo comes from leading others. Material wealth is sought after and frequently remarked on, but the truly wealthy are those who have activated social relationships and demonstrate a large number of loyal followers or dependants, what Africanist scholarship generally refers to as "wealth in people."[17] Becoming a *chef*, then, itself constitutes a form of individuation, one often closely associated with becoming a *star*. The possibility of one day realizing this dream keeps most musicians in a situation of bad working conditions, low pay, and subservience. The fact that most groups are formed by artists trying to establish themselves as independent stars means these artists often lose sight of what being a leader entails in terms of training and supervising young musicians. In this way the cycle of bad leadership reproduces itself, in spite of the fact that in many cases those breaking away have already had some experiences in leading others.

Throughout my training with the Big Stars, I had relatively little contact or interaction with Defao himself, who as the leader of the group was expected to maintain a certain distance between himself and his musicians. In fact, one of the musicians in the band told me that the reason Defao kept me at a safe distance was so that I could not see how he mistreated his musicians, a suggestion that regardless of its truth value says much about the level of mistrust among bandleaders and musicians. On more than one occasion, my position in the group became a topic of conversation among band members. There was a general belief among the musicians that my presence might attract the curiosity of a larger audience or increase our chances of getting noticed by important producers. Some musicians felt very strongly about my presence, saying that it was a "good thing for the group." Others fidgeted, presumably out of discomfort with the idea that I was being used to attract more attention to the group. As a white foreigner, I was not only a novelty but also a gimmick, or as Chef Maneko used to say about my role in the group: "C'est du marketing, quoi!" (It's like a kind of marketing!), an idea that invariably lead to complicit laughter among members of the band, myself included.

Somewhere hidden in this moment of humor was the irony of the idea that a local could exploit a white foreigner, but the idea of a *mundele* caught up in the frenzy of live performance also amused people. Though I had prepared for such an eventuality, it still came as a surprise when I was sprayed with money for the first time. It was a small concert in a remote neighborhood in Kinshasa, which made it possible for me to feel the full effect of this intimacy with the audience. People were sticking their hands in my pockets, putting things inside my shirt, opening and closing my hands, and rubbing pieces of paper across my by now very sweaty brow. It was a stage minute that seemed like an hour and left me with pockets full of crumpled Zairian banknotes, a US$100 counterfeit bill, and a feeling of giddy disorientation. At the end of the song, some of the musicians slapped their pockets and gave me the thumbs-up gesture for having attracted so much attention and presumably for the money I made. Judging from the number of requests I got for beer and soda, everyone in the band thought I had made a killing. "C'mon, Monsieur Bob," the keyboard player said to me at the end of the show, "I saw you out there, you're loaded!" Later that night I spoke with Chef Maneko and told him that I was thinking about giving the money to the other members of the band, especially the musicians in the rhythm section, who almost never got sprayed, in part because of their position on the stage. He assured me that it was my money and that I should do with it as I saw fit. "But if you want to give some of it to the other musicians," he said, "I don't think they would turn it down." So on the nights I made money, this is usually what I did, partly in the hopes that this might reduce the number of requests I received from fellow band members.

Of all the people in the band that asked for things, Koyo was by far the most memorable. He was short and skinny and wore a practiced expression of sadness on his face that became hungry when he tilted his head to the side and held his stomach, trying (as he often did) to get lunch money: "Monsieur Bob, j'ai faim" (Mr. Bob, I am hungry). On one occasion I gave Koyo some small bills, hoping this would be enough, but he continued, this time switching to Lingala for added emphasis: "Nzaya Monsieur Bob." I doubled the amount in his hand, and still he looked up at me with the same sad face, "Monsieur Bob, nzaaaayaaaah!" I could not believe my ears. Unlike most people with whom I came into contact, who would discreetly try to detract attention from the transaction, Koyo was holding it up in my face: he wanted more money, and he was going to continue asking until I gave it to him. I squinted and looked at him, completely incredulous, locked in a

Figure 52. Big Stars drummer Koyo "Nzaya" (he chose the backdrop).
PHOTO: BOB W. WHITE.

gaze that seemed to go on forever. Then suddenly something snapped as we both broke into laughter, and something seemed to have changed.

Following this incident, Koyo continued to ask me for things, but his requests took on a new meaning for me. I began to see them less as a threat and more as part of a game: Could he get money from me? Could I keep my cool? Could I master the gestures of giving and taking in this highly charged, unequal encounter? The humor that had laid bare the underlying relations of power between us continued to inform our interactions, eventually developing into our own inside joke, a running parody of humanitarian aid: he would perform hunger, I would call him Koyo Nzaya (Koyo the Hungry), and then I would proceed to buy him an orange soda, as much for me as for him. Gradually I came to realize that I had taken on the role of a small-time sponsor (figure 52). I gave money because I had money, and what I received in return was ongoing confirmation of this privileged status. This was an important lesson. It was important that I learn to disarm the feeling of panic that I often experienced in situations in which people asked me for money or food: "Why is he asking me for money? If I buy him a Coke, I'm going to have to do the same thing for everyone. I can't start doing this; I don't have the resources. What will happen if I say no?" It proved a challenge to view charity not as a sign of the other's weakness, but as a manifestation of resourcefulness or as part of an ethic of the redistribution of wealth. As Paulla Ebron writes: "We can tell that they are making personalistic connections with us that they hope will outlast any particular period of research. But we rarely know how to be . . . patrons" (2002, 125).

In time, I came to see Koyo's claims on my meager resources in much the same way as I had come to see *libanga*: formulaic, polysemic, and often with the intention of provoking an act of generosity. Gestures of praise implicitly urge those in positions of privilege to take action and reinforce networks of reciprocity (Appadurai 1990). These gestures are not to be read as acts of resistance, but as part of a political culture filled with pleas for superiors to fulfill unsatisfied social obligations and moral responsibilities. In this context it is not the privilege of a political big man or *chef* that is at issue, but rather the ability of the *chef* to live up to his responsibilities as a *responsable*. The question is not "Should there be a big man?" but rather, "Is he behaving like a big man?" Not "How did he come to be so important?" but "Will he deliver on his part of the deal?"

8

IN THE SKIN OF A CHIEF

POPULAR MUSICIANS IN MOBUTU'S ZAIRE DREW
from a variety of music-making strategies to soften the
impact of a mounting political and economic crisis. In
terms of the sound, they worked through compositional
structures that enabled them to lengthen songs, especially
during live performance, and this made it possible to increase audience participation, which in turn improved
musicians' access to financial support from fans and
sponsors. Together with the influence of state-sponsored
singing and dancing, declining record sales in the 1970s
favored the emergence of a new performative aesthetic,
one based on choreographed dancing, showmanship,
and *animation*. Faced with audiences increasingly distracted by the need to make ends meet, musicians developed narrative strategies focused on the deep-seated fear
of abandonment (both by loved ones and by the state),
but they also reactivated an age-old tradition of praise
singing, albeit in the uniquely modern form of *libanga*.
Like many forms of social organization in Kinshasa in the
1990s, popular music groups struggled with a "logic of
schism" (Bayart 1993, 229) that enabled the reproduction
of charismatic leadership but did very little to provide for

their members. As Zaire's most privileged form of cultural expression, popular music of the 1990s in Kinshasa acted as a mediating force between radically divergent socioeconomic worlds, but it also reinforced the symbols and structures of power that came to characterize the political culture of an authoritarian system of rule. This chapter will return to the question of political culture by examining a broad continuum of leadership strategies, the agonistic relations between popular musicians and the state, and debates among Congolese about what it means to be a *bon chef*, a good leader.

The Politics of Writing after Mobutu

When I first brought up the question of political culture to friends and colleagues in Kinshasa, I was specifically interested in understanding why popular music in Kinshasa in the 1990s so rarely referenced politics. Lye M. Yoka, a longtime observer of popular culture and politics in Kinshasa, showed some interest in my question. When I asked him to comment on the relative absence of political content in Congolese popular music, he immediately responded that political resistance came in many shapes and sizes, an idea he had been working on in a manuscript about popular music and contestation (Yoka and Kinkela forthcoming).[1] Indeed, more than one scholar has attempted to call attention to the subversive possibilities of Congolese popular music (Nkanga 1997; Ndaywel è Nziem 1993; Olema 1998; Pongo 2000).[2] In chapter 6, I discussed the way in which the metaphor of love is used to do the work of serious social critique. Thus I agree with Yoka's observation, but I argue that the idea of contestation, while it may satisfy the intellectual's vicarious need for resistance (Abu-Lughod 1990a; Mbembe 1992b; Ortner 1995), does very little to change a system of authoritarian rule. On the contrary, it may simply reinforce the system, especially in cases such as Zaire, where the state proved effective at keeping resistance in the realm of the unspeakable and the unsaid.

When I asked Yoka how Mobutu was able to stay in power for so long, he answered simply that Mobutu was *incontournable* (impossible to get around), and that even people with very strong political convictions found it difficult to resist the combination of threats and incentives that made the regime so powerful. People responded to these pressures in various ways. Those who saw the writing on the wall, and who had the means to leave, relocated their families to Belgium, France, the United States, and Canada (many of these families left Zaire in the early to mid-1970s). Others were forced into exile with not much more than the shirt on their backs because their political position put their lives in danger. Of those who stayed (and in the Zairian case this meant the vast majority) some did so out of personal ambition and some to ensure the survival of the people who depended on them. If leaving involved financial and political risks, staying involved risks of its own, since being in Zaire meant going along with a system of rule that was becoming increasingly intolerant of opposition. Thus the question for those who opposed the regime was not only whether or not to stay in Zaire but also how to stay in Zaire and remain true to their political convictions. Over time, many people in Zaire gave in to the temptation of being associated with the regime, and this would have long-term consequences in political terms. Yoka expressed this dilemma in terribly stark terms: "Inside each of us," he said, "there is a little Mobutu" (personal communication, August 20, 2003).

One year later, however, when I asked Yoka to read an early version of the introduction to my manuscript, a different set of issues emerged. "Listen. About your text . . . ," he said, fidgeting slightly. "It's interesting, but . . . well, I get the impression that Mobutu has cast a spell on you." His comment forced me to ask tough questions about the analytical frame I had chosen for my study, and it confirmed my suspicion that there might be problems with telling the story of Congolese popular music through the lens of political culture. "For Western researchers today," Yoka explained later in his written comments, "Mobutu has become a kind of formula, somewhere between 'gadget' and 'fashion,' between scientific curiosity and incantation. For me Mobutu is the very sign of a sinister process of covering up, of making over, of masking, of the cosmetics of power" (personal correspondence, August 31, 2004). As Yoka's comments suggest, when Western observers write about Mobutu, they tend to focus on the spectacular and monstrous aspects of the regime, and this emphasis reinforces the idea that the abuse of power only occurs outside the West. In the words of Jean-François Bayart, "the excess of power continues to have a deep rooted otherness in the eyes of western philosophers" (1993, 2). In Bayart's terms, corruption is not so much a political failure as it is a "method of social struggle" (236). To talk about corruption in relation to Zaire is so commonplace that it has become a journalistic cliché continuing to find an eager audience among Western consumers.³ When Congolese talk about this corruption, however, they invariably call attention to the fact that Mobutu was able to seize control of the Congo with military and financial support from governments in the West (especially from the United States and Belgium) and that this support continued well into the regime. Thus when Yoka talks about "covering up," he is referring not only to the "sinister processes" of the Mobutu regime. He is also arguing that by calling attention to Mobutu's atrocities we always run the danger of distracting attention from the atrocities of the West.

These are the politics of writing about Mobutu, after Mobutu. Now that Mobutu is gone (or at least no longer living; see White 2005), one would think that fewer risks would derive from talking about Mobutu's political practices and legacy in an openly critical way. For some people in the Congo, Mobutu and everything he represented is a recurring nightmare that they would just as soon forget. Others believe that people in the Congo must be constantly reminded of Mobutu's legacy to avoid making the same mistakes in the future. Given all we know about how the Mobutu regime squandered the potential of this resource-rich nation, and given the extent to which this abuse occurred under the watch (indeed with the material and symbolic support) of governments in the West, how can we write about the relationship between politics and popular culture without reproducing a narrative that ends up blaming the victim? How can we ensure that the stories we tell reflect the complexity and the dignity of a nation of people who never asked to be governed by a dictator? The answers to these questions are not easy, but there are several strategies that might point in the right direction.

First, it is important to remember that even in a context of generalized authoritarian rule there are leaders who consider themselves accountable to those they lead.⁴ They are constrained by the fact that they are not part of the political mainstream, but they coexist with other models or styles of leadership, and they must be named. Second, it is important to show that people living in authoritarian regimes do their best to eke out a living, in spite of serious obstacles. Among those struggling are those who attempt to make ends meet without compromising their political beliefs as well as those who participate more actively in the webs of political intrigue, either because they see no other option or because they imagine themselves benefiting from the exercise of power. Franco might serve as an example of the latter, and his case enables us to understand how musicians to some extent played out a dynamic of political conflict between insiders and outsiders in the overgrown "village of yesterday" called Kinshasa (Molei 1979). Third, it is important to show how the question of leadership constitutes a subject of critical reflection and debate among Congolese, increasingly in the final years of the Mobutu regime, and especially now that Mobutu is gone. In Kinshasa and abroad, I found Congolese very interested in this topic, and even when I approached the subject from an abstract point of view ("What does it mean to be a good *chef*?), the conversation was brought to life with concrete examples, vivid imagery, critical reflection, and humor.

Traditions of Leadership

In his landmark study *Paths in the Rainforest* (1990), Jan Vansina argues for the existence of a discrete "political tradition" in the equatorial region of Africa that spanned a period of more than four millennia. According to Vansina, this tradition was characterized by a system of social organization overseen by local big men who gained legitimacy by attracting and maintaining followers through the distribution of material forms of wealth and the management of perceptions about their personal qualities as leaders.[5] Vansina's methodology, a meticulous combination of linguistic and archaeological data (something he refers to as the "words and things" approach), enables him to show that the notion of lineage that has become so important to Africanist scholarship did not become operational as a political category until relatively late in the region's history, some time after 1000 AD. The central tension in Vansina's work—his attempt to formulate a model that accounts for continuity as well as change—makes for both a strength and a weakness; even the complexity of Vansina's data and methods are not enough to protect him from being criticized on this aspect of his work.[6] In Vansina's terms, traditions are "not just in the minds of observers. They are 'out there'" (258). "They must continually change to remain alive," but the particular path tradition will take cannot be predicted because "a tradition chooses its own future" and thus requires "power of self-determination" to thrive (259). When Vansina announces the "death" of this tradition, however, it is not clear what exactly has died, the tradition or the tradition's ability to determine its future.

Wyatt MacGaffey, in a recent book about the Kikongo-speaking peoples of the western Congo (2000) echoes Vansina in arguing for the existence of a "common core" of beliefs and practices that characterize the political culture of the region, principal among these being an idiom of witchcraft. While it may be true that witchcraft even today makes for an important aspect of explaining political success, it is not clear that "contemporary politics can only be understood by referring to beliefs in the occult" (16). People in Kinshasa often refer to witchcraft as one way of explaining success in music or politics (White 2004), but they are just as likely to talk about political economy and the dynamics of power under colonial rule. Much closer to my analysis is Nancy Rose Hunt's (1999) fascinating history of the medicalization of childbirth practices in the Belgian Congo, which focuses its attention on a number of "middle figures" (especially nurses and midwives) who mediated among local political traditions and the increasing presence of the colonial state. If these middle figures became local targets of resentment it was not only out of jealousy but also because they wielded the power of outsiders and used this power for personal gain, much like the Congolese officer in the widely circulated popular genre paintings known as la colonie belge (figure 53):

> The kapita were those who didn't have any real power, but they had power over their brothers, like the African who is using the whip in the colonie belge paintings.[7] Mobutu comes and destabilizes everything, just like the kapita. Mobutu is one of them, and the kapita have always been in Africa: Franco, Verckys, Tabu-Ley, Wemba, J. B. M'piana, Werra Son. Why are these people kapita? Because they seem to have control over their bands and their production, but in fact they don't. Instead of leading a productive life, you somehow know they won't end up like the Beatles. They come without a legacy and they don't leave one behind. Do you know how Mobutu's children live now? Now Grand Kallé, he was not a kapita, he was a genuine leader. (Mbala Nkanga, personal communication, July 10, 2006)[8]

The image of the kapita gives us some idea about the historical roots of corrupt leadership, and corruption in this context is not so much about the misappropriation of public funds as it is about the failure to "lead a productive life," either in material or moral terms. Thierry Nlandu Mayamba (2006) describes a painful scene in which the doyen of classic Congolese rumba, Lutumba Simaro (the leader of the still active Bana O.K. and Franco's only

Figure 53. *Colonie Belge, 1885–1959* (by Tshibumba Kanda Matulu, collection of Bogumil Jewsiewicki).

legitimate heir), buckles under the pressure and presents a line of scantily dressed female dancers during a private wedding party, much to the disappointment of the older people in the audience. Later in the same text, Nlandu Mayamba expresses his surprise at the lyrics of "Milonga ya kwango," a song composed by King Kester Emeneya, who, as a pivotal figure between the third and fourth generations, continues to cultivate an image of himself as the young Turk who broke away from Papa Wemba to make it on his own. In a wistful lament about the exploitation of ancestral lands by profiteers and speculators, Emeneya explains history in terms of a political legacy in which everything is for sale and the primary source of social mobility is the acquisition of wealth: "Our slaves have become our chiefs, they have become the most important chiefs." If Mayamba is as surprised with Simaro as he is with Emeneya, it is because generational chauvinism would have us believe that the past is somehow less corrupt. The author's analysis shows that every historical period has good and bad leaders. What changes are popular perceptions about the legitimacy of leaders, since by necessity they all claim to serve the public interest.[9]

My account of hierarchy in the organization of local dance bands (chapter 7) primarily focuses on charismatic figures who perpetuate bad leadership, but popular figures in the music scene in Kinshasa have a variety of strategies for establishing their legitimacy as leaders, and not all of them fall into this category. Some musicians are focused on their ability to create and influence trends and thus find it difficult to separate their image of themselves from that maintained by those who hold power in the political sphere. Others simply try to develop their careers as artists, drawing from the resources of local elites and politicians on a purely strategic basis. Others are more concerned with their role as providers and tend to see any investment in their music as an investment in their status as responsible members of society. These three styles of leadership constitute ideal types (rather than hard-and-fast categories), but they have surfaced in many of the conversations I have had about bandleaders and popular musicians in Kinshasa. Before concluding, I would like to discuss these categories in more detail.

Playing with Power

What are we to make of a form of popular performance that systematically avoids any direct reference to politics and yet constantly reappropriates the symbols of power? In Kinshasa musicians build up their personae by striking various poses intended to mark proximity with power and privilege. Koffi Olomide introduces a new persona with each new period of his career: Rambo (as in Sylvester Stallone), Papa Bonheur ("Father of Happiness"), le Roi du Tcha Tcho ("the King of Tcha Tcho"), Schwartzkopf (like the general), Papa Top ("#1 Father"), Mukolo Lupemba ("the Owner of Success"), and Quadra Cora Man ("Man with Four Coras," the African equivalent of a Grammy). The singer Kester Emeneya is also known to have a series of nicknames that invoke an image of personal power: King, Jésus, L'émerite ("Emeritus"), Docteur, and Ya Mokolo ("Big Brother"). And Papa Wemba who preceded both Olomide and Emeneya: le Chef Coutumier du Village Molokai ("The Traditional Chief of Molokai Village"), le Pape de la Sape ("The Pope of Fashion"), Foridole ("Starmaker"), and the King of Rumba Rock. Many of these self-fashioned layers of identity reference the world of politics and the language of power, using terms such as king, papa, grand, owner, or boss, and these words often come alongside images every bit as striking (figures 54 and 55). Even when musicians claim to remain outside the cycle of self-aggrandizement, they often reinforce the very narcissism they set out to criticize, as in the case of the title track from J. B. M'piana's album Toujours Humble (see chapter 1).

Figure 54. Wenge Music Maison Mère (Werra Son) (*A la queue Leu-Leu*, Groupe JPS, 2002).

The appropriation of symbols of power by musicians does not surprise fans in Kinshasa, who quite happily watch the controversy over narcissism and self-indulgence that characterizes the presence of popular musicians in the public sphere (White 2004) [video]. This type of gesturing is common in popular music elsewhere in the world (e.g., in the production of music videos in the hip-hop industry in the United States), but the tendency of musicians to appropriate official symbols of political power (as opposed to projecting an image of power as a "gangster" or a "rebel") may be unique to the Congo, and I would argue that this phenomenon must be understood in the larger context of the political culture of Mobutu's Zaire. When Koffi Olomide approved the layout for his hugely successful 1995 release V12, did he purposefully put himself in the clouds (figure 56)? If so, then we must read this album cover as a reference to the mystical power of Mobutu, who for many years descended from clouds at the beginning and end of every national newscast. If not, then some musicians appear to have unwittingly assimilated all the symbols and gestures politicians used to perform and

Figure 55. Koffi Olomide, "King Owner" (*Effrakata*, Next Music, 2001).

maintain political legitimacy. In this context, how can musicians like Olomide ever hope to separate their own status as *président* from that of the *président-fondateur* Mobutu?

Strategic Collaboration

When opportunities arise to benefit from connections with people in positions of power, most musicians will not turn up their nose. During a tour of the Bas-Congo region, one of the groups I was working with was invited to play a series of concerts in Matadi, the largest city in the region and the last stop of a long tour. It was probably for this reason that the musicians in the group were visibly disappointed to learn that an additional concert had been added on one of their only days off. The concert was organized by the Mobutu Youth League, otherwise known as FROJEMO (Front des Jeunes Mobutistes). The show started earlier than most since it was intended as entertainment for the FROJEMO meeting, which included a dinner and reception the same day. Before the group began to play, the person who had

Figure 56. Koffi Olomide descending from the clouds (*V12*, Sonodisc, 1995).

organized the event took the microphone to explain that FROJEMO was organized by the will of the people and thereby "apolitical." The musicians rubbed their eyes and yawned as he went through the group's painfully long mission statement, most of which was focused on demonstrating support for the government in Kinshasa. "Our objective is simple," he concluded nervously, standing up straight and adjusting the microphone in its stand. "It is summarized in the slogan of our organization. Please stand up and join me in reciting the slogan:

> FROJEMO! [group response:] O-yé!
> FROJEMO! [group response:] O-yé!
> FROJEMO Fraternity!
> Direct Action!
> Direct Action!

Earlier that afternoon, the bandleader had come to the hotel where the musicians were staying to practice a special song he had written for the occasion. He woke up the two guitarists who were catching up on sleep from the previous week, and he called them together with one of the singers to find some chords for the lyrics he had written on a napkin. The words were mostly forgettable, something about unity, fraternity, and the importance of respecting our ancestors. Later that night the song was performed with a slow, familiar rumba rhythm and was not received with a great deal of attention or interest, despite the fact that the lyrics were topped off with a generous smattering of *libanga* to immortalize the local FROJEMO representative, a few local dignitaries and wealthy businessmen, and of course President Mobutu. Several of the musicians were hiding behind the amplifiers squinting their eyes and covering their ears, crouched over slightly so that the people in the audience would not see them laughing about the ridiculous nature of the song. The idea of playing for a private party of Mobutistes seemed bad enough, but the bandleader had obviously been paid to compose and perform this song for the occasion.

The situation made most of the musicians uncomfortable, but they were powerless to do anything, and to avoid causing problems for their bandleader, they tried their best to hold back their laughter and embarrassment. The bandleader remained unfazed, and as soon as the song had ended he swung his arm in the air to signal the beginning of the real concert. I am sure he knew that his musicians found the situation ridiculous, especially since they were not going to receive any additional money for this political endorsement. At the same time, during the performance of the FROJEMO song he himself appeared visibly disinterested, consciously or otherwise signaling a certain distance from the organization that had paid him to compose the song and from the regime in Kinshasa. Regardless of his intentions, however, the bandleader's decision to accept the proposition represented a compromise. By participating in the sponsoring game, especially in the months leading up to the end of the regime, for what he gained in terms of money and connections, he sacrificed in terms of his artistic autonomy and integrity. He also set an example for the musicians in the band that put personal profit before political principle.

Putting Kinshasa on Your Head

The Congolese singer Pépé Kallé (also known as "The Elephant of Zaire") passed away in November 1998 in a Kinshasa clinic after suffering from a heart attack. The Congolese minister of culture asked for a temporary halt to all musical performance for several days until a public mourning ceremony could be held in his honor. Pépé Kallé toured across Africa with his group for many years, making him one of the country's best-known cultural ambassadors. Pépé Kallé's career began in the early 1970s, and he continued having hit songs well into the 1990s, but he will probably be most remembered for his generosity and thoughtfulness. When he passed away, he was touted as the most stable bandleader in the history of Congolese popular dance music. Empire Bakuba, the group that he co-founded with Papy Tex and Dilu Dilumona in 1974, lasted for twenty-five years without any form of splintering, an amazing accomplishment given that most groups with some degree of popularity have a hard time getting beyond ten years without a major reshuffling or restructuring. Under the leadership of Pépé Kallé, Empire Bakuba had become an institution and a model of organizational stability. In the context of the local music industry, the group was an exception to the rule, and it enjoyed a great deal of visibility and respect.

While preparing the music for an album of songs commemorating the fight against HIV-AIDS (see www.criticalworld.net, "Pardon, Pardon"), I was invited to the singer's house to work on his contribution to the project. Of all my encounters with musicians, the brief one with Kallé proved by far the most engaging. He began by asking me to play a blues progression on my guitar. He closed his eyes, thinking about one of the scenarios I had suggested (the story of a young boy who had lost his father to AIDS) and rocked back and forth improvising under his breath until he found a melody that pleased him. He then asked his arranger (the bass player Lofombo Gode) to transpose the melody into a Congolese chord structure and rhythm, and the song was born. The discussion that we had was centered on the lyrics of the song. He told me that the number of AIDS orphans in Kinshasa was alarming and that he wanted to make people more aware of the problem. "This is the kind of song that people expect from me. They know that I am close to the people. They know how much I care about children." He was particularly interested in explaining the song's central narrative, the story of a man who wanted to "put all of Kinshasa on his head," a man whom Pépé Kallé referred to as the "chef de quartier," or local big man, in this case a government-paid civil servant who died because he had one too many mistresses.

Pépé Kallé was a "chef de quartier" in another sense of the term. He lived in a medium-sized house in the central part of Bandal, a middle-class neighborhood in the newer part of Kinshasa. His decision to live in Bandal was itself revealing, since most famous musicians preferred to live in more remote, wealthier neighborhoods such as Limete or Macampagne. It was common upon entering his neighborhood to be escorted by a group of young children singing his name as far as the front door of his family compound. People in the neighborhood were accustomed to asking him for help to pay for school fees or for a sick family member, requests to which he invariably answered: "Okay, let me see what I can do." His generosity with friends and neighbors was legendary and most likely part of the reason that he was less conspicuous in his consumption practices. His vehicle was not very flashy, and he had a personal driver only because of a health condition that kept him from being able to drive (Kallé measured six-foot-three and weighed in at more than three hundred pounds, hence his nickname "the Elephant"). He dressed elegantly, very often in locally made clothes. He traveled more in Africa than in Europe or North America, he paid his musicians more regularly than most bandleaders, and he rarely became involved in the *polémique* of most of his colleagues. Indeed, one of his obituaries referred to him as "anti-polémique." Regardless of all his efforts, however, after Pépé Kallé's death Empire Bakuba broke up into several different groups (figure 57).With this unfortunate event, music and politics lost the most visible example of how Congolese could work toward a common goal. When Kallé passed away he was praised not only for his music but also for what he represented politically (figure 58).

Speaking with the Ghost of Franco

Of all the musicians I did *not* meet during my fieldwork, the one that I regret the most is Franco, one of the founders of the legendary O.K. Jazz and undoubtedly the most famous bandleader in the history of Congolese popular dance music. Franco, who passed away in 1989, is like a ghost floating over the music, in part because he took a number of important secrets with him to the grave.[10] According to urban legends in Kinshasa, Franco was given a special chair in Mobutu's presidential office, one that was used only by Franco and only during meetings in which Mobutu consulted Franco on questions of public opinion, rumors, witchcraft, and matters of state. Although people in Kinshasa believe that Franco's soul rests in peace, one wonders if such a

Figure 57. Local cartoon pamphlet after Pépé Kallé's death: "After Pépé Kallé does Empire belong to Djuna Mumbafu?"

thing is possible as long as Mobutu's body remains to be repatriated, and as long as so many people live with so much pain and suffering resulting from a political transition that has become a permanent way of life (White 2005). I have often thought about what I would have said to Franco if I had had the opportunity to speak with him in person: Does Wenge Musica deserve the title of fourth generation? What was he thinking when he sang before Mobutu's speeches? What does it mean to be a good leader? Who is responsible for the crisis in Zaire?[11]

The easy answer to this last question would be Mobutu. But even those who consider themselves to be among Mobutu's worst enemies know that problems of this depth and scale cannot be attributed to the actions of one person. The truth is that people at every level of Zairian society reinforced a particular way of managing resources and power, and whether or not we decide to call this a "political culture," it is clearly a legacy with which Congo-

Figure 58. Pépé Kallé's tombstone before the construction of the much larger monument in his honor at the Gombe Cemetery in Kinshasa. PHOTO: BOB W. WHITE.

lese have to contend. But it is also true that Zaire faced trouble long before it became known as Zaire. For more than a hundred years the Congo has been used as a playground for the rich and powerful—many of them ruthless in their disregard for local populations and culture (Hochschild 1998)—and this history has certainly contributed to a deep political cynicism among many Congolese. With respect to the emergence of a political culture, the role that popular music plays in this evolution is not necessarily encouraging. For generations, Congolese popular dance music has created possibilities for social mobility and collective pleasure, for artists as much as for fans. But through the performance of a particular style of artistic leadership, it has also reinforced the most negative aspects of charismatic leadership and authoritarian rule: divisiveness, narcissism, personal profit, neglect, and impunity.

Franco offered a perfect example of this paradox. He is remembered both as the musician who most criticized the abuses of Zaire's political bourgeoisie and as the official *griot* of the M.P.R. He is known for songs that are petty and vindictive (see for example the exchanges between Franco and Kwamy following their conflict, or a series of obscene songs Franco wrote to criticize a former lover, including "Hélène" [Stewart 2000; Walu 1999]), but he

CHAPTER EIGHT

is also credited with songs that are uplifting and educational (his extended monologue lecturing on the dangers of HIV-AIDS, "Keba na Sida," or his sympathetic tale of the challenges of life as a single woman, "C'est dur la vie d'une femme célibataire"). People often describe Franco as a consummate artist, not only for his talent as an observer of human behavior but also for his unique guitar style (Mumbanza 1999); yet just as often he is portrayed as a tyrant [video]. "Franco was a leader in musical terms," explained a Congolese man in his early fifties, "but he was just like Mobutu, he became important through a series of eliminations. In fact, I wouldn't say there is any difference [between the two], because Franco incorporated Mobutu's ways of doing politics into the life of the band . . . not only did he kick you out of the band, but he destroyed your career as well" (group interview, February 18, 2006). Another fan of the third generation expressed a similar opinion of Franco: "Franco and Mobutu are birds of the same feather. They have the same techniques, the same leadership style . . . and that's why I never listened to Franco, because [every time I heard his music] I just kept seeing Mobutu. If someone else tried to criticize people in positions of power, Mobutu would put him away immediately, but not Franco" (group interview, February 18, 2006). To lend a sense of legitimacy to a political system that increasingly became an object of public scrutiny, Mobutu needed a critic, but just one. This unwritten agreement between Franco and Mobutu was based not only on mutual admiration and fear, but also on their shared knowledge of the subtleties and vicissitudes of political life in Kinshasa.

In the final months before his untimely death in the Fall of 2003, the Congolese scholar and cultural critic T. K. Biaya was working on a text entitled "La Kinoiserie: The Sources of Contemporary Congolese Political Culture." Biaya's text is remarkable for its mere scope: it explains the culture of postcolonial politics in Zaire through an analysis of "la culture kinoise." It must be said that this is not Biaya's best writing. It is unfinished, undisciplined, and undocumented, in part because it was one of the last trains of thought he committed to paper. He maintains little or no distance from his object of study and his narrative reads like a delirious language game. Nonetheless I found myself returning to this text repeatedly. According to Biaya, the term *kinois* took on its most "vigorous form" during the early years of the Mobutu regime, when it came to refer not only to the residents of the huge, sprawling city of Kinshasa but also to a particular urban culture that opposed itself to the rectitude of colonial discipline and Christian morality. He explains that the term *kinoiserie* surfaced in the early 1980s and with a decidedly negative connotation that made it rhyme with deceit, opportunism, and hedonism. It was this term—*kinoiserie*—that Biaya argues lies at the core of post-colonial political culture in today's Congo.

In his analysis he sees *kinoiserie* as the result of a structural tension between the natives of Kinshasa (*lipopo*) and a group of ambitious latecomers (*kinois*) who were initially in competition with each other, but who eventually both lost political control of the capital to an uncultivated class of hardworking outsiders (*mbokatier*), and an educated class of upwardly mobile provincials (*kinshansois*) who would gradually displace the *kinois* as the key players in the regime. What emerged from this conflict, Biaya argues, was a deeply engrained political habitus that combined the art of politics with a particular form of hedonistic display ("l'art du bon vivant") that eventually became a central feature of the cultural and political landscape. This habitus was characterized by a strong emphasis on aggressive self-promotion ("O yebi ngai?"—'Do you know who I am?') and the subordination of political clients through a careful combination of magnanimity and humiliation. According to Biaya, this habitus expressed itself primarily through three phenomena that became integral to the performance of state-based power: the sexualization of political hierarchies, the distancing of politicians from their families, and the ostentatious display of high fashion known locally as *la sape*. The combination of these factors became an increasingly conspicuous form of political culture that Biaya would characterize as "governmentality without vision."

Further research and reflection will tell if Biaya got it right with this analysis. What he did get right is to suggest that the permanence of this political culture did not result from a series of political failures or the criminalization of the Zairian state (as much of the political science literature would have us believe), but from a complex political configuration that combined new forms of governmentality with the imperative of the street. According to Biaya, Mobutu's political genius derived not from his charisma (although this too was a necessary ingredient), but from his ability to take advantage of a structural tension that had characterized the organization of social and political life in Kinshasa since well before independence. Biaya's most important contribution, perhaps his last intellectual breath, was his decision to focus his attention on the question of political culture, and to locate the sources of this political culture in the historical processes of urbanization, class formation, and the politics of belonging (Geschiere 2005).

The tension between insiders and outsiders has also been a central feature of the music scene, and each new generation appears to play out this tension in strikingly similar ways. The excitement over a new (often modernist) sound fuels the imagination of a generation of youths that is coming of age and trying to imagine a place for itself in the political future (African Jazz with "Independence cha cha," Zaiko Langa Langa with "Onassis ya Zaire," Wenge Musica with "Kin e bouger"). Fans are struck by the fact that the creators of the sound seem to have emerged out of nowhere (White and Yoka 2006, 229), meaning that they are not the disciples of musicians from the previous generation, and that they display a relative degree of heterogeneity with regards to social class and ethnic origin. The group's innovation is related to its social organization and structure, but also to certain aspects of the sound, most notably the lead guitar of a heroic modernist figure who is known for his technical mastery of the instrument: Dr. Nico (African Jazz), Manwaku Waku (Zaiko Langa Langa), Alain Makaba (Wenge Musica). Eventually a conflict arises in the group (either over money, intellectual property, or artistic authority), and the guitarist leaves, generally together with a singer (Tabu Ley Rochereau, Chekedan, J.B. M'piana). Now faced with the prospect of their inability to share power, the initial splinter separates into smaller units and the cycle of "dislocation" continues. In each case some part of the conflict has to do with who is kinois and who is not, as in the case of Wenge Musica, where M'piana's increasing support from diamond traders in Kasai (his region of origin) put him at odds with Werra Son, whose cultural capital comes from his affinity with Kinshasa's disadvantaged youth, the majority of whom also trace their roots to the nearby region of Bandundu.

Each time a major separation occurs, young people are taken aback by the news. They struggle to find the language, even years later, to describe how the separation affected them personally, as in the case of these accounts of the 1979 split of Zaiko Langa Langa:

When Manuaku left, I never experienced anything like that.

It was very serious. I was in Matonge and all the taxis had stopped in the middle of the street. Pepe Fely [Manuaku] had left Zaiko. I didn't understand what was happening. In Matonge, even downtown, all the taxis just stopped in their tracks.

It's like you bring a baby into the world and then you reject it; it was a huge event.

I got sick that day. But we were all that way; we just couldn't imagine Zaiko without Pepe Fely.

It was the death of Zaiko. We couldn't see where Zaiko could find the strength to go on. (excerpts from group interview, February 18, 2006)

There are similar stories about the separations that came before and after, as young people looked around them and tried to figure out what impact these events would have on their personal relationships (White forthcoming), while elders attempted to intervene, each time in vain (see chapter 1). Arguably, the political culture of Kinshasa is not to be located in Biaya's *tryptique* of sexuality, family exile, and *sape*, but rather in the chauvinism and fear of autochthony, the drawing of lines between insiders and outsiders. In every generation, young people want to believe that they are different, that they, unlike their fathers and their fathers' fathers, will be able to rise above tribalism and corruption, and somehow remake the world (Jewsiewicki and White 2005). Unfortunately, they operate in a world in which they can, at best, remake themselves, and often—*par la force des choses*—they end up reproducing what came before, albeit with some variations in terms of language or sound.

While it is true that groups such as African Jazz, Zaiko Langa Langa, and now Wenge Musica have all been plagued with chronic splintering and division, in each case this dynamic has provided them with a built-in mechanism for renewal and thus a guarantee of maintaining the interest of audiences in Kinshasa. The same cannot be said for Franco's O.K. Jazz. As the torchbearer of the *ondemba* tradition, O.K. Jazz has simply not been able to reproduce itself. Bana O.K. continues to play and still has an impressive organization and live sound, but most fans agree that the group never really recuperated from Franco's death, and I do not know any young musicians today who explicitly identify themselves with the O.K. Jazz style or the *ondemba* aesthetic. In some sense, the only thing that remains of Franco's legacy is a particular big-man style of leadership. If Franco was able to stay on top of the music industry for so long, it was in part because of his sound, which was soulful, seductive, and punctuated with one of the best brass sections in the history of Congolese popular music. But it was also Franco's charisma and personality that made him so attractive to those in positions of power. Other musicians would not prove suitable, either because they were pro-Lumumba (such as Grand Kallé and Dr. Nico) or because they were not *kinois* enough, and Mobutu needed this legitimacy in order to build up and maintain his political base in the capital.

Mobutu's leadership, like that of Franco, was earthy and rough around the edges. Mobutu might have been the soldier to Franco's *hindubill*, but as Biaya has shown, these two expressions of masculinity clearly existed in a mutual gaze of admiration: musicians attracted the girls and soldiers brought the guns. Together they saw themselves opposing the clean modernism of the *évolués*, those upwardly mobile cosmopolitans wearing tuxedos and singing in Spanish (see chapter 2) who gave off an air of superiority because they had been to school ("ils ont été à l'école"). If Franco modeled himself on Mobutu, then the reverse also held true. They saw in each other a similar way of doing politics, one that was suspicious of cosmopolitan refinement and strategic in its proximity to "the people." In the words of V. S. Naipaul: "The African language the President had chosen for his speeches was a mixed and simple language, and he simplified it further, making it the language of the drinking booth and the street brawl, converting himself, while he spoke, this man who kept everybody dangling and imitated the etiquette of royalty and the graces of de Gaulle, into the lowest of the low. And that was the attraction of the African language in the President's mouth. That regal and musical use of the lowest language and the coarsest expressions was what was holding Metty" (1979, 213).

Mobutu consciously played with the image of the heroic marginal figure who because of his ambition is always in danger of becoming a witch (Mac-Gaffey 2000). By doing so he rejected the colonial model of modernity, which was the role assumed by his principal political rival, Patrice Lumumba. Franco, the quintessential ruffian, was the obvious choice as the primary spokesperson of Mobutu's policies, and he seemed to bask in the position of privilege that gave him a decided advantage over his rivals.[12]

Not all musicians during the Mobutu era allowed themselves to be co-opted by those in power. Grand Kallé and Dr. Nico, for example, saw their musical careers seriously threatened by their association with the former prime minister Patrice Lumumba, and their reluctance to sing the praises of the Mobutu regime further limited their professional possibilities as the musical and political landscape rapidly evolved in the first half of the 1970s.

A recent interview with Wendo Kolosoy by the African music critic Banning Eyre suggests that this legacy of affiliation with Lumumba's progressive politics continued to haunt musicians even into the twenty-first century:

> Banning Eyre: You mentioned the other day that you were friends with Patrice Lumumba. When was that?
>
> Wendo Kolosoy: Ohhhh. Lumumba, 1940s. We were together all the time, the same generation. Often he came to my place, and he slept. We slept together. We drank together. We ate together.
>
> BE: Did you talk about independence?
>
> WK: No. I'm not a politician. I'm a composer of songs. I am a musician.
>
> BE: Right, but surely you must have talked about things.
>
> WK: Yes, he talked about politics, but me: no.
>
> BE: But it's not just a political idea. It concerned everyone, didn't it?
>
> WK: I wasn't there. That didn't interest me. We ate together. I played my music. That was it. I was not a politician. Politics, no. If you want to come to my place, Papa Wendo, for the songs "Marie Louise," and "Albertina," I was spending my time with that. But as far as politics go, I never thought about that. I didn't concern myself with that. I ate. I thought about my music. We were here in town. He was from there, and I was from the lake. We were almost related by blood. We were brothers. But why are you interested in Lumumba?
>
> BE: He's someone important.
>
> WK: No. Leave that. Leave that. You can ask me why Papa Wendo composed this or that song. . . . [sings] I'm proud to talk about that. But if you want to ask about politics, I am very afraid.
>
> BE: Allright, but let me ask you this. Why did you stop recording and performing during the 1960s?
>
> WK: As I said, before, the fundamental reason for this is politics. The fact that there was a time when I didn't sing much, politics is at the base of it. Because political men at the time wanted to use musicians like stepping stones. That is to say, they wanted musicians to sing their favors. Me, I did not want to do that. That's why I decided it was best for me, Wendo, to pull myself out of the music scene, and stay home. Now, by the grace of God, I am having a reprise. So if there was a time when I did not sing it was because politicians wanted to use me. They wanted me to sing their praises. They wanted to use me as a stepping stone,

and I did not want to be involved in politics. I stayed home, and it was only later that things got better, which meant that I, Wendo, receive you today to talk about music, not about politics. (excerpt from www .afropop.org, consulted December 2002)[13]

"To Be a Chef Is an Agreement"

For obvious reasons, such as personal security and access to state-owned media, successful musicians need to be extremely careful about how they position themselves politically. Fans of popular music, however, have less to lose, and they are much more interested in discussing the symbolic and material links that make musicians and politicians part of the same moral universe. Since completing my initial fieldwork in Kinshasa, the question of leadership has become increasingly explicit in my research.[14] When I ask questions about how Congolese define the notion of leadership, the answers I get vary somewhat, but the question almost always elicits an interested response. Very often I hear that Congolese have come to expect authoritarian behavior from people in positions of authority: "People in Zaire want to be led poorly. If as a leader you're not hard, they call you *yuma*, or someone who is afraid and weak. They need a strong leader with a strong hand . . . [they think that] a *chef* is someone who dictates the law of the land. We learned this from Mobutu, that's the way he used to talk. If you listen to him talking to his subordinates, it sounds like he's always angry, but this is the only way that people will respect you" (J. P. Busé, August 25, 1997). This authoritarian style of leadership is seen as an aspect of everyday social organization that is difficult to shake, even within Congolese communities living abroad. Here is an excerpt from an exchange with Congolese living in Montreal (group interview, February 18, 2006):

> Participant 1: When someone is a *chef*, he doesn't want to hear anyone else's voice . . . if someone starts contradicting him, he will automatically be taken for the enemy (ibid).

When my questions challenge this observation, the discussion comes back to national politics and the cynicism that invariably accompanies the mention of Mobutu's legacy.

> BW: But there are so many people in the Congo with conviction and good ideas . . .

Participant 2: If there are no good leaders this is because there are no good thinkers; all the good thinkers were kicked out [reference to waves of exile during the 1970s and 1980s]. The population has been so corrupted that people do not see any other way of doing politics. The model we had for x number of years, was Mobutuism; it took over our lives. It's unfortunate, but it must be said.

There is not always agreement about the source of this problem. Some participants believe that the inability to effectively transfer power is simply a question of political will ("Politicians make no effort to prepare the leaders of tomorrow"), while others view this phenomenon as a deep cultural trait ("it is in our culture"). When pushed on this point, some research participants enthusiastically shared examples of model leadership in the world of popular music. From the same interview:

Participant 3: All the musicians, even the worst ones like Koffi, whenever there was a conflict, musicians used to go see Pépé Kallé for advice. Every one of them, without exception. If there was problem between Wemba and Olomide, the only one who could fix the problem was Pépé Kallé.

Participant 4: Manwaku [one of the founding members of Zaiko Langa Langa] really made me think. He held on to his principles and he supported the people in the band that were in the minority, people that were not even stars yet. With some hindsight I think that it was a meaningful gesture. So why am I talking to you about Manwaku? It's because he put his foot down and said 'that's it.' It was the first time someone had the strength to do this and it is rare in our culture for someone to step down from a position of power.

When asked about the characteristics of a good leader, most participants' answers had clear and concise answers, as if they had already given considerable thought to the topic:

Participant 4: In our country it is difficult to find a good leader, because our model is Mobutu and Mobutu was not a good leader. A good leader for me is someone that works for those under him. Instead of them working for him, he should be working for them. That's what makes a good leader.

Participant 1: A good leader is someone who listens. He shouldn't be someone who simply imposes his will. He should not impose his will, he should work together with others. He should be able to listen and work together.

Participant 2: He has to show an ability to differentiate right from wrong, good judgment, critical judgment. When someone says something to him, he has to be able to see the positive and negative aspects of what he has been told.

The most compelling answer to this question came during a cold winter day in Montreal, when I was sitting in a hotel room speaking with a Congolese musician who was touring Canada with his band and who had decided to extend his stay following changes in the tour schedule. "What does it mean to be a *chef*?" I asked him. Without missing a beat he began putting on his jacket and answered as if what he had to say was completely obvious: "To be a *chef* is an agreement, otherwise we would call him a 'house.' But he's a *chef* and we decided that" (interview with Lokassa ya Mbongo, January 17, 1998). With that he stood up, patted down his hair in the mirror, and opened the door for me, motioning for us to go.

From the point of view of the people I interviewed, the elements that characterize good leadership (the ability to listen, critical judgment, a sense of accountability) are things that would make sense to people in any part of Africa, or for that matter, in any part of the world: "To be a *chef* is an agreement." Given this political ideal, how did things get so out of control in Mobutu's Zaire? I have attempted to work through this question by showing how popular music and politics acted together to reinforce a uniquely modern tradition of authoritarian rule. Popular musicians' constant back and forth movement over the "frontiers of the moral and the immoral" (Nlandu Mayamba forthcoming) makes them extremely entertaining to watch, but at a certain point their movements are no longer funny: "Unable to understand what is happening to us, musicians today avoid the workshops and conferences in which we talk about them, most likely afraid of becoming the scapegoats of a society that blames them for all its ills" (Nlandu Mayamba forthcoming). But musicians cannot be blamed for all of society's ills. The problems with Koffi Olomide began with Papa Wemba and those of Wemba began with Franco, whose complicity with Mobutu was based on a particular style of big-man leadership that was opposed to any form of opposition.

This tradition of impunity would go down in history as one of Mobutu's only contributions to Congolese politics, but Mobutu was not alone. Mobutu's power, as people in the Congo constantly reminded me, was based on a long-term complicity with the Western governments that conveniently put aside democratic principles in order to guarantee that he would seize control of the country and keep it. For some musicians, following in the footsteps of this political legacy is nothing more than a survival strategy, but for others it eventually becomes part of their personal identity and their image of themselves. Just like politicians, they begin to imagine themselves as different from others, somehow above the law. They lose their ability to listen, and before they know it, they become "just like Mobutu, exactly like Mobutu."

The question that we have to ask about political culture in Mobutu's Zaire is not whether its roots are to be found in traditional African culture or in the culture of colonialism (Mamdani 1996), but rather to understand how it is that one particular style of leadership came to be accepted as the dominant order of the day, what Achille Mbembe has described as the complex relationship between colonial political culture and the "the most despotic aspects of ancestral traditions" (2001, 42). Popular music forms part of the people's answer to this question, and each generation has tried to find an answer that makes sense within its own "moral imagination" (Beidelman 1993). In Mobutu's Zaire, music is not simply a reflection of politics. It is a complex field of action in which popular culture and politics prop each other up and fix each other into place: "The real inversion takes place when, in their desire for splendor, the masses join in madness and clothe themselves in the flashy rags of power so as to reproduce its epistemology; and when, too, power, in its own violent quest for grandeur and prestige, makes vulgarity and wrongdoing [délinquance] its main mode of existence. It is here, within the confines of this intimacy, that the forces of tyranny in Africa must be studied" (Mbembe 2001: 133). This contamination is reciprocal because music provides a space for people in socially marginal positions—not just musicians, but also entrepreneurs, pirates, and promoters—to play out a heroic scenario with deep historical resonance. The recurring motif of Lumumba in Congolese popular painting shows the extent to which past heroisms are imagined as part of the present (Jewsiewicki 1999), but when people in the Congo remember Patrice Lumumba, the image they have is that of a martyr and not that of a big man (figure 59). With Lumumba's assassi-

Figure 59.
Patrice Lumumba,
"National Hero"
(by Tshibumba
Kanda Matulu,
collection
of Bogumil
Jewsiewicki).

nation the Congolese will to be modern was shattered, and a rich tradition
of leadership with the potential for responsibility was put in the hands of
people whose only legacy was to drive the country into the ground.

One of my objectives in writing this book has been to try to convey something about the experience of living in Mobutu's Zaire. How do people give
meaning to their lives after more than thirty years of dictatorship and despo-
tism? How do people navigate their way through a political reality that can
only be described as "incontournable" without compromising their dreams?
Popular music in Zaire, with all of its possibilities for social mobility and collective pleasure, is not to be construed as an answer to people's problems. If
it were, then music would have done more to undermine Mobutu's machine,
and the political landscape of today's Congo would not look as troubled as
it does today. Nor should popular music be seen as a simple form of escape,
since as this research shows, the social organization of popular music is

tied up in a particular way of doing politics. In the political and cultural complexity of Mobutu's Zaire, popular music mediates between people and various institutions of power, and the tension in this relationship creates something both painful and problematic, but also beautiful. If this book evokes a sense of what it is like to be musical—or at least to love music—in Mobutu's Zaire, it is because the stories it tells are shot through with suffering, joy, irony, and wonder. This is what it felt like to watch popular music at a time that many Congolese hope will be remembered as the end of an era.

NOTES

Chapter 1: Popular Culture's Politics

1. These words referenced a series of popular French films from the 1950s and 1960s featuring the well-known French comedian Louis de Funès, who plays a bumbling police commissioner who spends most of the film in pursuit of the masked public enemy known as Fantomas.

2. The texts that I have found most useful in constructing my own version of this complex narrative are Callaghy 1984, Ndaywel è Nziem 1998, Schatzberg 1988, Vellut 1974, and Young and Turner 1985.

3. I am grateful to Leonard Buleli N'sanda for having brought this term to my attention.

4. The *Titanic* album cover features the pictures of a sinking cruise ship and in the foreground the members of M'piana's Wenge floating in the water, each with a life buoy around his smiling face. Audiences in Kinshasa understood the message clearly: the "original" Wenge was a sinking ship, and M'piana and his allies were the only true survivors.

5. See a painting by Cheri Samba entitled *Lutte contre les moustiques* (Jewsiewicki 1995, 50).

6. Recent uses of the term *political culture* generally exclude a body of writing about traditional or customary authority, much of which was influenced by E. E. Evans-Pritchards and Meyer Fortes's pioneering comparative work on politics in Africa entitled *African Political Systems*, first published in 1940. I view Fabian's (1990) monograph *Power and Performance* as a conceptual bridge between the classic texts of British social anthropology and the more recent postmodernist interest in the ethnography of states. I have also benefited from the writing of Mbembe (1992a), Schatzberg (1988), and Averill (1997), who place a strong emphasis on the way that state-based power is translated and negotiated in everyday, local settings.

7. Much of this recent literature is based on research in sub-Saharan Africa. For some recent examples see Abélès 2000, Biaya n.d., Cefai 2001, Gupta 1995, Hasty 2005, Martin 2002, Mbembe 2001, McGovern 2002, Monga 1996, Nkanga 1999, Richards 1996, Rubango 2001, Schatzberg 2001, Taussig 1997, Werbner and Ranger 1996, and White 2005. A particularly interesting example of this field is a series of recent collaborations between Bennetta Jules-Rosette and David B. Coplan on the topic of the South African national anthem; see etudesafricaines.revues.org/document4631 .html (accessed July 27, 2007). For an excellent collection of articles related specifically to questions of identity and power in contemporary Africa, see Biaya and Bibeau (1998).

8. In a debate with Noam Chomsky in 1971, Michel Foucault elegantly expressed the idea that power must be understood by examining the social formations and institutions that seem on the surface to have nothing in common with politics: "Le pouvoir, il s'exerce encore, il s'exerce en outre, de plus, par l'intermédiaire d'un certain nombre d'institutions qui ont l'air comme ça de n'avoir rien de commun avec le pouvoir politique, qui ont l'air d'en être indépendants et qui ne le sont pas." For a video excerpt see http://www.dailymotion.com/related/966262/video/x43qe_ noam-chomsky-vs-michel-foucault (consulted February 8, 2008).

9. Attempts to define *ambiance* have mostly failed, but the term generally refers to the city's particular combination of sexuality, spectacle, and dance music. There have been many attempts to elaborate a formula for *ambiance*, most of which clearly reflect a male bias (see, e.g., Biaya 1994). For other references on this topic, see Biaya 1997, Tchebwa 1996, and Trefon 2004.

10. To read further on the history of Kinshasa, see Gondola 1997, Ndaywel è Nziem 1998, and Ngimbi 1982.

11. In their recent book on Kinshasa, De Boeck and Plissant examine this question by looking at "the imaginative ways in which local urban subjects continue to make sense of their worlds and invent cultural strategies to cope with the breakdown of urban infrastructure" (2005, back cover).

Chapter 2: The Zairian Sound

1. Apart from what it tells us about popular music, Bemba's text constitutes a valuable piece of information about the political context in the early to mid-1980s, especially with regard to the political relations between Congo-Brazzaville and Zaire. A number of texts have discussed music as a bridge between the two Congos (Gondola 1990 and 1997; Tchebwa 1996).

2. I use the term *genre* in two ways. The first usage—genre as an identifiable set of intrinsic aesthetic or formal traits—attempts to explain what the music sounds like and how this sound has evolved over the past fifty years or so. The second usage views genre as the expression of a community of taste organized around a particular category or style of popular music.

3. Nyandu Rubango's important work on political discourse in the Congo (2001)

shows how rhetorical motifs from religious discourse are used to activate and maintain postcolonial political networks. Johannes Fabian, in his writing on the Congolese popular painter Tshibumba (1996), shows not only how genre can be an impediment to creative expression (and thus the ability to survive) but also how the relative success of local artists depends on their ability to reference other genres of popular culture.

4. On the question of sound in anthropological analyses of music, see Feld 1982, Feld and Brenneis 2004, and Meintjes 2003.

5. This does not include less visible types of music (marching band music or *fanfare*, missionary music, and, of late, rap music); the styles I have chosen are those that meet the informal criterion of being available both in local record stores and with roving vendors of prerecorded music.

6. Outside the Congo in many other French-speaking parts of Africa, this music is simply referred to as *la musique zaïroise* or Congolese rumba, a strange label given that most world music styles carry genre-specific (not national) names (zouk, reggae, soca, polka, salsa, isicathimiya, etc.).

7. Afro-Cuban recordings of various types were relatively available and extremely popular by the time that Congolese started composing and performing nontraditional music of their own. More research is required to determine why the label *rumba* in particular became associated with these styles, but it does seem that Afro-Cuban music in general constituted for many Congolese an expression of their urban, cosmopolitan lifestyle (White 2002; see also Shain 2002).

8. On the analysis of layering in non-Western music, see Feld and Brenneis 2004.

9. In 1995, Radio Matanga, a traditional cassette distributor, sold music from seven to eight different ethnic groups in Congo-Brazzaville, each cassette for 3,000 CFA, the equivalent of about US $6, about twice the price of modern music cassettes. The cassettes were made from live performances, and they did not include the name of the group or the song titles, only the ethnic label (e.g, Lari, Mbochi, Kongo, Teke, etc.). Commercially recorded *folklore* cassettes are also available. These usually feature a particular group, somewhat modernized songs, and a more polished sound.

10. The recent "Congotronics" series, produced by Vincent Kenis of Crammed Discs, provides the most detailed account of urban traditional music in Kinshasa to date. For more information see www.crammed.be.

11. By following the process through which young men in Pendeland try to make a name for themselves as innovators, not only of masks but of dances and rhythms, Zoe Strothers (1997) shows how the aesthetics of traditional performance is also subject to the cycles of trends and fashion.

12. Variations on the *fanfare* ensemble (or mini marching band) can also be considered a form of religious-based music. Although this genre is less common in Kinshasa, *fanfares* are used in some local churches (Kimbanguiste, Salvation Army, etc.) and for various types of life-cycle ceremonies. I have also not discussed the missionary-sponsored dancing choirs for which Père Van den Boom was so well known in the

1970s. The most famous of these groups, Petits Chanteurs et Danseurs de Kenge, prepared many young musicians for a career in music, among them Reddy Amisi of Papa Wemba's Viva La Musica.

13. Many of the songs in this genre use extended choruses, while modern compositions vary between verses and choruses. In most cases they retain the transition to the *seben* (discussed later in this chapter) and the characteristic snare-drum rhythm, as well as the layered, flowing electric guitars. On the complex relationships, both musical and social, between these two genres, see Pype (2006).

14. Manda Tchebwa (1996) inserts an additional generation at the end of the second one (musicians such as Ntesa Dalienst, Sam Mangwana, and Dino Vangu), but most popular discourse about generation places these musicians cleanly within the second one. It is also interesting to note that instead of using the term *generation*, Tchebwa describes the changes in terms of "waves," a strategic move that, as he explained to me, kept him from getting caught up in the debate about generations.

15. Jewsiewicki 2003b contains a series of texts about the emergence and performance of urban popular music in the Katanga region. Low 1982 is a firsthand account of life with popular musicians in the Shaba region at the end of the 1970s.

16. According to Phyllis Martin, Brazzaville (at that time part of French Equatorial Africa) had civil servants from as far as Guadeloupe and Martinique (1995, 127). She also discusses the Cabindans and Senegalese soldiers (*tirailleurs*) who had probably participated in the construction of the Matadi-Leopoldville railroad. She attributes the distinctive palm-wine guitar style (an essential influence for early Congolese guitarists) to the Kru of Liberia and Sierra Leoneans also present in Brazzaville during these years. Presumably these same musicians, or at least their musical styles, were present at roughly the same time in Leopoldville.

17. Literally, "The Time of the Wendos," inspired by the most well-known musician from the period, Wendo Kolosoy. This expression is also the title of a film that traces Wendo's life and times (Popovitch and Zinga 1993).

18. For historical material on Congolese popular music outside Kinshasa, see Jewsiewicki 2003b, Low 1982, Rycroft 1962.

19. Radio Brazzaville opened in 1943, and by the late 1950s Congolese guitar music had become the craze in Lagos: "Almost everybody loved Congo music. And if you bought a radio set then you bought it because you wanted to learn to tune to Congo-Brazzaville" (Waterman 1990, 93).

20. To my knowledge, Bokasi 1990 is the only piece of social scientific writing devoted solely to the Zaiko phenomenon. In addition to a history of the group's evolution, and some thematic analysis of song lyrics (including a brief analysis of the shouts in Zaiko's repertoire), the author also presents the results from a series of interviews about perceptions of popular music and morality.

21. These are the names of the two corresponding styles. The label *fiesta* was a popular stylish word at the time and would become permanently associated with the music

of Kallé and African Jazz after his protégés Dr. Nico and Tabu Ley Rochereau separated from him to start African Fiesta in the mid-1960s.

22. According to one informant, Dr. Nico played his guitar with a regular tuning, but Franco often used an adapted tuning, known as *mi-composé*, in which the first string on the guitar is effectively doubled by retuning the fourth string.

23. The practice of keeping an *orchestre amateur*, or training group, was common during this period and still continues today, although more recruitment seems to happen informally through friends or during open-mike auditions.

24. This sentenced was uttered by Mbuta Mashakado, the Zaiko Langa Langa singer/dancer most well known for imitating the dance steps of James Brown (*Super Stars*, p. 7, c. 1988).

25. For early recorded examples of this rhythm, listen to the 1973 Zaiko Langa Langa recordings "Eluzam," "Beya mbeya," and "Amoureux deçu."

26. For an explanation of the Cuban clave rhythm (including tablatures), see the website of the percussionist Alex Pertout: pertout.customer.netspace.net.au/lclaveac.htm (accessed August 28, 2007).

27. Some groups use a fourth guitar, called *mi-solo*, which usually plays in the mid-register between rhythm and lead but can also double the lines of either.

28. Given this history, it is perhaps no coincidence that Kintambo has produced a disproportionate number of *folklore* or urban-traditional music ensembles, most notably the Swede Swede family of music groups, which took Kinshasa by storm for the first time in the late 1980s. Kintambo also produced a large number of individual musicians who would later go on to work as *atalaku* on a professional basis (the most well-known being Choc Stars' Ditutala, Empire Bakuba's Djuna Mumbafu, and Robert Ekokota from Wenge Musica).

29. For a discussion of the content of Zaiko's shouts, see Bokasi 1990.

30. This structure is often compared with the two-part structure of Cuban *son-montuno* music that tends toward an upbeat rhythmic section referred to as *descarga*.

Chapter 3: Made in Zaire

1. See Askew 2002, Guilbault 1993, Jones 2001, Moore 1997, Pacini Hernandez 1995, Turino 2000, Vianna 1999, and Wade 2000. Gage Averill's (1997) study of popular music in Haiti shows a striking number of similarities with Zaire, particularly his discussion of the Duvalier dictatorship, which (like that of Mobutu) combined the strategies of thuggery, patronage, and indigenist politics to consolidate the authority of his regime (see esp. his chap. 3).

2. Thomas Turino's (2000) analysis responds to the nationalism literature by showing how cosmopolitanism, generally viewed as antithetical to the emergence of modern nations, is actually an integral part of nationalist movements in this part of the world. Kelly Askew (2002) examines the case of Swahili *taarab* music in Tanzania, showing how this genre, previously shunned by cultural policy initiatives under

Julius Nyerere, was suddenly incorporated as a manifestation of national culture at exactly the same time that multiparty politics emerged in the early 1990s. Another example is Peter Wade's fascinating study of the emergence of national identity and popular music in Colombia, which shows how national elites "resignify a diversity which they also partly construct" (2000, 7). Several recent studies (Moore 1997; Wade 2000; Vianna 1999) call attention to way in which debates about this diversity are grounded in historically specific configurations of race and class.

3. Ndaywel è Nziem (1998, 706–26) provides a thorough overview of the state initiatives in the domains of literature, theater, and the plastic arts, some of which have remained intact since Mobutu's departure.

4. By 1975 UNESCO had already commissioned more than thirty country-based studies of cultural policy, including that of Zaire by Bokongo Ekanga Botombele (1975). For a more critical perspective on cultural policy issues, see Bennett 1998, especially the chapter entitled "Culture and Policy."

5. For a recent discussion of the relationship among anthropological and other uses of the term *culture*, see White 2006c.

6. According to Jan Vansina, "Unlike the case of other colonies, 'cultural policy' in the Belgian Congo was not unified, nor even agreed on. It is a subject in its own right" (personal correspondence, April 19, 1998).

7. For a more elaborate discussion of cultural policy during the Mobutu regime, see White 2006a.

8. Many of these ideas are articulated in the political science literature of the 1980s, which displayed a peculiar obsession with classifying the Mobutu regime. "The Mobutu regime has a vague and eclectic legitimating 'mentality'—an eclectic and often haphazard blend of ambiguous, fluctuating, and often derivative legitimating formulas or doctrines (as opposed to a coherent ideology)—which includes notions from liberal democracy, revolutionary populism, even socialism. Above all, however, it is organic-statist in orientation, drawing on traditional African notions of community, equity, authority, and power, particularly pre-colonial concepts of kingship, chiefship, and the 'big man'" (Callaghy 1984, 6).

9. Crawford Young and Thomas Turner (1985, 213) argue that not only the writing of Placide Tempels but also that of Jan Vansina (see chapter 8) inspired thinking about *authenticité*.

10. Zenda Mukulumanya wa N'Gate (1982) offers a preliminary reading of the relationship between Zairian authenticity and various Western philosophical traditions. For a brief history of the concept of authenticity in Zaire, see Ndaywel è Nziem 1998, 675–81.

11. In the words of Jean-Claude Willame, "A partir de 1978, on ne discerne plus de projet de société, même dans le verbe, mais un discours du pouvoir sur lui-même" ("Starting in 1978, Mobutu's discourse is no longer a question of society, not even at the level of language, as much as it is a discourse about its own power"; 17).

12. In a speech addressed to the first session of the Makanda Kabobi Institute, Mobutu explained that Mobutuism was not to be seen as a substitute for what had come before, but as its logical culmination: "Authentic Zairian nationalism, authenticity, recourse to authenticity, and now Mobutuism are not simply new words intended to replace old ones. It is indispensable to understand the logical relation between them" (Mobutu n.d., vol. II:525). "Nationalism," he went on to explain, "is the doctrine of the MPR. Authenticity is its ideology and Recourse to Authenticity is its method. Taken together, all of these concepts can be seen as the "teachings and thoughts of the President-founder, i.e. 'Mobutuism.'"

13. The term *abacost* (or *abacoste*) was an abbreviation of the French expression "à bas les costumes" (down with Western-style suits). Neologisms such as this one were common also in the creation of "authentic" proper names. I. Ndaywel è Nziem gives examples of how these name changes involved a certain degree of irony and subversiveness (1998, 679).

14. In what Crawford Young and Thomas Turner have aptly referred to as the government's "episodic quest for relegitimation" (1985, 220), the Mobutu regime was terribly skilled at keeping control through the appearance of renewal at the level of both rhetoric and policy. More than one scholar has remarked on the way that *authenticité* seemed to fade in and out of the foreground of Zairian political discourse (see Kapume 1978).

15. One of the most complex aspects of the story of *animation politique* is the extremely ambiguous document left behind by Kapalanga, who passed away under mysterious circumstances (i.e., he disappeared without a trace). The political implications of this document are enormous since it attempts to analyze the extent to which *animation politique* constitutes an organic expression of authenticity. According to my sources in Kinshasa, the original version of this text (which included some material critical of the regime's cultural policy) was censored, and certain sections of the text were destroyed.

16. For a discussion of the importance of mass media to the development of *animation politique*, see Kapalanga 1989.

17. Zaire, in turn, would have significant influence on various types of political performance elsewhere in Africa. C. Toulabor (1986) has discussed the extent to which Mobutu's policies served as a model for President Eyadema of Togo, who at one point decided to send *animateurs* to Kinshasa for training. Toulabor also alludes to a link between Zaire and Guinea, though more research is necessary to establish a connection between Mobutu and Sekou Touré.

18. Some examples include the Red Cross, Xaveri, and FEBOSCO (the Congolese Federation of Boy Scouts). On this topic see Charles Tshimanga's (1999) article on the history of the scouting movement and its relationship to the emergence of nationalist political parties of the period.

19. One of the best descriptions we have of Mobutu's speeches during this period

comes from V. S. Naipaul's *A Bend in the River*: "The themes were not new: sacrifice and the bright future; the dignity of the woman of Africa; the need to strengthen the revolution, unpopular though it was with those black men in towns who dreamed of waking up one day as white men; the need for Africans to be African, to go back without shame to their democratic and socialist ways, to rediscover the virtues of the diet and medicines of their grandfathers and not to go running like children after things in imported tins and bottles; the need for vigilance, work and, above all, discipline" (1979, 214).

20. *Salongo* refers to the mandatory public works programs Mobutu initiated as part of *authenticité*. Most people living in Kinshasa during this period remember the feeling of collective energy that went along with this activity, which required all citizens to devote part of each Saturday to cleaning public spaces and thoroughfares. For information about how *salongo* functioned outside of Kinshasa (in the context of public education), see Muhima 1975.

21. For more information on the famous "lettere ouverte" addressed to Mobutu in 1980, see Ndaywel è Nziem (1998).

22. For an example of how these measures were enforced arbitrarily, see Roberts 1984.

23. This motif harkens back to Mobutu's famous political rallying slogan: "How many nations? One! How many chiefs? One! How many governments? One! How many Congos? One!" (Mobutu n.d., vol. I:311).

24. During the Mobutu years successful bands were rather commonly called on by the office of the president to entertain at official events, many of which took place outside of Kinshasa. Groups such as Zaiko Langa Langa and the hugely popular Swede Swede Boketchu Premier were jetted off to presidential family weddings and birthday parties in Europe and then flown back the next day, regardless of their own concert or recording schedule.

25. Franco was the first musician to receive money from the newly created Fonds Mobutu Sese Seko (1972), a fund intended to help writers, musicians, and other performing artists. In 1973 he was appointed the director of the first Zairian musicians' union, Union des Musiciens du Zaïre (UMUZA), and in 1974 he was awarded ownership and management of MAZADIS, the record-pressing plant that was one of the last foreign-owned companies to be transferred during the nationalization measures of the 1970s. In 1976 he was inaugurated into Mobutu's prestigious Order of the Leopard, an honor that would be taken away because of the Kengo scandal in the 1980s, and then reinstated after Franco's death in 1989.

26. For more about Mobutu's secret service, see Schatzberg 1988 (chap. 3, "The State as Ear").

27. Franco was also known for his uncanny ability to imitate Mobutu, not only in terms of voice but also of his ticks and nervous gestures (see Kapalanga 1989, 160, 170).

28. In the notes to the second installment of the government-sponsored music collection *Anthologie de la musique zaïroise moderne*, Wendo Kolosoy is remembered for having composed a song entitled "Papa Mobutu apika bendele" ("Papa Mobutu Plants the Flag"): "This patriotic hymn in honor of Mobutu is an expression of gratitude from Zairian musicians to their patron, but also of their feeling of affection for the homeland that he has given them. It is well known that artists who live without constraints are able to sing about what people think" (Bureau du Président de la République du Zaïre 1974).

29. Even in 1966 a hit song such as Tabu Ley's "Mokolo na ko kufa" managed to sell two thousand copies per week.

30. According to Christopher Waterman, recording companies in Nigeria would often release records with one side in standard Yoruba and the other in a regional dialect (1990, 95–96).

31. On the affects and uses of cassette technology in developing economies, see also Abu-Lughod 1990b, Diawara 1997, and Manuel 1993.

32. I have chosen to refer to this category of cultural operators as redistributors rather than as pirates because they are not all pirates, and they are not always selling pirated products. The term *pirate* will be used where it applies more specifically to the illegal duplication and sale of musical products.

33. The first copyrights office in the Congo was opened under the name of SACO (Société d'Auteurs Congolaises), but it later changed its name to SONECA. In the period from 1970 to 1978 SONECA's activities were unstable, with seven changes in director and nine changes in executive committees. In 1978, the singer Tabu Ley assumed the direction and was succeeded some time later by a Mr. Engwandu, who would serve as the director until the end of 1996, when increasing dissatisfaction with his management forced him to resign.

34. To avoid pursuit, many of the vendors specialize mainly in "golden oldies" (*merveilles du passé*) which are much less contentious than newly or recently released albums. Several mobile vendors told me that they are sometimes required to pay small sums of money to local police in exchange for the latter's inattention to pirate cassette sales.

35. Under the supervision of Jean Pierre Gombe (Tamaris), a young producer and promoter in Brazzaville named Lascony Balloux set up the first mobile cassette sales system, a system he referred to as the *démarcheurs* (walkers). Balloux's walkers were equipped with a so-called Super Cassette carrying case, matching hat and T-shirts, and a rubber band on the arm for grouping series of cassettes. Vendors would literally pass from door to door and neighborhood to neighborhood, a technique completely unheard of for products of this type in Brazzaville. This approach was innovative not only for the way that it attempted to bring the product in direct contact with the customer but also because vendors were trained in how to present arguments about the issue of piracy. Vendors (mostly young men) were also offered

incentive programs in the form of bonuses. Balloux later went on to work with Amadou Ndiaye, a Senegalese businessman who (thanks in part to Balloux) became the primary cassette producer and distributor in the region.

36. The largest vendor association I found (Ecurie SKC, named after a brand name of blank audio cassettes) was based in Matonge, generally considered the most important urban zone in terms of music production and consumption. Members numbered around twenty, and meetings were held on a monthly or bimonthly basis. I was not able to attend any meetings of this sort, but I was told that meeting agendas included electing officers, discussing developments in the association's territory, and organizing rotating savings.

37. Apart from urban mobile vendors, there is a special category of mobile vendors who operate across much greater distances. Often shuttling back and forth between Kinshasa (or other major urban centers) and the diamond-producing regions of Kasai in southern Congo or the borderland area between Congo and Angola, many diamond traders have taken up the practice of buying large quantities of cassettes to sell to obtain seed money for other activities.

38. This is not to say that the music business has never had local brokers; the two most common examples would be Henri Bowane and Kiamanguana Verckys (see Stewart 2000).

Chapter 4: Live Time

1. This writing strategy, which was at the center of the debates about ethnographic representation in the middle of the 1980s (Clifford and Marcus 1986), has been severely criticized as a means through which western scholars distance themselves from their subjects through the subtle use of metaphors of space and time (see also Fabian 1983). Despite these critiques, I have maintained the use of the present tense to draw out and accentuate the immediacy of live performance.

2. *Performativity* is a term first articulated by Judith Butler in her controversial and widely read *Gender Trouble* (1990). In reality this text, more often cited than analyzed in the performance literature, is not about performance per se. As Butler herself admits (1990, 192), her theory of performativity (gender's constructedness expressed primarily through a stylized repetition of acts) more closely resembles Pierre Bourdieu's theory of habitus than any theory of performance.

3. On Cheri Samba, see Jewsiewicki 1993, 1995.

4. Thompson is the name of a small fish that has become something of a staple food in Kinshasa because of its low price and easy availability.

5. Manda Tchebwa also translates this term as "curious" and provides a nice picture of *ngembo* in action in the 1950s (Tchebwa 1996, second page of third picture set).

6. Tchebwa estimates the number of neighborhood bands (*orchestres des jeunes*) in Kinshasa to range between six and seven hundred (1996, 173,192). Other estimates I heard go as high as three thousand (Zachary Bababaswe, personal communication,

April 10, 1996), which would be the equivalent of one group every two or three square kilometers. This estimate is probably high and most likely includes all types of music groups, not just those playing popular dance music. In any case, neighborhood bands have limited exposure in the sprawling urban center that is Kinshasa. My questions about the bands playing before us usually fell on deaf ears. No one seemed interested, and no one, not even Chef Maneko, knew who the band was. He would invariably answer, "Some group of kids from the neighborhood."

7. Short for *fondateur*, or "founder," this is the term that most band members use when addressing Defao.

8. Men in Kinshasa often greet each other by gently bumping the corners of their foreheads, alternating sides as they shake or hold hands. This form of greeting, which uses the same gestural motion as do kisses on the cheek common in many parts of Europe, seemed to be most pronounced among men in positions of wealth and power, such as wealthy businessmen or well-placed civil servants.

9. As Paul Berliner has described regarding the performance of *mbira* music in Zimbabwe (1978, 111), a cyclical song structure means that the group leader calls the end of a particular song when he sees fit. To signal the end of the song, most bands in Kinshasa use a standard musical motif or tag usually sung by the *atalaku*. In Zaiko Langa Langa, for example, the *atalaku* will roll a long, loud r into the microphone after having seen the leader's signal to end the song.

10. I have used the term *cosinger* instead of *backup singer* since the latter usually refers to completely secondary musicians who complement the lead singer but never take the lead or sing solos themselves. In Zairian music, cosingers, although usually part of a hierarchy, often have the opportunity to sing alone, at which time other singers (including the lead singer) will back off from the microphone. Their position onstage (four microphones equally spaced for equal importance) also reflects their unique place in the band.

11. There are some exceptions. Certain well-known guitarists (Boeing 737 and Lofombo from Empire Bakuba, Alain Makaba and Burkina Faso from Wenge Musica BCBG) are appreciated for their occasional forays into the dance section, their animated dance moves, and their facial expressions during performance.

12. I attended one wedding concert to which Defao was invited as the entertainment and during which the female dancers were encouraged to dance with other musicians or guests during classic rumba numbers.

13. In the Big Stars, six of the eight *danseuses* used similar tactics on a regular basis. Informal observation suggests similar ratios for other bands as well.

14. The wall-of-dance phenomenon is less developed in other well-known groups; most groups have anywhere from one to four *danseuses*. Groups such as Empire Bakuba, Zaiko Langa Langa, and Super Choc will have on occasion large *danseuse* troupes, but this requires considerable resources and preparation. Two groups in particular, Rajakula's Station Japana and the group of the Geneva-based musician

Jolino, experimented with even larger group dance formations (eight to sixteen dancers apart from the musicians), but this style of performance is limited to large stage shows and music videos because of its space requirements. Another variation involves several female dancers performing on either side of the lead singer, a common formation in Defao's stage show.

15. There are of course some exceptions. Nostalgia groups such as Afrique Alliance and Mathieu Kuka's Afrique Ambiance make very little use of choreographed dances and their accompanying shouts. Although Bana O.K. has been influenced by the multipart song structure and *animation* of the new wave movement, the dances they use are of their own creation and reflect the taste and age of their mostly older audience. Another important exception is the music of Viva La Musica (led by Papa Wemba), the only well-known band to resist the use of other groups' dances and shouts. "We want to do something different," Wemba once told me in an interview (January 15, 1996). Other established bands such as Zaiko Langa Langa, renowned for their creative energy in this area, are more and more often forced to give in to pressure from fans to use the shouts and dance steps created by younger artists.

16. The most well-known example is Koffi Olomide, who actually began his career as the *parolier* for Papa Wemba. Tabu Ley also apparently supplied lyrics to Grand Kallé before joining African Jazz (Lonoh 1969, 68).

17. Some photographers will also take more standard concert photos at certain events, focusing primarily on well-known singers or stars, since these photos can be sold later as individual prints to the general public.

18. For discussions of spraying elsewhere in Africa, see Waterman 1990 and Askew 2002.

19. On the distinction between singers and instrumentalists in popular music in general, see Frith 1989.

Chapter 5: Musicians and Mobility

1. For a discussion of musicians' professional trajectories in the context of the English-speaking Caribbean, see Stolzoff 2000.

2. Justin-Daniel Gandoulou has written extensively on this subject (see 1989). Although his work provides some important sociological detail, other writing on the subject has gone further in analyzing the historical, political, and symbolic aspects of this unique form of urban social organization. Phyllis Martin (1994) looks at the historical relationship between clothes and local notions of individual force or power. Jonathan Friedman (1990) gives a semantic reading of the relationship of style to personal identity and political economy. R. Bazenguissa-Ganga (1992) argues that la *sape* must be understood in terms of Congo-Brazzaville's complex history of politicized ethnic relations between the primarily Kikongo-speaking peoples of the south and Bangala ethnic groups from the north who dominated national politics during the period of Gandoulou's study. David Hecht and Maliqalim

Simone (1994) view the *sapeur* as a challenge to the political order and class-based state rule, while Didier Gondola (1999) examines the way that *la sape* represents a statement of defiance in relation not only to the state but also to the legacy of colonial rule.

3. John Low's (1982) account of his time spent playing music and living with musicians (especially the legendary Jean Bosco Mwenda) in and around the Shaba region offers a fascinating example of the foreign music aficionado who travels to the Congo to learn about the music firsthand. Low's story, "not just a 'musical field-trip'" (9), is filled with specialized information about musical technique, compositional practice, and research methods, but it also provides a good deal of ethnographic information about everyday life in this part of Zaire at the end of the 1970s.

4. I am not saying that the idea came from Heath but wish to compare our two somewhat similar experiences.

Chapter 6: Live Texts

1. Compare with the notion of *ukumbusho*, the Swahili word often translated as "memory" or "purposeful reflection." For a discussion of this concept for the Congo, see Fabian 1996.

2. Other accounts of the social dynamics of live performance have been described by Coplan 1994, Erlmann 1996, Fabian 1990, and Waterman 1990. For a more general discussion of theories of performance, see Ebron 2002.

3. Some of the most innovative work on the meaning of sound is being done by Philip Tagg. For an excellent recent example, see Tagg and Clarida 2003.

4. Compare with Unni Wikan's (1992) discussion of an interpretivist bias in American anthropology in which she criticizes Clifford Geertz (among others) for being "wordstruck" and analyzes how this fixation on our own words keeps us from being able to capture the nuances of nonverbal cues and emotional response.

5. For a good analysis of the relevance of Williams's work to critical approaches in anthropology, see the useful text of Camille Brochu (2005). Ortner 1973 provides a valuable overview of the key-symbols approach in anthropology.

6. Compare with Johannes Fabian's (1996) discussion of "deception" and "loss" in the context of his analysis of the work of the popular painter Tshibumba Kanda Matulu. Though this part of Fabian's analysis is concerned primarily with the colonial period, Fabian himself shows how memory mediates between past and present. Whereas the idea of loss seems more appropriate to popular thinking about the colonial period, the idea of deception (meaning "disappointment") is close to my discussion of abandonment.

7. Here I am referring to the cultural-models approach elaborated in Holland and Quinn 1987. For a more recent overview of discourse analysis in cultural anthropology, see Quinn 2005.

8. The French term *immortaliser* is also used.

9. I am grateful to Serge Makobo for this observation.

10. Certain strands of linguistic anthropology have taken seriously M. M. Bakhtin's notion of "addressivity," much more so than our colleagues in comparative literature: "In point of fact '*word*' *is a two-sided act.* It is determined equally by *whose* word it is and *for whom* it is meant. As word, it is precisely *the product of the reciprocal relationship between the speaker and listener, addresser and addressee.* Each and every word express the 'one' in relation to the 'other'; I give myself verbal shape from another's point of view, ultimately form the point view of the community to which I belong. A word is a bridge thrown between myself and another" (Volosinov 1973, 86; original emphasis).

11. Musicians calling out each others' names or nicknames makes for common practice in many African musical styles (see, e.g., Waterman 1990). As Paul Berliner (1978) has shown, this practice has a stimulating effect on musicians while they play. In the early years of Congo-Zairian music, shouts were almost exclusively made up of other musicians. In live performance in the 1990s, lead guitarists and drummers are most often those who are "thrown" by fellow band members. For example, Defao created a special shout for the lead guitarist that he had "stolen" from Wenge Musica at about the same time that I joined the band: "Burkina Faso! [variation on the guitarist's name] Faso na Faso-eh!"

12. A special category of sponsor songs focusing on commercial products seemed more common in the first few decades of Congolese music. Leon Bukasa sang a song about the founder of the Ngoma record label, and a certain Mokoko sang about Bata shoes in the 1950s. In the 1970s Tabu Ley sang for Skol beer, Omo soap, and FNMA refrigerators. During the same time period, Franco sang for Primus and Kronenburg beers. Both Tabu Ley and Franco sang songs for Azda, a well-known importer of inexpensive European cars in Kinshasa in the 1970s. See chapter 4 for a discussion of the relationship among popular musicians and large-scale commercial sponsorship in the 1990s.

13. The vast majority of people attending concerts of groups from Kinshasa are Congolese.

14. In addition to Waterman 1990, the extensive literature on the politics of griot praise and performance in West Africa is also pertinent (see Ebron 2002; Schulz 1999).

15. Some of the most common names cited during the 1990s: Saddam Hussein (Mobutu's son), Manda Tchebwa (a TV announcer), Bolowa Bonzakwa (a TV announcer), Alain St. Pierre (a radio announcer), Jean-Jacques Bayonne (a nightclub owner and music producer), George Weah (a soccer player), Mutombo Dikembe (a basketball player), Alain Mbiya (a music promoter), Eric Kenzo (a music promoter), Bob Maswa (a music promoter), Gaby Shabani (a music promoter), Mère Kosala (a bar owner), Africa #1 (a radio station in Libreville), and Antenne A (a radio station in Kinshasa).

16. I am grateful to Peter Seitel for suggesting that shouting and throwing may serve as speech genres.

17. Corinne Kratz's analysis of song in the context of ritual initiation among the Okiek of Kenya analyzes pragmatic sung language in similar terms: "Each directive line of each group is an individual hook with a particular rhetorical barb and phrasing, but all have a single pragmatic focus, encouragement, and a specific temporal focus, the operation at dawn" (1994, 271). For discussions of the use of hooks in popular music, see Burns 1987, Middleton 1990, and Waterman 1990, 18.

18. For more details on the question of masked messages and subversion in the lyrics of Congolese popular dance music, see Yoka and Kinkela (forthcoming).

19. For more information on audience-based approaches to the ethnographic study of popular music, see www.atalaku.net/listening, which also includes data on the most popular songs and lyrics from more than fifty years of popular music production in Congo-Zaire.

20. Camille Kuyu Mwissa's (1993) analysis uses a number of widely recognized song texts to understand the norms and values regulating relations between the sexes. The first case presented by Mwissa—Luambo Makiadi's "La vie des hommes"— tells a story of conjugal breakdown resembling that told in "Famille Kikuta."

21. In this research, Lye M. Yoka and I are also investigating a practice I call "cross-singing," in which a male singer or composer sings from the perspective of a woman. The fact that this practice is very common suggests a complex three-way dynamic among musicians, female fans, and male fans, but research on this topic currently remains in its preliminary stages. For more information on the question of popular music and gender, see Engundu Walu's (1999) research on the representation of feminine beauty and sexuality in popular song lyrics during Mobutu's rule.

Chapter 7: The Political Life of Dance Bands

1. Gage Averill reports a similar phenomenon in his analysis of popular music and power in Haiti (1997, 10).

2. This term has been used in a number of different readings of contemporary political life: those that look at the individual faced with impersonal institutions of various sorts (Certeau 1984), especially the state (MacGaffey 1991; Mbembe 1992a); those concerned with relations among social classes (Bourdieu 1984); the reactions of peasants to various forms of authority (De Boeck 1999); the reaction of indigenous peoples to encroaching capitalist economies (Taussig 1980); political differentiation within indigenous or tribal societies (Gluckman 1949; Turner 1957); and political relations among them (Evans-Pritchard 1940).

3. In trying to understand these issues, my research has benefited from the rich body of literature on indigenous notions of power and authority in an African context, but I am especially interested in scholarship with an historical (Packard 1981) or social anthropological emphasis (Karp 1989; Turner 1969).

4. I am referring to Mbembe's discussion of the "ruler" and the "ruled," which does not refer directly to Gramsci's writing on this subject. On the dialectical nature of

charismatic leadership, see Martin 2006. A similar dialectic is suggested by Ivan Karp's (1989) distinction between power (or the power to rule over others) and capacity (the power or ability to do something).

5. Though what is potentially the most interesting about Fabian's research on this topic is that he was unable to find an exact equivalent to this expression in local African languages. On metaphors of eating or consumption in African political discourse, see also Bayart 1993, Cohen and Odhiambo 1989, Mbembe 1992a, Schatzberg 1993.

6. Frederic Cooper has challenged Foucault's notion of diffuse power by arguing that power in colonial societies in Africa was more concentrated in social and spatial terms, making it "arterial" instead of "capillary." Power, he argues, is always "in need of a pump to push it from moment to moment and place to place" (1994, 1533).

7. As I am primarily concerned with the working structure of the musical group, my focus in this discussion will be on hierarchies of a professional nature. In this context, professional hierarchies are more operational than those based on social class or ethnicity. The role of gender in these hierarchies is more complex, an issue to which I will return later in this chapter. Veit Erlmann (1992) discusses many of these issues in his work on Zulu migrant workers in South Africa, and Christopher Waterman (1990) has examined band structure and hierarchy among juju musicians in Nigeria.

8. Some bands have special dance coaches (e.g., Lambio Lambert, the well-known dance master of Viva La Musica), and in some cases the *animateur* will serve as a sort of dance supervisor (e.g., Djuna Mumbafu of Empire Bakuba).

9. Zaire's real GDP per capita in 1992 was US$380, placing it at 127 of 140 countries on the United Nation's Human Development Index (United Nations Development Program 1993).

10. Although suspensions happen regularly in most bands, there is some effort to hide their occurrence. Suspensions that turn into dismissals invariably become important local news items.

11. It is common practice for suspended musicians to make a request through the band manager for the suspension to be lifted; otherwise it will last indefinitely. If the initial request is refused, the suspended musician will usually try to activate other social networks (friends of the bandleader, important friends or family members, etc.) to make a case for themselves. Musicians excluded from the band altogether have to go through the same steps, but their reintegration process is longer and much more difficult.

12. Compare this with J. P. Busé's assessment of the splintering that occurred in Zaiko Langa Langa: "It was so big that everybody knew something was going to happen. They just didn't think about where they were going" (interview, August 25, 1997).

13. Thus it is possible to talk about a kind of fission, in which elements of the organism separate to form distinct independent organisms while still retaining something of

the original, a process Manda Tchebwa has described as *scissiparité* (1996, 175). The opposite process, that of fusion, rarely occurs. If musicians attempt to rejoin a band they have left, they invariably do so individually and not as a unit. They are usually put on probation before being able to take back their previous full-time position.

14. Ilo Pablo, one of the driving forces behind this splinter group, explained to me that the suffix Familia Dei was chosen to create an image separate from the original Zaiko, which was known for its involvement in various "ungodly" practices, especially the use of sorcery.

15. This warning, however, may be nothing more than a claim to leaders' control over female sexuality. One group found an innovative solution to this problem by putting into effect an official band policy that restricted band members from dating or having sexual relations with the same women: "If I like her and she doesn't like me, then the other musicians can't go after her" (interview with Lokassa ya Mbongo, January 17, 1998).

16. Christopher Waterman shows that the distribution of money is a common focus for gossip and recrimination, and the most frequent cause of breakups among *juju* groups in Nigeria. His informal observations suggest that more than 50 percent of band earnings are kept by the bandleader for his own purposes (1990, 159).

17. On the topic of wealth among people in the Central African region, see Guyer 1993, Guyer and Belinga 1995, and Vansina 1990.

Chapter 8: In the Skin of a Chief

1. Often-cited examples include "Ata Ndele" (Adou Elenga), "Nakomitunaka" (Verckys), and "Indépendance Cha Cha" (African Jazz). Elsewhere I address this question more explicitly, see my analysis at www.atalaku.net

2. Much of this writing has focused on social and political protest in the context of popular religious song: see Ndaywel è Nziem 1993, Pongo 2000, and Tshijuke 1988. On the question of religious or church-based political opposition more generally, see Schatzberg 1988.

3. The most recent example is Michela Wrong's *In the Footsteps of Mr. Kurtz* (2000). The summary on the back cover reads: "A sparkling account of the rise and fall of Mobutu Sese Seko, the charismatic dictator who plundered his country's wealth and indulged a passion for pink champagne, gold jewellery and chartered Concordes. Absurdity, anarchy, and corruption run riot in Michela Wrong's fascinating dissection of the Congo; a story of grim comedy amidst the apocalypse and a celebration of the sheer indestructibility of the human spirit."

4. Camile Kuyu Mwissa discusses popular musicians' potential to move from a position of power to one of "moral authority" (1993, 426).

5. Jane Guyer and S. M. Eno Belinga (1995) argue that the accumulation model that dominated most early writing on this topic is in need of revision and that one aspect missing from most formulations of people's wealth is that of knowledge.

6. In a review of Vansina's book, David Cohen (1991) plays out the postmodernist de-

bate of the early 1990s when he criticizes Vansina for having resuscitated the "quest for continuity" and "yearning for a lost order." Cohen's critique, whose aggressive tone is embedded in a language of praise, points out that Vansina's distinction between "cognitive reality" and "physical reality" is under-theorized and that Vansina tends to use the terms "past" and "history" interchangeably.

7. On the *colonie belge* motif in Congolese popular painting, see Fabian 1996 and Jewsiewicki 2003a.

8. Presumably the term "kapita" comes from the French word "capitaine," an intermediate position of authority in the colonial armed forces (personal communication, Mbala Nkanga, July 10, 2006).

9. "Servir et non se servir" (Serve others but not yourself) was an often heard political slogan during Mobutu's period of "self-criticism" following the disastrous nationalization schemes during the second half of the 1970s.

10. Franco has been the subject of several theses and monographs. Ewens 1994 is a good overview of the artist and the period, with a great deal of original research. Olema 1998 examines Franco's political and artistic legacy through a sophisticated analysis of the use of political satire. Mumbanza 1999 examines among other things Franco's contribution as a bandleader and manager.

11. In the song "Kashama Nkoy," Tabu Ley speaks to a deceased friend who fell victim to the political upheaval of the early years of the Mobutu regime. "What would you say if you could meet Lumumba?"

12. Engundu Walu writes about the complex way in which male rivalry is played out through the appropriation of female sexuality. See for example her discussion of two of Franco's most controversial songs, "Jacky" and "Hélène" (1999, 164–68).

13. One of the pictures featured in the interview shows Wendo dressed in a shirt bearing the image of the former president Laurent Kabila.

14. Some of the material in this section is drawn from more recent interviews conducted as part of a project entitled "Ethnographies of Listening," a comparative audience-based study in collaboration with Lye M. Yoka that took place simultaneously in Kinshasa and Montreal between 2002 and 2005. For more information about this project, see www.atalaku.net/listening.

BIBLIOGRAPHY

Abélès, Marc. 2000. *Un ethnologue à l'Assemblée*. Paris: Odile Jacob.

Abu-Lughod, Lila. 1990a. "The Romance of Resistance." *American Ethnologist* 17 (1): 41–55.

———. 1990b. "Shifting Politics in Bedouin Love Poetry." In *Language and the Politics of Emotion*, ed. Catherine A. Lutz and Abu-Lughod, 24–45. Cambridge: Cambridge University Press.

———. 2005. *Dramas of Nationhood: The Politics of Television in Egypt*. Chicago: University of Chicago Press.

Adorno, Theodor W. 1973. *The Jargon of Authenticity*, trans. Knut Tarnowski and Frederic Will. Evanston, Ill.: Northwestern University Press.

Appadurai, Arjun. 1986. *The Social Life of Things: Commodities in Cultural Perspective*. Cambridge: Cambridge University Press.

———. 1990. "Topographies of the Self: Praise and Emotion in Hindu India." In *Language and the Politics of Emotion*, ed. Catherine A. Lutz and Lila Abu-Lughod, 92–112. Cambridge: Cambridge University Press.

Appadurai, Arjun, and Carol A. Breckenridge, eds. 1995. *Consuming Modernity: Public Culture in a South Asian World*. Minneapolis: University of Minnesota Press.

Askew, Kelly M. 2002. *Performing the Nation: Swahili Music and Cultural Politics in Tanzania*. Chicago: University of Chicago Press.

Averill, Gage. 1997. *A Day for the Hunter, a Day for the Prey: Popular Music and Power in Haiti*. Chicago: University of Chicago Press.

Badibanga, Ne-Mwine. 1992. "Sortir du sinistre culturel." In *Quelle politique culturelle pour la Troisième République du Zaïre?*, ed. I. Ndaywel è Nziem, 117–24. Kinshasa: Bibliothèque Nationale du Zaïre.

Bakhtin, M. M. 1986. *Speech Genres and Other Late Essays*, trans. Vern W. McGee. Austin: University of Texas Press.

Balandier, Georges. 1957. *Ambiguous Africa: Cultures in Collision*, trans. Helen Weaver. New York: Pantheon.

———. [1955] 1985. *Sociologie des Brazzavilles noires*. Paris: Fondation Nationale des Sciences Politiques.

Barber, Karin, ed. 1997. *Readings in African Popular Culture*. Bloomington: Indiana University Press.

Barlow, Sean, and Banning Eyre, with Jack Vartoogian. 1995. *Afropop! An Illustrated Guide to Contemporary African Music*. Edison, N.J.: Chartwell.

Bauman, R., and C. L. Briggs. 1990. "Poetics and Performances as Critical Perspectives on Language and Social Life." *Annual Review of Anthropology* 19:59–88.

Bayart, Jean-François. 1993. *The State in Africa: The Politics of the Belly*. New York: Longman.

Bazenguissa-Ganga, Rémy 1992. "La sape et la politique au Congo." *Journal des africanistes* 62 (1): 151–57.

Beidelman, T. O. 1993. *Moral Imagination in Kaguru Modes of Thought*. Washington: Smithsonian Institution Press.

Bemba, Sylvain. 1984. *Cinquante ans de musique du Congo-Zaire (1920–1907): De Paul Kamba à Tabu Ley*. Paris: Présence Africaine.

Bender, Wolfgang. 1991. *Sweet Mother: Modern African Music*. Chicago: University of Chicago Press.

Bennett, Tony. 1998. *Culture: A Reformer's Science*. Thousand Oaks, Calif.: Sage.

Berliner, Paul. 1978. *The Soul of Mbira: Music and Traditions of the Shona Peoples of Zimbabwe*. Berkeley: University of California Press.

Berman, Marshall. 1988. *All That Is Solid Melts into Air: The Experience of Modernity*. New York: Penguin.

Biaya, T. K. n.d. "La kinoiserie: Aux sources de la culture politique congolaise contemporaine." Unpublished manuscript.

———. 1985. "La 'cuistrerie' de Mbuji Mayi (Zaïre): Organisation, fonctionnement et idéologie d'une bourgeoisie africaine." *Genève-Afrique* 23 (1): 65–84.

———. 1992. "Et si la perspective de Tshibumba était courbe?" In *Art pictural zaïrois*, ed. Bogumil Jewsiewicki. Sillery, Que.: Septentrion.

———. 1994. "Mundele, ndumba et ambience: Le vrai 'Bal blanc et bal noir(e).'" In *Belgique/Zaïre: Une histoire en quête d'avenir*, ed. Gauthier de Villers. Paris: L'Harmattan.

———. 1997. "Kinshasa: Anomie, 'ambiance' et violence." In *Youth, Street Culture, and Urban Violence in Africa*, ed. Georges Hérault and Pius Adesanmi, 329–82. Ibadan: IFRA.

Biaya, T. K., and Gilles Bibeau, eds. 1998. "L'Afrique revisitée." Special issue, *Anthropologie et sociétés* 22 (1).

Bokasi, Mula Ebolabi. 1990. *La symbolique de la production discographique de Zaiko Langa-Langa: Une socio-analyse de la musique zairoise moderne*. Master's thesis, Department of Sociology, University of Lubumbashi.

Botombele, Bokongo Ekanga. 1975. *La politique culturelle en République du Zaïre*. Paris: Unesco.

Bourdieu, Pierre. 1984. *Distinction: A Social Critique of the Judgement of Taste*, trans. Richard Nice. Cambridge: Harvard University Press.

Braeckman, Collette. 1992. *Le dinosaure: Le Zaïre de Mobutu*. Paris: Fayard.

Briggs, Charles L., and Richard Bauman. 1992. "Genre, Intertextuality, and Social Power." *Journal of Linguistic Anthropology* 2 (2): 131–72.

Brochu, Camille. 2005. "The Keywords Methodology." http://www.criticalworld.net/tool.php?type=9&id=102.

Bureau du Président de la République du Zaïre. 1974. *Anthologie de la musique zaïroise moderne.*

Burns, Gary. 1987. "A Typology of 'Hooks' in Popular Records." *Popular Music* 6 (1): 1–20.

Butler, Judith. 1990. *Gender Trouble: Feminism and the Subversion of Identity*. New York: Routledge.

Callaghy, Thomas. 1984. *The State-Society Struggle: Zaire in Comparative Perspective*. New York: Columbia University Press.

———. 1987. *Politics and Culture in Zaire*. Ann Arbor: Center for Political Studies / Institute for Social Research, University of Michigan.

Castaldi, Francesca. 2006. *Choreographies of African Identities: Négritude, Dance, and the National Ballet of Senegal*. Urbana: University of Illinois Press.

Cefai, Daniel, ed. 2001. *Cultures politiques*. Paris: Presses Universitaires de France.

Certeau, Michel de. 1984. *The Practice of Everyday Life*, trans. Steven Rendall. Berkeley: University of California Press.

Chernoff, John Miller. 1979. *African Rhythm and African Sensibility: Aesthetics and Social Action in African Musical Idioms*. Chicago: University of Chicago Press.

Cheyney, Tom. 1989. "Loketo: Shake Your Hips." *Beat* 8 (6): 23–25.

Chiwengo, Ngwarasungu. 1997. "Congolese Women in Popular Fiction, TV, and Politics." Paper presented at the "Politics, Culture, and Youth in the New Congo" conference, Ann Arbor, Michigan, October 26–28.

Clifford, James, and George E. Marcus, eds. 1986. *Writing Culture: The Poetics and Politics of Ethnography*. Berkeley: University of California Press.

Cohen, David. 1991. "Historicizing a Regional Cultural Tradition." *Current Anthropology* 32 (3): 363–64.

Cohen, David William, and E. S. Atieno Odhiambo. 1989. *Siaya: A Historical Anthropology of an African Landscape*. Athens: Ohio University Press.

Cooper, Frederic. 1994. "Conflict and Connection: Rethinking Colonial African History." *American Historical Review* 99 (5): 1516–43.

Coplan, David. 1985. *In Township Tonight: South Africa's Black City Music and Theater*. New York: Longman.

———. 1994. *In the Time of Cannibals: The Word Music of South Africa's Basotho Migrants*. Chicago: University of Chicago Press.

Corin, Ellen. 1998. "Re-figuring the Person: The Dynamics of Affects and Symbols in an African Spirit Possession Cult." In *Bodies and Persons: Comparative Perspectives from Africa and Melanesia*, ed. Michael Lambek and Andrew Strathern, 80–102. Cambridge: Cambridge University Press.

Dangaremba, Tsitsi. 1988. *Nervous Conditions*. New York: Seal.

Das, Veena, and Deborah Poole, eds. 2004. *Anthropology in the Margins of the State*. Santa Fe: School of American Research.

De Boeck, Filip. 1998. "Beyond the Grave: History, Memory, and Death in Postcolonial Congo/Zaire. In *Memory and the Postcolony: African Anthropology and the Critique of Power*, ed. Richard Werbner. London: Zed.

———. 1999. "Domesticating Diamonds and Dollars: Identity, Expenditure, and Sharing in Southwestern Zaire." In *Globalization and Identity: Dialectics of Flow and Closure*, ed. Birgit Meyer and Peter Geschiere. Oxford: Blackwell.

———. 2005. "The Apocalyptic Interlude: Revealing Death in Kinshasa." *African Studies Review* 48 (2): 11–32.

De Boeck, Filip, and Marie-Françoise Plissart. 2005. *Kinshasa: Tales of the Invisible City*. Brussels: Royal Museum for Central Africa and Ludion.

Devisch, René. 1995. "Frenzy, Violence, and Ethical Renewal in Kinshasa." *Public Culture* 7 (3): 593–629.

———. 1996. "'Pillaging Jesus': Healing Churches and the Villagisation of Kinshasa." *Africa* 66 (4): 555–86.

Diawara, Mamadou. 1997. "Mande Oral Popular Culture Revisited by the Electronic Media." In *Readings in Popular Culture*, ed. Karin Barber. Bloomington: Indiana University Press.

Diawara, Manthia. 1992. *African Cinema: Politics and Culture*. Bloomington: Indiana University Press.

Duranti, Alessandro, and Charles Goodwin, eds. 1992. *Rethinking Context: Language as an Interactive Phenomenon*. Cambridge: Cambridge University Press.

Durham, Deborah. 2002. "Democratizing Dance: Institutional Transformation and Hegemonic Re-ordering in Postcolonial Jamaica." *Cultural Anthropology* 17 (4): 512–50.

Ebron, Paulla A. 2002. *Performing Africa*. Princeton: Princeton University Press.

Erlmann, Veit. 1992. "'The Past Is Far and the Future Is Far': Power and Performance among Zulu Migrant Workers." *American Ethnologist* 19 (4): 668–709.

———. 1996. *Nightsong: Performance, Power, and Practice in South Africa*. Chicago: University of Chicago Press.

Evans-Pritchard, E. E. 1940. *The Nuer: A Description of the Modes of Livelihood and Political Institutions of a Nilotic People*. Oxford: Clarendon.

Ewens, Graeme. 1991. *Africa O-ye! A Celebration of African Music*. London: Guinness.

———. 1994. *Congo Colossus: The Life and Legacy of Franco and OK Jazz*. North Walsham, Norfolk: Buku.

Fabian, Johannes. 1978. "Popular Culture in Africa: Findings and Conjectures." *Africa* 48 (4): 315–84.

———. 1983. *Time and the Other: How Anthropology Makes Its Object*. New York: Columbia University Press.

———. 1986. *Language and Colonial Power: The Appropriation of Swahili in the Former Belgian Congo (1880–1938)*. Cambridge: Cambridge University Press.

———. 1990. *Power and Performance: Ethnographic Explorations through Proverbial Wisdom and Theater in Shaba, Zaire*. Madison: University of Wisconsin Press.

———. 1996. *Remembering the Present: Painting and Popular History in Zaire*. Berkeley: University of California Press.

———. 1998. *Moments of Freedom: Anthropology and Popular Culture*. Charlottesville: University Press of Virginia.

Feld, Steven. 1982. *Sound and Sentiment: Birds, Weeping, Poetics, and Song in Kaluli Expression*. Philadelphia: University of Pennsylvania Press.

———. 2001. "A Sweet Lullaby for World Music." In *Globalization*, ed. Arjun Appadurai, 189–216. Durham: Duke University Press.

Feld, Steven, and Donald Brenneis. 2004. "Doing Anthropology in Sound." *American Ethnologist* 31 (4): 461–74.

Fortes, Meyer, and E. E. Evans-Pritchard. 1940, *African Political Systems*. London: Oxford University Press.

Friedman, Jonathan. 1990. "The Political Economy of Elegance: An African Cult of Beauty." *Culture and History*, no. 7:101–25.

Frith, Simon. 1996. *Performing Rites: On the Value of Popular Music*. Cambridge: Harvard University Press.

———, ed. 1989. *World Music, Politics, and Social Change: Papers from the International Association for the Study of Popular Music*. New York: Manchester University Press.

Gandoulou, Justin Daniel. 1989. *Dandies à Bacongo: Le culte de l'élégance dans la société congolaise contemporaine*. Paris: L'Harmattan.

Gellner, Ernest. 1994. *Encounters with Nationalism*. Oxford: Blackwell.

Geschiere, Peter. 1997. *The Modernity of Witchcraft: Politics and the Occult in Postcolonial Africa*, trans. Peter Geschiere and Janet Roitman. Charlottesville: University Press of Virginia.

———. 2005. "Funerals and Belonging: Different Patterns in South Cameroon." *African Studies Review* 48 (2): 45–64.

Giddens, Anthony. 1991. *Modernity and Self-Identity: Self and Society in the Late Modern Age*. Cambridge: Polity.

Gluckman, Max, with J. C. Mitchell and J. A. Barnes. 1949. "The Village Headman in British Central Africa." *Africa* 19 (2): 89–101.

Goffman, Erving. 1959. *The Presentation of Self in Everyday Life*. New York: Doubleday.

Gondola, Ch. Didier. 1990. "Kinshasa et Brazzaville: Brève histoire d'un mariage séculaire." *Zaïre-Afrique*, November–December, 249–50.

———. 1992. "Ata Ndele . . . et l'indépendence vint: Musique, jeunes et contestation politique dans les capitales congolaises." In *Les Jeunes en Afrique*, ed. Hélène d'Almeida-Topor et al., 463–87. Paris: L'Harmattan.

———. 1997. *Villes miroirs: Migrations et identités urbaines à Kinshasa et Brazzaville (1930–1970)*. Paris: L'Harmattan.

———. 1999. "Dream and Drama: The Search for Elegance among Congo Youth." *African Studies Review* 42 (1): 23–48.

Gramsci, Antonio. 1971. *Selections from the Prison Notebooks*. New York: Internation.

Guilbault, Jocelyne. 1993. *Zouk: World Music in the West Indies*. Chicago: University of Chicago Press.

Gupta, Akhil. 1995. "Blurred Boundaries: The Discourse of Corruption, the Culture of Politics, and the Imagined State." *American Ethnologist* 22 (2): 375–402.

Guyer, Jane I. 1993. "Wealth in People and Self-Realization in Equatorial Africa." *Man*, n.s., 28 (2): 243–65.

Guyer, Jane, and S. M. Eno Belinga. 1995. "Wealth in People as Wealth in Knowledge. Accumulation and Composition in Equatorial Africa." *Journal of African History*, no. 36:91–120.

Hannerz, Ulf. 1992. *Cultural Complexity: Studies in the Social Organization of Meaning*. New York: Columbia University Press.

Hansen, Thomas Blom, and Finn Stepputat, eds. 2001. *States of Imagination: Ethnographic Explorations of the Postcolonial State*. Durham: Duke University Press.

Hasty, Jennifer. 2005. *The Press and Political Culture in Ghana*. Bloomington: Indiana University Press.

Haugerud, Angelique. 1995. *The Culture of Politics in Modern Kenya*. Cambridge: Cambridge University Press.

Heath, Deborah. 1994. "The Politics of Appropriateness and Appropriation: Recontextualizing Women's Dance in Urban Senegal." *American Ethnologist* 21 (1): 88–103.

Hebdige, Dick. 1979. *Subculture: The Meaning of Style*. New York: Methuen.

Hecht, David, and Abdou Maliqalim Simone. 1994. *Invisible Governance: The Art of African Micropolitics*. Brooklyn, N.Y.: Autonomedia.

Hochschild, Adam. 1998. *King Leopold's Ghost: A Story of Greed, Terror, and Heroism in Colonial Africa*. New York: Mariner.

Holland, Dorothy, and Naomi Quinn. 1987. *Cultural Models in Language and Thought*. Cambridge: Cambridge University Press.

Hountondji, Paulin J. 1992. "Daily Life in Black Africa." In *The Surreptitious Speech: "Présence Africaine" and the Politics of Otherness, 1947–1987*, ed. V. Y. Mudimbe, 344–64. Chicago: University of Chicago Press.

Hunt, Nancy Rose. 1999. *A Colonial Lexicon of Birth Ritual, Medicalization, and Mobility in the Congo*. Durham: Duke University Press.

———. 2002. "Tintin and the Interruptions of Congolese Comics." In *Images and Empires: Visuality in Colonial and Postcolonial Africa*, ed. Paul S. Landau and Deborah D. Kaspin, 90–123. Berkeley: University of California Press.

Inongo, Sakombi. n.d. *Regards sur Kinshasa*. Kinshasa: Éditions Réunies.

Jewsiewicki, Bogumil. 1992a. *Art pictural zaïrois*. Sillery, Que.: Septentrion.

——. 1992b. "Jeux d'argent et de pouvoir au Zaïre: La 'bindomanie' et le crépuscule de la Deuxième République." *Politique africaine*, no. 46:55–70.

——. 1993. "Cheri Samba and the Postcolonial Reinvention of Modernity." *Callaloo* 16 (4): 772–95.

——. 1995. *Cheri Samba: The Hybridity of Art*. Montreal: Galérie Amrad African Art Publications.

——. 1996. "De l'art africain et de l'esthétique: valeur d'usage, valeur d'échange." *Cahiers d'études africaines* 141–42:257–69.

——. 2003a. *Mami Wata: La peinture urbaine au Congo*. Paris: Gallimard.

——, ed. 1999. *A Congo Chronicle: Patrice Lumumba in Urban Art*. New York: Museum for African Art.

——, ed. 2003b. *Musique urbaine au Katanga: De Malaika à Santa Kimbangu*. Paris: L'Harmattan.

Jewsiewicki, Bogumil, and Bob W. White. 2005. "Mourning and the Imagination of Political Time in Contemporary Central Africa: Introduction." *African Studies Review* 48 (2): 1–9.

Jones, Andrew F. 2001. *Yellow Music: Media Culture and Colonial Modernity in the Chinese Jazz Age*. Durham: Duke University Press.

Jules-Rosette, Bennetta. 1984. *The Messages of Tourist Art: An African Semiotic System in Comparative Perspective*. New York: Plenum.

Jules-Rosette, Bennetta, and Denis-Constant Martin. 1997. *Cultures populaires, identités et politique*. Paris: Cahiers du CERI.

Kambo, K. M. 1974. "Autour d'une mesure." *Zaïre*, June 3.

Kangafu, Kutumbagana. 1973. "Discours sur l'authenticité: Essai sur la problématique idéologique du recours à l'authenticité." Kinshasa: Presses Africaines.

Kapalanga, Gazungil Sang'Amin. 1989. *Les spectacles d'animation politique en République du Zaïre*. Louvain-la-Neuve: Cahiers théâtre Louvain.

Kapume, Kongha. 1978. "Constat de l'authenticité zaïroise aujourd'hui: Analyses et réflexions critiques." *Zaïre-Afrique*, no. 127:411–16.

Karp, Ivan. 1989. "Power and Capacity in Rituals of Possession." In *Creativity of Power: Cosmology and Action in African Societies*, ed. W. Arens and Ivan Karp, 91–112. Washington: Smithsonian Institution Press.

Kasongo, Émile L. 1997. "Affaire Wenge Musica: L'immaturité des musicians à la base de l'imbroglio." *La société*.

Kazadi, Wa Mukuna. 1979. "The Origin of Zairean Modern Music: A Socio-economic Aspect." *African Urban Studies*, no. 6:31–39.

Keil, Charles, and Steven Feld. 1994. *Music Grooves: Essays and Dialogues*. Chicago: University of Chicago Press.

Kenis, Vincent. 1995. Liner notes to CD "Roots of Rumba Rock 2: Zaire Classics, 1954–1955." Crammed Discs.

Kopytoff, Igor. 1986. "The Cultural Biography of Things: Commoditization as Process." In *The Social Life of Things: Commodities in Cultural Perspective*, ed. Arjun Appadurai, 64–94. Chicago: University of Chicago Press.

———, ed. 1987. *The African Frontier: The Reproduction of Traditional African Societies*. Bloomington: Indiana University Press.

Kratz, Corinnne A. 1994. *Affecting Performance: Meaning, Movement, and Experience in Okiek Women's Initiation*. Washington: Smithsonian Institution Press.

———. 2002. *The Ones That Are Wanted: Communication and the Politics of Representation in a Photographic Exhibition*. Berkeley: University of California Press.

Kulabakwenda, Tulengi. 1992. "Les animateurs culturels." In *Quelle politique culturelle pour la Troisième République du Zaïre?*, ed. I. Ndaywel è Nziem, 71–80. Kinshasa: Bibliothèque Nationale du Zaïre.

Larkin, Brian. 2002. "The Materiality of Cinema Theaters in Northern Nigeria." In *Media Worlds: Anthropology on New Terrain*, ed. Faye D. Ginsburg, Lila Abu-Lughod, and Brian Larkin, 319–36. Berkeley: University of California Press.

Lienhardt, Godfrey. 1958. "The Western Dinka." In *Tribes without Rulers*, ed. John Middleton and David Tait, 99–135. London: Routledge and Kegan Paul.

Likaka, Osumaka. 1997. *Rural Society and Cotton in Colonial Zaire*. Madison: University of Wisconsin Press.

Liyolo, Limbe M'Pwanga. 1992. "La culture, moteur du développement." In *Quelle politique culturelle pour la Troisième République du Zaïre?*, ed. I. Ndaywel è Nziem, 45–50. Kinshasa: Bibliothèque Nationale du Zaïre.

Lokele. 1985. *Hommage à Grand Kallé*. Kinshasa: Lokele.

Longa, Fo Eye Oto. 1992. "Les conditions d'une politique culturelle nationale. In *Quelle politique culturelle pour la Troisième République du Zaïre?*, ed. I. Ndaywel è Nziem, 193–98. Kinshasa: Bibliothèque Nationale du Zaïre.

Lonoh, M. B. 1969. *Essai de commentaire sur la musique congolaise moderne*. Kinshasa: S.E.I./A.N.C.

———. 1990. *Négritude, africanité et musique africaine*. Kinshasa: Centre de Recherches Pédagogiques.

Low, John. 1982. *Shaba Diary: A Trip to Rediscover the "Katanga" Guitar Styles and Songs of the 1950s and '60s*. Vienna: Elisabeth Stiglmayr.

Luzibu, Basilua. 1973. "L'évolution de la mentalité zaïroise perçue dans sa musique." *Zaïre-Afrique*, no. 79:531–41.

Mabika, Kalanda. 1967. *La remise en question, base de décolonisation mentale*. Brussels: Remarques africaines.

MacDougall, Jill. n.d. "Authentic Terrorists: The 'Balubwila' and the President's Ballet." Unpublished manuscript.

———. 1991. "The Tie and the Bra: Constructing the 'Postcolonial Body' in Zaire." Paper presented at the seminar "Identity, Rationality, and the Postcolonial Subject," Columbia University, February 28.

MacGaffey, Janet, ed. 1991. *The Real Economy of Zaire: The Contribution of Smuggling and Other Unofficial Activities to National Wealth*. Philadelphia: University of Pennsylvania Press.

MacGaffey, Janet, and Remy Bazenguissa-Ganga. 2000. *Congo-Paris: Transnational Traders on the Margins of the Law*. Bloomington: Indiana University Press.

MacGaffey, Wyatt. 2000. *Kongo Political Culture: The Conceptual Challenge of the Particular*. Bloomington: Indiana University Press.

Makobo, Serge. 1996. "Les noms dans la musique zaïroise: Tous, ils sont des sponsors." *Ndule Magazine*, November 15, p. 27.

Mamdani, Mahmood. 1996. *Citizen and Subject: Contemporary Africa and the Legacy of Colonialism*. Princeton: Princeton University Press.

Mankekar, Purnima. 1999. *Screening Culture, Viewing Politics: An Ethnography of Television, Womanhood, and Nation in Postcolonial India*. Durham: Duke University Press.

Manuel, Peter. 1993. *Cassette Culture: Popular Music and Technology in North India*. Chicago: University of Chicago Press.

Marcus, George, and Michael Fischer. 1986. *Anthropology as Cultural Critique*. Chicago: University of Chicago Press.

Martin, Denis-Constant. 2006. "Le charisme d'Ambedkar." *Anthropologie et sociétés* 30 (2): 27–42.

————, ed. 2002. *Sur la piste des OPNI (Objets politiques non identifiés)*. Paris: Karthala.

Martin, Phyllis M. 1994. "Contesting Clothes in Colonial Brazzaville." *Journal of African History* 35 (33): 401–26.

————. 1995. *Leisure and Society in Colonial Brazzaville*. New York: Cambridge University Press.

Mbembe, Achille. 1992a. "The Banality of Power and the Aesthetics of Vulgarity in the Postcolony." *Public Culture* 4 (2): 1–30.

————. 1992b. "Prosaics of Servitude and Authoritarian Civilities." *Public Culture* (5) 1: 123–48.

————. 2001. *On the Postcolony*. Berkeley: University of California Press.

McCracken, Grant. 1988. *Culture and Consumption: New Approaches to the Symbolic Character of Consumer Goods and Activities*. Bloomington: Indiana University Press.

McGovern, Michael. 2002. "Conflit régional et rhétorique de la contre-insurrection: Guinéens et réfugiés en septembre 2000." *Politique africaine*, no. 88:84–102.

Meintjes, Louise. 2003. *Sound of Africa: Making Music Zulu in a South African Studio*. Durham: Duke University Press.

Merriam, Alan P. 1964. *The Anthropology of Music*. Evanston, Ill.: Northwestern University Press.

Middleton, Richard. 1990. *Studying Popular Music*. Philadelphia: Open University Press.

Mikanza, Mobyem. 1992. "Pour une politique culturelle nationale." In *Quelle politique culturelle pour la Troisième République du Zaïre?*, ed. I. Ndaywel è Nziem, 199–220. Kinshasa: Bibliothèque Nationale du Zaïre.

Miller, Daniel. 1994. *Modernity: An Ethnographic Approach; Dualism and Mass Consumption in Trinidad*. Oxford: Berg.

Mobutu, Sese Seko, n.d. *Discours, allocutions et messages.* Kinshasa: Bureau du Président-Fondateur du Zaïre.

———. 1982. "Discours du Président-Fondateur du Mouvement Populaire de la Révolution, président de la République, le citoyen Mobutu Sese Seko Kuku Ngbendu Wa Za Banga." In *Authenticité et développement: Actes du Colloque national sur l'authenticité,* ed. Union des Écrivains Zaïrois. Paris: Présence Africaine.

Molei, Molanga. 1979. *Kinshasa: Ce village d'hier.* Kinshasa: SODIMCA.

Monga, Celestin. 1996. *The Anthropology of Anger: Civil Society and Democracy in Africa.* Boulder: Lynne Rienner.

Moore, Robin. 1997. *Nationalizing Blackness: Afrocubanismo and Artistic Revolution in Havana, 1920–1940.* Pittsburgh: University of Pittsburgh Press.

Muhima, Sebisogo. 1975. "Le rôle du 'salongo' (travail manuel) dans les écoles." *Zaïre-Afrique,* no. 95:273–92.

Mukulumanya wa N'Gate, Zenda. 1982. "Authenticité: Mythe ou identité?" In *Authenticité et développement: Actes du Colloque national sur l'authenticité,* ed. Union des Écrivains Zaïrois, 65–96. Paris: Présence Africaine.

Mumbanza, Mondo. 1999. "Luambo Franco: Artiste et manager." M.A. thesis, Institut National des Arts, Kinshasa.

Murphy, John. 1999. "Kinshasa's Music, Congo's War." BBC online, November 11.

Mwissa, Camille Kuyu. 1993. "Musique et regulations des relations entre les sexes à Kinshasa." Ph.D. diss., Université Paris I, Panthéon-Sorbonne.

Naipaul, V. S. 1979. *A Bend in the River.* New York: Penguin.

Ndaywel è Nziem, I. 1993. "La société zaïroise dans le miroir de son discours religieux (1990–1993)." *Cahiers Africains / Afrika Studies* 6:39–50.

———. 1998. *Histoire générale du Congo: De l'héritage ancien à la République Démocratique.* Brussels: Duculot.

Ngangura, Mwenze, and Benoit Lamy, dirs. 1987. *La vie est belle.* VHS, California Newsreel.

Ngimbi, Mbumba. 1982. *Kinshasa, 1881–1981: Cent ans après Stanley.* Kinshasa: Centre de Recherches Pédagogiques.

Ngoye, Achille. 1993. *Kin-la joie, Kin-la folie.* Paris: L'Harmattan.

Nkanga, Dieudonné Mbala. 1992. "'Radio Trottoir' in Central Africa." *Passages,* no. 4:4–5, 8.

———. 1999. "Touma et Atalaku, un aspect de la dynamique du spectacle dans *Qui a mangé Madame d'Avoine Bergotha?*" In *Francophonie littéraire africaine en procès: Le destin de Sony Labou Tansi,* ed. Drocella Mwisha Rwanika and Nyunda ya Rubango. Paris: Silex / Nouvelles du Sud.

Nkashama, P. Ngandu. 1979. "Ivresse et vertige: Les nouvelles danses des jeunes au Zaïre." *L'Afrique littéraire et artistique,* no. 51:94–102.

———. 1992. "La chanson de la rupture dans la musique zaïroise moderne." In *Papier blanc, encre noire: Cents ans de culture francophone en Afrique centrale (Zaïre, Rwanda et Burundi),* ed. Marc Quaghebeur and Emile van Balberghe, 477–89. Brussels: Labor.

Nlandu Mayamba, Thierry. Forthcoming. "La musique congolaise: Entre le miroir cassé et le miroir recollé." In *L'Ethnographie de l'écoute*, ed. Lye M. Yoka and Bob White. Paris: L'Harmattan.

Nlandu-Tsasa, Cornelis. 1997. *La rumeur au Zaïre de Mobutu: Radio-trottoir à Kinshasa*. Paris: L'Harmattan.

Ntondo, Ladji. 1997–98. "La piraterie c'est le SIDA de la musique en Afrique centrale." *Afro-Vision*, December–February, 21–22.

Olema, Debhonvapi. 1984. "Société zaïroise dans le miroir de la chanson populaire." *Canadian Journal of African Studies* 18 (1): 122–30.

———. 1998. "La satire amusée des inégalités socio-économiques dans la chanson populaire urbaine du Zaïre: Une étude de l'oeuvre de Franco (François Luambo) des années 70 et 80." Ph.D. diss., Université de Montréal.

Ortner, Sherry B. 1973. "On Key Symbols." *American Anthropologist* 75 (15): 1338–46.

———. 1984. "Theory in Anthropology since the Sixties." *Comparative Studies in Society and History* 26 (1): 126–66.

———. 1995. "Resistance and the Problem of Ethnographic Refusal." *Comparative Studies in Society and History* 37 (1): 173–93.

Pacini Hernandez, Deborah. 1995. *Bachata: A Social History of a Dominican Popular Music*. Philadelphia: Temple University Press.

Packard, Randall. 1981. *Chiefship and Cosmology: An Historical Study of Political Competition*. Bloomington: Indiana University Press.

Paine, Robert. 1971. "A Theory of Patronage and Brokerage." In *Patrons and Brokers in the East Arctic*. St. John's: Institute of Social and Economic Research, Memorial University of Newfoundland.

Pongo, Martin Kalulambi. 2000. "Dires, délires et extases dans la chanson de la rupture." *Ethnologies* 22 (1): 115–38.

Popovitch, Mirko, and Kwami Zinga. 1993. "Tango ya Ba Wendo." Brussels: Ti-Suka.

Powdermaker, Hortense. 1966. *Stranger and Friend: The Way of an Anthropologist*. New York: W. W. Norton.

Prezio, Mac. 1996. "Reddy Amisi: Je ne suis pas maître de mon destin." Unpublished manuscript.

Pwono, Damien M. 1992. "The Institutionalization of African Popular Music in Zaire." M.A. thesis, University of Pittsburgh.

Pype, Katrien. 2006. "Dancing for God or the Devil: Pentecostal Discourse on Popular Dance in Kinshasa." *Journal of Religion in Africa* 36 (3–4): 296–318.

Quinn, Naomi. 2005. *Finding Culture in Talk: A Collection of Methods*. New York: Palgrave.

Radio France International. 1992. "Rumba cha-cha: Musiques des deux Congos (1950–1960)." CD liner notes. Paris: RFI.

République du Zaïre. 1979. *Actes du Deuxième Congrès Ordinaire du M.P.R., 23–27 novembre*. Kinshasa: Institut Makanda Kabobi.

Richards, Paul. 1996. *Fighting for the Rain Forest: War, Youth, and Resources in Sierra Leone*. Oxford: James Currey.

Roberts, Allen F. 1984. "The Comeuppance of 'Mr. Snake,' and Other Tales of Survival from Contemporary Rural Zaire." In *The Crisis in Zaire: Myths and Realities*, ed. Georges Nzongola-Ntalaja, 113–22. Trenton: Africa World.

Rubango, Nyunda ya. 2001. *Les pratiques discursives du Congo-Belge au Congo-Kinshasa: Une interprétation socio-linguistique.* Paris: L'Harmattan.

Rycroft, David. 1962. "The Guitar Improvisations of Mwenda Jean Bosco (Part II)." *African Music* 3 (1): 86–102.

Sahlins, Marshall. 1961. "The Segmentary Lineage: An Organization of Predatory Expansion." *American Anthropologist*, no. 63:322–44.

Schatzberg, Michael G. 1978. "Fidelité au guide: The J.M.P.R. in Zairian Schools." *Journal of Modern African Studies* 16 (3): 417–31.

———. 1988. *The Dialectics of Oppression in Zaire.* Bloomington: Indiana University Press.

———. 1993. "Power, Legitimacy, and Democratization in Africa." *Africa* 63 (4): 445–61.

———. 2001. *Political Legitimacy in Middle Africa: Father, Family, Food.* Bloomington: Indiana University Press.

Schulz, Dorothea. 1999. "Pricey Publicity, Refutable Reputations: *Jeliw* and the Economics of Honour in Mali." *Paideuma*, no. 45:275–92.

Seitel, Peter. 1999. *The Powers of Genre: Interpreting Haya Oral Literature.* London: Oxford University Press.

Senghor, L. S. 1976. "Authenticité et négritude." *Zaïre-Afrique*, no. 102:81–86.

Shain, Richard M. 2002. "Roots in Reverse: Cubanismo in Twentieth Century Senegalese Music." *International Journals of African Historical Studies* 35 (1): 83–101.

Spitulnik, Debra. 2002. "Mobile Machines and Fluid Audiences: Rethinking Reception through Zambian Radio Culture." In *Media Worlds: Anthropology on New Terrain*, ed. Faye D. Ginsburg, Lila Abu-Lughod, and Brian Larkin, 337–54. Berkeley: University of California Press.

Steiner, Christopher B. 1994. *African Art in Transit: The Production of Value and Mediation of Knowledge in the African Art Trade.* Cambridge: Cambridge University Press.

Stewart, Gary. 2000. *Rumba on the River: A History of the Music of the Two Congos.* New York: Verso.

Stolzoff, Norman. 2000. *Wake the Town and Tell the People: Dancehall Culture in Jamaica.* Durham: Duke University Press.

Strother, Zoe S. 1997. *Inventing Masks: Agency and History in the Art of the Central Pende.* Chicago: University of Chicago Press.

Tagg, Philip. 1989. "Open Letter: Black Music, Afro-American, and European Music." *Popular Music* 8 (3): 285–98.

Tagg, Philip, and Bob Clarida. 2003. *Ten Little Title Tunes.* Montreal: Mass Media Music Scholars' Press.

Taussig, Michael. 1980. *The Devil and Commodity Fetishism in South America.* Chapel Hill: University of North Carolina Press.

————. 1997. *The Magic of the State*. New York: Routledge.

Taylor, Charles. 1991. *The Malaise of Modernity*. Toronto: House of Anansi.

Taylor, Julie. 1998. *Paper Tangos*. Durham: Duke University Press.

Taylor, Timothy D. 2007. "The Commodification of Music at the Dawn of the Era of 'Mechanical Music.'" *Ethnomusicology* 51 (2).

Tchebwa, Manda. 1996. *La terre de la chanson: La musique zaïroise hier et aujourd'hui*. Brussels: Duculot.

Tempels, Placide. 1949. *La philosophie bantoue*. Paris: Présence Africaine.

Toulabor, C. 1986. *Le Togo sous Eyadéma*. Paris: Karthala.

Trefon, Theodore, ed. 2004. *Reinventing Order in the Congo: How People Respond to State Failure in Kinshasa*. New York: Zed.

Tsambu Bulu, Léon, 2004. "Musique et violence à Kinshasa." In *Ordre et désordre à Kinshasa: Réponses populaires à la faillite de l'état*, ed. Theodore Trefon, 193–212. Paris: L'Harmattan.

Tshijuke, K. 1988. "De l'abbé Charles Mbuya à Mukwa Bumba: L'histoire religieuse dans la chanson populaire." In *Dialoguer avec le léopard*, ed. Bogumil Jewsiewicki and H. Monot, 131–41. St. Foy: SAFI.

Tshimanga, Charles. 1999. "Scoutisme et formation de l'élite au Congo-Kinshasa, 1920–1960." *Congo-Afrique*, no. 333:161–75.

Tshonga, Onyumbe. 1982. "Nkisi, nganga, et ngangankisi dans la musique zaïroise moderne de 1960 à 1981." *Zaïre-Afrique*, no. 169:555–68.

————. 1983. "Le thème de l'argent dans la musique zaïroise moderne de 1960 à 1981." *Zaïre-Afrique*, no. 172:97–111.

————. 1984. "La femme vue par l'homme dans la musique zaïroise moderne de 1960 à 1981." *Zaïre-Afrique* 184:229–43.

————. 1988. "La société à travers la chanson zaïroise moderne." In *Dialoguer avec le Léopard*, ed. B. Jewsiewicki and H. Moniot, 150–78. St. Foy: SAFI.

————. 1994. "Urban Music and Public Rumor: Popular Expression against Political Authority in Zaire." Paper presented at the Institute for Advanced Study and Research in the African Humanities, Northwestern University, Evanston, Ill.

Tumba, Kekwo. 1992. "Guérir du kwashiorkor culturel." In *Quelle politique culturelle pour la Troisième République du Zaïre?*, ed. I. Ndaywel è Nziem, 89–92. Kinshasa: Bibliothèque Nationale du Zaïre.

Turino, Thomas. 2000. *Nationalists, Cosmopolitans, and Popular Music in Zimbabwe*. Chicago: University of Chicago Press.

Turner, Victor. 1957. *Schism and Continuity in an African Society: A Study of Village Life*. New York: Humanities Press.

————. 1969. *The Ritual Process: Structure and Anti-structure*. Chicago: Aldine.

Tutashinda, N. 1974. "Les mystifications de l'authenticité." *La Pensée*, no. 175:68–81.

Union des Écrivains Zaïrois. 1982. *Authenticité et développement: Actes du Colloque national sur l'authenticité*. Paris: Présence Africaine.

United Nations Development Program. 1993. *Human Development Index*. New York: United Nations.

Vansina, Jan. 1982. "Mwasi's Trials." *Daedalus* 3 (2): 49–70.

———. 1990. *Paths in the Rainforest: Toward a History of Political Tradition in Equatorial Africa*. Madison: University Wisconsin Press.

Vellut, J. L. 1974. *Guide de l'étudiant en histoire du Zaïre*. Kinshasa: Centre de Recherches Pédagogiques.

Vianna, Hermano. 1999. *The Mystery of Samba: Popular Music and National Identity in Brazil*. Chapel Hill: University of North Carolina Press.

Volosinov, V. N. 1973. *Marxism and the Philosophy of Language*. Cambridge: Harvard University Press.

Wade, Peter. 2000. *Music, Race, and Nation: Musica Tropical in Colombia*. Chicago: University of Chicago Press.

Walser, Robert. 1993. *Running with the Devil: Power, Gender, and Madness in Heavy Metal Music*. Hanover, N.H.: Wesleyan University Press.

Walser, Robert, and Susan McClary. 1990. "Start Making Sense! Musicology Wrestles with Rock." In *On Record: Rock, Pop, and the Written Word*, ed. Simon Frith and Andrew Goodwin. New York: Routledge.

Walu, Engundu. 1999. "Images des femmes et rapports entre les sexes dans la musique populaire du Zaïre." Ph.D. diss., University of Amsterdam.

Waterman, Christopher. 1990. *Juju: A Social History and Ethnography of an African Popular Music*. Chicago: University of Chicago Press.

Werbner, Richard, and Terence Ranger, eds. 1996. *Postcolonial Identities in Africa*. Atlantic Highlands, N.J.: Zed.

White, Bob W. 1999. "Modernity's Trickster: 'Dipping' and 'Throwing' in Congolese Popular Dance Music." *Research in African Literatures* 30 (4): 156–75.

———. 2000. "Soukouss or Sell-Out? Congolese Popular Dance Music on the World Market." In *Commodities and Globalization: Anthropological Perspectives*, ed. Angelique Haugerud, M. Priscilla Stone, and Peter D. Little. New York: Rowman and Littlefield.

———. 2002. "Congolese Rumba and Other Cosmopolitanisms." *Cahiers d'études africaines* 62 (4) 168: 663–86.

———. 2004a. "The Elusive *Lupemba*: Rumors about Fame and (Mis)Fortune in Mobutu's Zaire." In *Reinventing Order in the Congo: How People Respond to State Failure in Kinshasa*, ed. Theodore Trefon, 174–91. New York: Zed.

———. 2004b. "Modernity's Trickster: 'Dipping' and 'Throwing' in Congolese Popular Dance Music." In *African Drama and Performance*, ed. John Conteh-Morgan and Tejumola Olaniyan. Bloomington: Indiana University Press.

———. 2005. "The Political Undead: Is It Possible to Mourn for Mobutu's Zaire?" *African Studies Review* 48 (2): 65–85.

———. 2006a. "L'incroyable machine d'authenticité: L'animation politique et l'usage public de la culture dans le Zaïre de Mobutu." *Anthropologie et sociétés* 30 (2): 43–64.

————. 2006b. "Pardon, Pardon." Multimedia project, Critical World, www.critical world.net.

————. 2006c. "Pour un lâcher prise de la culture." *Anthropologie et sociétés* 30 (2): 7–26.

————. Forthcoming. "Écouter ensemble, penser tout haut: La musique populaire et l'émergence des consciences politiques au Zaïre de Mobutu." In *L'Ethnographie de l'écoute*, ed. Lye M. Yoka and Bob W. White. Paris: L'Harmattan.

White, Bob W., and Lye M. Yoka. 2006. "Audience-Based Research in the Era of Democratization." *Civilisations* 55 (1–2): 223–36.

Wikan, Unni. 1992. "Beyond the Words: The Power of Resonance." *American Ethnologist* 19 (3): 460–82.

Willame, Jean-Claude. 1992. *L'automne d'un despotisme*. Paris: Karthala.

Williams, Raymond. 1976. *Keywords: A Vocabulary of Culture and Society*. New York: Oxford University Press.

————. 1997. *Marxism and Literature*. New York: Oxford University Press.

Wrong, Michela. 2000. *In the Footsteps of Mr. Kurtz: Living on the Brink of Disaster in the Congo*. London: Fourth Estate.

Yoka, Lye M. 1995. *Lettres d'un Kinois à l'oncle du village*. Paris: L'Harmattan.

————. 2000. *Kinshasa, signes de vie*. Paris: L'Harmattan.

Yoka, Lye M., and Vi Kan'sy Kinkela. Forthcoming. *Cinquante ans de contestation dans la musique populaire au Congo-Zaïre*.

Young, Crawford, and Thomas Turner. 1985. *The Rise and Decline of the Zairian State*. Madison: University of Wisconsin Press.

DISCOGRAPHY

Adou Elenga. "Ata Ndele." *Rumba Cha Cha Cha: Musique des Deux Congos* (RFI, 1992).

African Jazz. "Indépendance Cha Cha." *Succès des années 50–60 (vol. 1)* (Sonodisc, 1997).

Bana O.K. "Tu es mon seul problème." *Tonnere Show* (Sonodisc, 1997).

Delta Force. "Charly la suissesse." *Confirmation* (Clarys Music, 1999).

Empire Bakuba. "Dieu seul sait." *Dieu Seul Sait* (Empire Flash Diffusion Business, 1997).

Général Defao et les Big Stars. "Alain Mbiya," " Ya Gégé." *Dernier Album* (Antabel Production, 1995).

———. "Famille Kikuta." *Famille Kikuta* (Defao Production, 1995).

———. "Hitachi." *Hitachi* (AN0908DF, 1990).

Koffi Olomide et Quartier Latin. " Fouta Djallon." *V12* (Sonodisc, 1995).

———. "Ko ko ko ko." *Affaire d'État* (Sonodisc, 2003).

———. "Papa na Roissy." *Ultimatum* (Sonodisc, 1997).

———. "Zaniha." *Droit de véto* (Sonodisc, 1999).

Lofombo. "Femme infidèle." *Lofombo "Kamola Basse"* (B. Mas Production, 1995).

O.K. Jazz. "Coupe du monde." *Franco et Josky, Pepe Ndombe en Compagnie du T.P. O.K. Jazz* (Sonodisc, 1994).

———. "La Vie des Hommes." *Franco et le Tout Puissant O.K. Jazz* (Sonodisc, 1989).

Pépé Kallé. "Chef de quartier." *Pardon, Pardon* (Unicef, 1996).

Reddy Amisi. "Libala." *Prudence* (Galaxie Productions, 1994).

Super Choc. "Shabani." *Mandundu* (B. Mas Production, 1996).

Tabu Ley Rochereau. "Kashama." *Bel Ley (Mpeve ya Longo)* (Edition Verckys, 1984).

Verckys Kiamanguana. "Nakomitunaka." *Bankoko Baboyi* (Sonodisc, 1998).

Viva La Musica. "Jeancy." *Nouvelle Écriture* (Sonodisc, 1997).

———. "Perdue de vue." *Pôle Position* (Sonodisc, 1995).

———. "Phrase." *Mzee Fula-Ngenge* (Sonodisc, 1999).

Wenge Musica B.C.B.G. "Feux de l'amour." *Feux de l'Amour* (Simon Music, 1996).

———. "Kin é bouger." *Kin é Bouger* (B. Mas Production, 1991).

———. "Libération." *Titanic* (Simon Music, 1998).

———. "Serge Palmi." *Titanic* (Simon Music, 1998).

———. "T.H." *T.H.* (Simon Music, 2000).

Wenge Musica Maison Mère. "Treize ans." *Kibuisa Mpimpa* (JPS Production, 2001).

Zaiko Langa Langa. "Amoureux Décu." *Hits Inoubliables Volume VIII* (Éditions Imbuma, 1997).

———. "Eluzam." *Les Éveilleurs de l' Orchestre Zaiko Langa Langa* (Éds. Ngoyarto, 1996).

———. "Persévérer." *Nous y Sommes* (Établissements N'diaye, 1998).

———. "Reviens Shaaly." *Backline Lesson One* (Sonima Music, 1997).

INDEX

Page numbers in *italics* refer to illustrations.

Anthropologists (continued)
phers, 69; arrogance avoided by, xv; ethnographic present used by, 98; as instrument of knowledge, 132; as "natives," 16

Askew, Kelly, 68, 99, 164, 166, 257 n. 2

Atalaku, 27, 59–64, 103, 110–12, 116, 119, 121, 151, 159, 163, 170, 174, 176, 206, 263 n. 9; *animation* and, 63; cultural policy and, 11; marginal status in band of, 58, 152, 157; mood of *seben* and, 58, 113; origins of term, 58; shouts vs. sung-shouts, 51; "traditional" music and, 152; training to become, 152–58. See also Animation

Audience-performer interactions, 98, 107, 123, 152, 193; accommodating audiences, 125–27, 128–29; *atalaku* and, 113, 116–19, 221; auditions and, 145–46; co-construction of narratives and, 135–36; dancing and, 145–46; fans and fan clubs, 137, 138–39, 161; *libanga* as form of, 162–64; 170–77; musicians in public, 138–41, 238; picture taking, 125–27; song requests, 124; songs by commission, 173, 190, 236. See also Spraying

Audiences, xv, 25, 79–80, 100, 114, 116–19, 123, 126–29, 165–94, 247–50; *animation politique* experienced by, 73; expectations of, 108, 120, 127, 178; female, 193; foreign, 66; participation of, 34, 48, 49, 55, 109–10, 120, 124, 225; response to dancing of, 146; response to first *atalaku* of, 61–62

Authenticité, 25, 27, 64, 65, 69, 78; changing names and, 71; conference on, 76; explaining, 79; as ideology, 72; responses to, 259 n. 14; theories of culture and, 70; women and, 72

Authenticity, 70, 157, 174, 259 n. 12

Averill, Gage, 13, 99, 257 n. 1, 267 n. 1

Bakhtin, Mikhail, 30, 176, 266 n. 10

Balandier, Georges, 16–18

Balloux, Lascony, 261 n. 35

Bana Odeon, 34, 60–61

Bana O.K., 23, 56, 177, 244, 264 n. 15. *See also* O.K. Jazz

Bandalungwa (Bandal), xiv, 17, 34, 133, 143, 145, 238

Bandleaders, 10–11, 37–54; 108, 196, 204, 214–23; authority delegated by, 208–11; junior, 144, 159, 200–202, 207–13; leadership qualities of, 243–48; leadership styles of, 232–38; loyalty tested by, 211–13; musicians vs., 200; musicians reprimanded by, 205–7; treatment of musicians by, 149, 195, 197–99, 203, 238. *See also* Leadership

Bars, 22, 40, 103–4, 121, 125, 137, 138

Bas-Congo (Bas-Zaïre; Lower Congo), 4, 34, 39, 74, 83, 121, 229–30, 234

Batêtes (Junior Leaders), 144, 159, 200–202, 207–13

Bavon Siongo ("Bavon" Marie Marie), 53

Bayart, Jean-François, 214, 225, 227

Bayouda du Zaïre, 35

Beatles, 230

Bébé Atalaku, 59–62, 63, 153–56

Beer, 103, 104, 120, 128, 138, 176

Belgian Congo, xxi, 39, 40–42, 68–69, 82, 230, 231, 240

Belgicains, 45, 47

Belgium, 42, 45, 46, 66, 94, 226

Bholen, Léon, 52–53

Biaya, T. K., 23, 241–43, 245, 254 n. 8

"Big man" leadership, 7, 15, 122, 170, 219–23, 229, 243

Big Stars, xii, 100–107, 108, 115, 116–19, 121–25, 128–29, 141–53, 155–64, 175, 188–90, 199–204, 219–23

"Bill Clinton" (Didier Kalonji), 59, 62

Bleu de Bleu, 121

Bowane, Henri, 41, 262 n. 38

Brazzaville, 16–19, 39, 141; Kinshasa vs., 20–21, 28

Brussels, 171, 172

Brown, James, 39

Bukasa, Leon, 40

Bumbu (neighborhood in Kinshasa), 17, 133, 204

Busé, J. P., 59, 175, 215–16, 247, 268 n. 12

Canada, 2, 216, 226, 249

Capitalism, 18

Cassettes, 33, 37, 84, 261 n. 31; duplication of, 85, 88–89; prices of, 87; sale of, 86–93; types of, 86–87

Catholic Church, 36; musical training and, 52

Cavacha rhythm, 56–57

Celebrity, 61–64, 131–41; being, 37–51, 134, 135, 136, 144, 198, 199; gestures of, 104–5, 134; narratives of, 135–36

Censorship, 68

Chefs. See Leadership

China, 74

Cities, 16–24

Clave rhythm, 40, 57

Clothing, 78, 133, 142–43, 160; in context of live performance, 101–2, 106, 107, 109, 110; *sape* phenomenon and, 141; as source of income, 100

Colonialism, 34, 76, 231, 250; Belgian, 68–69; cultural policy and popular culture under, 69; French, 39; French vs. Belgian, 18

Colonie Belge, 230, 231, 270 n. 7

Conflict, 1–2, 4–8, 69, 195–223; as form of analysis, 16

Congo, Democratic Republic of (Congo-Zaïre; Congo-Kinshasa), 4, 17; name changed by, xxi, 196; perceptions of, 63; stereotypes of, 3, 9, 18

Congo, Popular Republic of (Congo-Brazzaville), 16–21, 39–40, 141, 177,
208, 254 n. 1, 255 n. 9; 256 n. 19, 264 n. 2

Congolese diaspora, 37, 65–66, 226–27, 247–49

Congolese people: ethnic identity and, 69; ideas about *poto* (abroad) among, 22; perceptions abroad of, 3, 9; self-perceptions of, 19, 63; stereotypes of, 9, 18. *See also* Audiences

Congo River, 4, 101; crossing of, 19–20

Consumption, 42, 91, 166; *sape* phenomenon and, 141

Copyrights, 84, 85, 122, 261 n. 33

Corps des Volontaires de la République (CVR), 74

Corruption, 65, 71, 82, 227–28, 230; *animation politique* and, 79; upon entering country, 19

Cosmopolitanism, 52, 255 n. 7, 257 n. 2

Crisis, economic and political, xiii, 9–10, 13, 23, 35, 81, 93, 165, 189, 192–93, 225

Culture: definitions of, 13–14, 68–69; emergent cultural forms, 167; mobilization for political purposes of, 64, 67–82, 97; popular culture vs., 14; as source of happiness, 80; as source of national pride, 71, 81

Cultural borrowing, 27, 120, 122

Cultural brokers, 91–93. *See also* Distributors and redistributors

Cultural commodities, xv. *See also* Cultural Products

Cultural policy: during colonial period, 69, 75; during Mobutu era, 11, 43, 54, 64, 65, 66–79, 97, 193; music industry and, 81–82; tradition in, 11, 34, 42, 69–70; UNESCO publications on, 68

Cultural products, xiii, xv, 8, 14

Cultural stereotypes, 9

CVR, 74

119, 120, 123, 124, 128–29, 138, 141, 144, 158–59, 161–63, 173, 175, 180, 183, 188–90, 199–200, 201, 203, 216, 218, 220

Generations, 39–46, 52, 169, 197, 231; biological and musical, 37, 256 n. 14; fourth, 38, 47–51, 54; seniority and, 37; "spiritual ancestors," 198; tension between, 62, 243–44

Genres: differentiation of, 30, 38, 51; in popular music, 25, 29–32; speech and, 30, 176; work of, 177; of writing about popular music, 28

Ghenda, Raphael, 5–6

Globalization: foreign musics and, 11, 39, 42, 45, 255; "larger impersonal systems" and, 14; western presence in Congo, 71, 131–32, 227–28, 250

Gluckman, Max, 16

Gombe (neighborhood in Kinshasa), 17, 153, 240

Gramsci, Antonio, 196–97

Grand Kallé (Kabasele, Joseph), 42, 43, 51, 198, 230, 245

Grand marché (central market), 86, 89

Grand Zaiko Wawa, 215–16

Griots, 79, 173, 240, 266 n. 14

Grooves, 55, 108

Guidomanie, 3–8

Guitars, 50, 53, 55, 100, 105, 109, 114, 129, 133, 134, 146; drums vs., 32, 58; first-generation musicians and, 40; layering of, 32, 58; learning to play, 148–52; *ondemba* vs. *fiesta* styles and, 52; palm wine style, 56, 256 n. 16; polyrhythms and, 148–49; rhythm vs. lead, 148; *seben* and, 56, 57–58

GV series, 39–40

Hair salons, 22, 23

Hegemony, 72, 196

Heidegger, Martin, 70

Herder, J. H., 70

Hierarchies, 197–212, 231; terms of address in, 203

"Hit songs," 107, 169, 182–94

Hunt, Nancy Rose, 14, 230

Ideology, 69, 72, 75, 76

Ilo Pablo, 20, 91, 216

Improvisation, 108

Independence, 36, 44, 69, 71, 147, 242

Informal economy: diamond trade and music, 262 n. 37, musicians' dependence on, 25; music industry and, 66, 84–92, 105

Jackson, Michael (artist), xii, 39

Jewsiewicki, Bogumil, 3, 15, 231, 244, 250, 251, 253 n. 5, 256 n. 15, 256 n. 18, 262 n. 3

Journée des trois Z, 71

Kabasele, Joseph (Grand Kallé), 42, 43, 51, 198, 230, 245

Kabasele, Yampanya (Pépé Kallé), 133, 236–38, 239, 240, 248

Kabila, Laurent Désiré: popular musicians and, 1–3; rebel mouvement led by, 5

Kabosé, 159

Kaludji, Tutu, 59

Kapalanga, Gazungil Sang'Amin, 73, 75, 76, 259 n. 15

Kapita, 230

Kasanda, Nicolas (Dr. Nico), 42, 45, 52, 132, 133, 199, 243, 245

Kenis, Vincent, 59, 255 n. 10

Keywords approach, 167

Kikongo, 32, 58, 59, 80, 229–30

Kinois, 21, 28, 156, 241, 245

Kinoiseries, 241–43

Kinshasa, 4, 16–19, 46, 60, 66, 101, 140, 142, 153, 165, 171, 178, 183, 194, 229;

Male-female relations, 11, 111, 267 nn. 20–21; couples dancing, 109–10; female dancers as scapegoats, 202, 216–17; male artists and female audiences, 193; marriage, 180, 185–87, 188–89; romantic love in song lyrics, 178–94

Malueka (neighborhood in Kinshasa), 183, 185

Manchester School, 16–18

Maneko, Chef, 100, 102, 105, 146, 148–50, 152, 159, 221

Mangwana, Sam, 101, 198

Manwaku, Fely, 243–44, 248

Maracas (spray can), 11, 12, 60; learning to play, 153–55

Marxism, 98

Matadi, xii, 200, 234

Matanga (public mourning ceremony), 33, 73, 237

Matonge (neighborhood in Kinshasa), 21, 34, 37, 66

Matou, Samuel, 38

Mayamba, Thierry Nlandu, 230–31, 249

MAZADIS (*Manufacture Zaïroise du Disque*), 82, 84, 94

Mbala, Théo, 163

Mbemba, Shora, 137–39

Mbembe, Achille, 15, 16, 196, 219, 226, 250, 267 n. 2, n. 4

Mbongo, Lokassa ya, 150

Mediation, 16, 24

Micropolitics, 195–23, 267 n. 2

Military, 3, 175, 203; musicians and, 245

Mining industry, 39

Ministry of Culture, 5–6, 19, 237

Missionaries, 36, 69, 75

Mobile vendors, 92–93, 104, 105; authorities avoided by, 89, 90, 91; sales and income of, 90; sales strategies of, 91

Mobutu, Mwenze Kongolo ("Saddam Hussein"), 5, 175

Mobutu Sese Seko, 70; associations with, 227; authenticity politics under, 64, 69–79; authoritarian rule and, 45, 77, 249; corruption under, 65, 71, 82, 227–28, 230; cultural policy under, 66–78; divisiveness exploited by, 7; Franco and, 238–41; FROJEMO, 234–36; as head of MPR, 3; as head of Zaïre, 77; as heroic figure, 75, 233, 243; honorific titles of, 7; intellectuals and, 78; as *kapita*, 230; legacy of, 3, 25, 228, 230, 239, 247, 249; longevity of, 226; monuments to, 77; nationalism and, 69; opposition to, 79, 80; perceptions of, 24; popular musicians and, 1–3, 24, 45, 79–82, 238–41, 245; removal from power of, 1; resistance to, 226–27; rhetorical strategies of, 8; secret service of, 79; singing and dancing as tools of, 69, 80; Southeast Asia visited by, 74–75; speeches of, 72, 75, 80, 245, 259 n. 19; Western representations of, 227–28; Zaïre under, 131, 165, 174, 178, 192, 195, 225, 233, 249, 250, 252

Mobutisme, 4, 71, 77, 248, 258 n. 12

Modernism: *passion moderniste*, 17; *ondemba* vs. *fiesta* schools, 51–54

Modernity, 42, 152; symbols of, 18; nation-state as symbol of, 69

Money, 182; as source of conflict in musical groups, 218–19, 221–23; songs by commission, 173, 190, 236. *See also* Spraying

Montana, 102, 103, 106, 144–47, 159, 200

Montreal, 2, 216, 247, 249

MOPAP, 81

Mouvement Populaire de la Révolution (M.P.R.), 71, 73, 78; formation of, 3; one-party rule and, 240

M'piana, J. B., 5–6, 7–8, 9, 50, 138, 183–85, 230, 232, 243, 253 n. 4. *See also* Wenge Musica

Mumbafu, Djuna, 59, 61, 120, 239, 257 n. 28. *See also* Empire Bakuba

Mundele, 143, 147

Musical equipment, 53, 104, 133, 142, 204

Musical groups: amateur, 104–5, 120, 257 n. 23; auditions for, 145–47; band meetings, 205–7; hierarchy within, 140; 197–213, 231; in Kinshasa, 262 n. 6; offspring of, 52, 244; promotional strategies of, 93; seniority within, 197; size of, 43, 197, 208; social organization of, 33, 25, 43, 46, 99, 195–223

Musical instrumentation, 32, 34, 36, 40, 43, 57, 197

Musicians: amateur, 104–5; *animation politique* and, 75; arrogance and humility of, 139–41; auditions by, 145–47; biographies of, 28; claims to innovation by, 197–98; crises and, 225; dependence on bandleaders of, 149; dependence on the state of, 11, 67, 81, 97; honorific titles used by, 232; as mediating figures, 166, 178, 185, 226, 230; military and, 175, 245; Mobutu likened to, 10, 233–34, 250; Mobutu regime and, 24, 45, 79–82; morality of, 113, 249; perceptions of, 136; political culture and, 192; politicians and, 246–47; professionalization of, 40, 82, 104–5, 136; in public, 101, 103, 238; salaries of, 210, 218; social mobility and, 2, 25; social responsibility of, 165; suspensions of,

208–13. *See also* Audience-performer interactions

Music industry, xiv, 38, 84–96; cultural policy and, 81–82; decline in, 10, 25, 65–66, 67, 83, 225; foreign music and, 11, 39, 42, 45, 47, 255; formative years of, 40–44; mismanagement in, 82; Mobutu regime's neglect of, 67, 81, 83, 97; music journalism and, 28; optimism about, 83; religious music and, 37

Music producers, 161–62; lack of, 204; musicians recruited by, 83; organizational strategies of, 94; sales strategies of, 83–84, 93. *See also* Sponsors

Music stores, 67

Music videos, 7, 23, 121

Musique de variétés, 105

Musique moderne, 25, 27, 31, 36, 54, 62

Musique religieuse. 35–37, 38, 269 n. 2

Musique traditionnelle. *See* Traditional music

Musique zaïroise, 31, 255 n. 6

National identity, xv, 8, 14, 68, 182; Congolese perceptions of, 18–19

Nationalism, 19, 68, 69, 71, 81, 257 n. 2; economic, 70–71

Nationalization measures, 45, 65, 67, 71, 80, 84; *zaïrianisation*, 3, 82

Ndombolo (dance), 20, 120, 121

Ndule (live concert atmosphere), 98

Negritude, xii

Negro Succès, 52–54

Ngembo, 103

Ngiri Ngiri (neighborhood in Kinshasa), 17, 101, 102, 143, 145

Nkashama, Pius Ngandu, 29, 182, 193

Nkisi (charms, magic), 182

Nono Atalaku, 59, 60, 63

North America, 85

North Korea, 74
Nouvelle Image, 120, 122
Nouvelle vague, 45–47
Nyamabo, Ben, 83, 216

Oil crisis, 3
O.K. Jazz, 136, 179, 214, 238, 244; African Jazz vs., 42–45, 51–54; formation of, 44
Olema, Debhonvapi, 80
Olomide, Koffi, 48, 49, 52, 56, 59, 85, 135, 177, 179, 180, 181, 183, 190–92, 199, 232, 233, 234, 235, 248, 249, 264 n. 16
Olympia Theater (Paris), 7, 114
Ondemba school, 51–54, 243. *See also* O.K. Jazz

Papa Noel, 53
Papa Wemba, 22, 48, 52, 56, 75, 135, 138, 147, 171, 176, 177–78, 179, 198, 219, 230, 231–32, 248, 249. *See also* Viva La Musica
Paroliers (ghost writers), 48, 122
Patron-client relations, 2, 10, 15, 33, 96, 127–29, 170, 219–22; political economy of clientage, 24, reciprocity and, 25, 179, 193, 223, 249
Pépé Kallé, 133, 236–38, 239, 240, 248
Performance, 25, 108–9, 114–26, 195, 225; language and, 99; mental preparation before, 105; rehearsal vs., 100, 143; ritual and, 99; space on stage during, 110–13, 112, 119, 125, 144, 150; spraying money during, 34, 96, 107, 117, 118, 127–29, 134, 137, 146, 221; taking pictures during, 125–27; theories of, 98–99, 166. *See also* Audience; Audience-performer interactions
Pillage, 3, 90
Piracy, 81, 84–93

Political culture: 26, 192, 242; anthropology of, 14–15, 253 n. 6; cynicism and, 240, 247; impunity, 250; insiders vs. outsiders and, 243–44; *kinoiseries* and, 241–43; Mobutu regime and, 95, 99, 195, 219, 226, 233, 239; political convictions and, 228, 236, 247; popular culture vs., 15; sources of, 229–30, 248. *See also* Leadership; Power
Political economy: ethnography and, 168; music and, 25, 67, 84, 93, 96
Politics: elites and, 24, 80, 242; participation in, 24; popular music and, 1–26; rallies and, 34; sexualization of, 79, 242. *See also* Cultural policy; Leadership; Mobutu Sese Seko
Popular culture: defined, 13; intellectual discomfort with, 16; national identity and, 14; political culture vs., 15; politics vs., 68
Popular music: circulation of, 31; cultural policy and, 65; external influences on, 11, 39, 42, 45, 255 n. 7; formal characteristics of, 30–31; as form of escape, 251; as form of political satire, 80; as form of social mobility, 24, 251; genre and, 25, 29–32; history of, 27, 37–64; Kinshasa and, 20, 22; monotony in, 93, 108; origins of, 29, 38; politics and, xv, 8–16, 26, 79–82, 238–52; power of, 14; in public sphere, 20, 22, 34, 233; religious music and, 36; reproduction of political culture and, 240; as source of livelihood, 20; subversive possibilities of, 80, 226; study of, 13, 28; as urban phenomenon, 39
Popular painting, 15, 231, 251, 253 n. 4
Popular press, 137, *138*, 168
Popular theater, 99
Postcolonial period, 25, 26, 29, 65–96, 80, 196, 219, 241–42

Bob W. White is an associate professor of anthropology at the University of Montreal.

Library of Congress Cataloging-in-Publication Data
White, Bob W., 1965–
Rumba rules : the politics of dance music in Mobutu's Zaire / Bob W. White.
p. cm.
Includes bibliographical references (p.) and index.
ISBN-13: 978-0-8223-4091-1 (cloth : alk. paper)
ISBN-13: 978-0-8223-4112-3 (pbk. : alk. paper)
1. Popular music—Political aspects—Congo (Democratic Republic) 2. Popular music—Social aspects—Congo (Democratic Republic) 3. Music and state—Congo (Democratic Republic)—History—20th century. 4. Mobutu Sese Seko, 1930–1997.
I. Title.
ML3917.C67W45 2008
306.4´8423096751—dc22   2007044862